Religious Atheism

SUNY series in Theology and Continental Thought

Douglas L. Donkel, editor

Religious Atheism
Twelve Philosophical Apostles

ERIK MEGANCK

Cover: Wilfried Op't Eynde

First published in The Netherlands by Uitgeverij Damon, Eindhoven.
Religieus atheïsme: (Post)moderne filosofen over God en godsdienst © 2021,
Erik Meganck

Published by State University of New York Press, Albany

© 2023 Erik Meganck

All rights reserved

Printed in the United States of America

No part of this book may be used or reproduced in any manner whatsoever without written permission. No part of this book may be stored in a retrieval system or transmitted in any form or by any means including electronic, electrostatic, magnetic tape, mechanical, photocopying, recording, or otherwise without the prior permission in writing of the publisher.

For information, contact State University of New York Press, Albany, NY
www.sunypress.edu

Library of Congress Cataloging-in-Publication Data

Name: Meganck, Erik, author.
Title: Religious atheism : twelve philosophical apostles / Erik Meganck.
Description: Albany : State University of New York Press, [2023] | Series: SUNY series in Theology and Continental Thought | Includes bibliographical references and index.
Identifiers: ISBN 9781438495248 (hardcover : alk. paper) | ISBN 9781438495262 (ebook) | ISBN 9781438495255 (pbk. : alk. paper)
Further information is available at the Library of Congress.

10 9 8 7 6 5 4 3 2 1

Contents

Introduction 1

1 Reflection: Feuerbach 11

2 Opium: Marx 21

3 Leap: Kierkegaard 37

4 Dead: Nietzsche 51

5 Neurosis: Freud 67

6 Primitive: Russell 79

7 Silence: Wittgenstein 91

8 Nothing: Heidegger 105

9 Unfree: Sartre 121

10 Face: Levinas 135

11 Metanarratives: Lyotard 147

12 Silent: Derrida 163

Extroduction 183

Notes	201
Bibliography	223
Index	229

Introduction

God is back!

No, not quite like before, thank God. Why? Well, God does not come back from being away, like when we return from vacation or from prison. God returning is not a god from the ancient world or the pre-modern God of the Middle Ages. If God returns, this does not mean that history is reversed. That would imply a certain betrayal, for after all, God must also go through history in the right direction.[1] So God returns through modernity. More than that, God returns through his own death. A philosophical resurrection, so to speak. God is dead, long live God!

When God comes back, he obviously brings along an appropriate vocabulary, even if the meanings have undergone a notable change—after all, "to mean" is a verb. It is then up to philosophy to open itself to the strong theological signs that profoundly signify the present. This implies that kenosis, i.e., humiliation/exaltation (see extroduction), plays a crucial role in the rapprochement between philosophy and theology. God also brings with him an appropriate grammar. This in turn means that the death of God, which thoroughly marks our time, directs the rapprochement. This rapprochement marks actuality. It is therefore in a sense itself the return—and vice versa. God returns in the rapprochement, in the event of philosophy and theology befriending each other. The rapprochement registers the return where postmodern thought leaves behind any hard rational resistance to God.

The modern opposition between philosophy and theology, between reason and faith, is actually a surface phenomenon, a caricature, an ideological strategy, suitable for textbooks and introductions. The relationship was turbulent, notably but not exclusively during modernity. Tertullian already claimed (ca. 200 AD) that Athens had nothing to do with Jerusalem. But a marriage crisis does not necessarily end in a messy divorce. Even though modern philosophy has viewed the church, religious practice, and theology with suspicion, it has never fully eliminated religion from thought—some have tried to do so, but they turn out not to be the great ones. By "religious," I mean not denominational but rather receptive thinking that confesses to being recalibrated by hope, trust, and openness—and of these three, the last one is most important (if this sounds familiar: 1 Cor 13:13).[2]

In any case, one of the modern ambitions did include the reckoning with the God of faith—attempts that were rather carelessly lumped together under the vague heading of "secularization." God was conceptually inserted into cosmological and ethical theory. This insertion eventually killed God. Surprisingly, this death did not erase the name "God." Current events actually testify to the opposite: God was never eliminated, though this was an effect or sometimes even an intention of modernity, at least of Enlightenment.

Such persistence deserves at least our interest. If God keeps returning, we must take this return seriously. Then something noble like philosophy must not cycle cowardly around it, as it has actually done for a long, modern time. Then it should urgently confer with that part of theology that also takes this return seriously. Academic philosophy had got into the habit of leaving God up to theologians and surreptitiously hooking up with both human and natural sciences. This means that the dead God had to molt into a marginal research topic. Science as mummification.[3]

This "exuviation" is indeed clearly an echo of God's death. After all, God's death is an event that manifests itself through many facts. Those facts are usually gathered under the term "atheism" and arranged according to the already cited denomination "secularization." Perhaps, however, the term "atheism" in its current sense is not broad or deep enough. Perhaps there is more meaning hidden inside it than can be discerned on the surface. After all, facts never exhaust the sense of an event. Philosophy and theology reach beyond science. The latter calculates (on) facts; the former deals with what happens behind, inside, beyond those facts. Well, then it certainly cannot hurt to examine this so-called atheism in depth. Who knows, a philosophical atheism may turn out not to be atheistic in the superficial, factual sense—spoiler alert: it is not. For this book does not seek to deny that modernity thinks atheistically; it does argue that its "flat" determination does atheism philosophical injustice. It is precisely where philosophy abandons or avoids this flat atheism that it becomes interesting for and relevant to the purpose of this book.

Philosophical Apostles

I introduce twelve philosophical apostles, great modern thinkers, each of whom has bent and shifted the path of philosophy. Most of them are also called "atheist"—to a greater or lesser degree. This raises some thorny questions. First of all, how come these twelve heavyweights have not succeeded in pushing God completely and definitively out of the world, or at least out of Western culture?[4] Except for Kierkegaard and Levinas, they all seem to have tried to do so.[5] At least so the textbook caricatures teach us. But take Marx, for instance. He did not want to banish religion at all. He wanted to banish the reason why people sought solace there. Nor did Sartre want to throw God out of the world; he advised humanity to exist as if God did not exist. These are just two examples of important nuances that are usually left out of textbooks and introductions. The answer to the question why these guiding thinkers did not help religion out of the world therefore cannot simply be "because people are too stupid." For that matter, that might as well be the answer to the question of why, after 2000 years, people still have not understood the message of Christianity. Rather, the answer is that these thinkers aimed their critique at something other than religion. Thus, they are all critical of traditional metaphysics to a greater or lesser degree.

This leads me to yet another pertinent question. How is it that the thoughts of these supposedly Godless giants nevertheless breathe religiosity, even emphatically Christianity? In one way or another, sometimes firmly disguised, they each thematize a longing for God, a redemption from a state of decay, philosophy's receptivity to the "other," a hope for a better future, and so on. These are all recognizable religious traces, traces that point to a name, God, without ever ending up with something or someone called God. None of the philosophers gathered here, by the way, has ever unequivocally claimed that God does not exist. After all, it is characteristic of great thinkers, unlike their disciples, that they at least think in nuances. Shouting "God doesn't exist, period!" comes down to "meatball thinking." That is what I call "flat" atheism. Unfortunately, this is the most widespread form of it. By the way, the same goes for "God exists, period," which is just "flat" theism.

The philosophical giants in this book are not to blame for this. They never lowered themselves to such a caricature—although it sometimes took them until the end of their lives to correct their own version of the caricature. This was the case with Sartre, for example, although his Simone tried to hush it up. Marx also denounced the caricature that was spread among his comrades of his thoughts on religion even during his lifetime. Heidegger, on the other hand, made a fascinating circumambulatory movement from the Catholic to the Protestant God and farther along a consistent philosophical atheist path to the "last god" that will arrive to save us. Derrida's thought path also exhibited ever more religious traits after he was accused of trivial speculation. Even Kierkegaard, like Augustine, led a fairly debauched life before trying to devote his existence to Christ.

I present each of the twelve philosophical apostles in his own unique way. They are virtually lured out of their atheist camp. I do not turn them into "Bible thumpers" but I will highlight some nuances of their thinking. This will reveal how the stereotypical determination of atheism will not fit them. Instead of proving the existence or non-existence of God in a glass-hard, ice-cold, one-sided, detached—in short, objective-rational—way, I present them on a philosophical and theological eggshell plate of religious, even Christian-motivated thinking that seems to seek a philosophical answer to Eckhart's well-known plea to God to deliver us from God. They do not, therefore, propose yet another divine substance. They do ask difficult questions and propose answers that raise even more questions—but is that not precisely what is expected of a philosopher?

I would like to insert a term here that I borrow from the greatest theological rascal of our time, John Caputo, who speaks of "hier*an*archy." This should be read positively and affirmatively as when and where Christ repeatedly challenges and undermines moral complacency, which could count as a possible philosophical interpretation of original sin. In this way, the apostles in this book bring a traditional way of thinking to a standstill, which is experienced as liberating by all those who do not avoid the deeper questions and are not (or are no longer) satisfied with the traditional answers in the guises of Grand Narratives and Strong Systems.

It begins with Feuerbach undoing the hitherto obvious identification of God and Supreme Being. Nietzsche then suddenly declares the very position of the Supreme Being itself invalid. Kierkegaard and Wittgenstein strip the divine of any theory. Marx and Freud find a $_l$owest $_b$eing that resides beyond the reach of those theories. Heidegger suddenly dismantles all traditional metaphysics, courtesy of Nietzsche. Metaphysics never recovered from all this critique, but that turns out to be precisely what offers the most fascinating perspectives regarding the relationship between philosophy and theology. Each in his own way, Sartre, Levinas, Lyotard, and Derrida elaborate on an aspect of Heidegger's track.

On that track, rather unexpectedly, theology comes into view. This is no longer the triumphant, glorious theology that engages philosophy in the name of a powerful world church. Rather, it is a theology that by the middle of last century has learned, step by step, to be a little more modest as far as its truth claims are concerned. This theology finds that it can learn something from a philosophy that is inclined toward a certain atheism. Philosophy finds that it can cooperate with this theology, humble rather than triumphant, rather of the Cross than of the Glory. "As is the case in friendship, both show the greatest respect for each other, support each other where necessary, and lay no claim on each other. One stimulates, provokes, nurtures the other, but at the same time knows that each must do his own work, have his own style." In such words, spoken at a conference, Jean-Luc Nancy described his friendship with Derrida, but these words apply just as well to the relationship between philosophy and theology that I have in mind here.

Religious Atheism

This "other" atheism no longer avoids the name of God. Until not so long ago, it was not done in philosophical circles to speak benevolently about God. However, now that "otherness" or alterity has become a basic term in thought—we will run into differential thought step by step along the path of our twelve philosophers—God, as "Other," (re)enters. This philosophy does not pronounce on the existence or the unity or the height of God and is essentially religious in register, even if it rarely acknowledges this. It is a philosophical atheism that, with an open mind and in close friendship, allows itself to be informed by theology—and vice versa, of course. This philosophy does not start from an image of God or from the idea that there must be a God who has revealed himself, but from the incontrovertible fact that the name "God" (still) circulates. This may count as a "minimal" revelation in philosophy upon which theology builds lustily. Heidegger speaks of "publicity" (*Offenbarkeit*), the worldly framework in which a manifestation of the divine becomes conceivable, receivable. The circulation of the name is thus also a public event, a revelation or publication.

Where does this name get its obstinacy to "last"? The name—for philosophy has no other "beginning," no other material in the form of concepts or things to start from—continues to circulate without ever falling back on something as a referent—for this referent is rather a matter for theology, after a long time finally the best friend of philosophy. God may no longer exist, but he can insist (again Caputo) and persist—at least insofar as he may be (Richard Kearney here). Only theology and philosophy that have won through to the "other" side of metaphysics can and have indeed become good friends. Within metaphysics, philosophy can choose between service either to theology or to scientific rationality. In the latter case theology is usually rejected; in the former case scientific rationality is not necessarily rejected—at least if philosophy follows in the footsteps of Thomas Aquinas rather than Augustine. This picture is somewhat clouded, however, by the rise of the universities. Whereas previously theology, with or without any help from philosophy, provided the clarification of religious experience and practice, theology then moved to the university, where it became an independent variety of scholarship, leaving faith orphaned in the abbey.

Religious experience succumbed to the rigid schemes of metaphysics. Now, metaphysics has long espoused a two-world model: this world of appearance and transience (nature) versus the other, eternal and true world (supernatural). Theology was concerned with the supernatural, and philosophy (which then included the natural sciences) with nature. Once the domain of theology, especially that of the supernatural, lost its credibility, philosophy turned its back on the queen of the sciences and hooked up with the natural and human sciences. These conformed even better to the rigors of metaphysics than theology with its revelation truths.

It seemed as if philosophy traded its position of maid for that of judge and thus no longer served theology but since then judged it on its reasonableness. But it is also true that philosophy traded its position of servant of theology for that of servant of science. Enlightenment agreed that reason took over from faith and thereby disenchanted the world; that transcendence imploded into pure immanence and so enclosed the world in one final scientific explanation; that no longer that other but this world had become the "true" world. These claims were then cast in (mostly one-sided) models of secularization.[6] In the brilliant fourth chapter of *Twilight of the Gods*, Nietzsche "unmasks" the notion of the "true" world, thereby stopping the process of persistent falsification of one world in favor of yet another "true" world, over and over again. Actually, Nietzsche unmasks this unmasking at its very core. Real unmasking does not replace one mask with another.

In any case, the aforementioned double switch significantly muddied the relationship between philosophy and theology for three centuries. Philosophy did not feel called upon to save the household and left theology. The latter apparently could not continue on its own—only a giant like Kierkegaard could still pull both philosophy and theology up together and light the fire underneath. Western culture noted that both discourses concerning the ultimate questions had failed. Mystery was outsourced to hopeless romantics. Here, the modern division between faith and reason silently manifests itself. Philosophy turned to science and theology committed itself to socio-ethical engagement. For philosophy, the true world became the scientific-technical world, and for theology, the true world became the third and later the fourth world. They no longer shared a world. They no longer even wrote each other a Christmas card.

Now philosophers no longer get around to thinking because the academy demands publication and promotion. Theologians no longer get around to praying because abbeys have become tourist attractions where you can buy beer and cheese and practice yoga. Bishops have become managers with troubling bank accounts and even more troubling scandal records.

But that's not the reason why the miracles have left this world. Looking back over the last half century, it is safe to say that this was not a case of final separation, of drifting further and further apart, but rather one of reshuffling the cards and a few sessions of marriage counseling. Philosophy and theology learned to listen to each other again, began to read and write to each other again, and lo and behold: it works. They dare to speak each other's language again. Suddenly words like "hope," "trust," "hospitality"—the theological virtues from above, still from 1 Cor 13:13—find their way into philosophy, without meeting any headstrong resistance.

I contend that philosophy and theology, like thinking and believing, are not opposites. It is not even easy to delineate believing and knowing in opposition to each other. Thinking and believing each presuppose the other. They relate as each other's extensions, as poles of thinking/believing. No thinking without believing, no believing without thinking—though the respective doses may vary. A religious philosophy is not thought that is being outsourced to institution and dogmatics (metaphysical or natural theology) or to evidence and method (scientific reason). On the contrary, it experiences thinking as an event of receiving and giving back that never allows itself to be fixated in a comprehensive system, but always maintains a modest openness. The twelve apostles in this book bring, mostly unintentionally, philosophy back to theology.

The introduction is circular. God comes back into philosophy, but (of course) not as before. God does not come back from being-away. If God is coming back into philosophy along the tracks of the critique of metaphysics by the twelve philosophers here presented, then this return is at the same time a retreat. God does not become present except as absent. You will notice that both traditional metaphysics and analytic philosophy, with their rather rigid views on the logical consistency of thought, cannot deal with this kind of statement.

This Book, Then

I start from the legacy of Immanuel Kant and Georg Wilhelm Friedrich Hegel. These are the two summits of high modernity. Kant radically broke with the crucial scholastic evidence that God is beyond the reach of knowing. We can speak meaningfully about God only within the moral register. Theology becomes ethics. Even though we can never know God, we recognize that without God any ethical qualification of our existence remains meaningless. Hegel called Christianity the epitome of religious truth, but not of truth as such. Full truth is only attainable by philosophy. After all, religion works with vague representations (images, stories . . .) whereas philosophy deals with clear and lucid concepts. It is only in philosophy, in rational concepts, that the world comes to full self-understanding. You see that theology no longer plays the first violin here as it did with Augustine and Thomas Aquinas. The roles are even reversed: it is now philosophical reason that assigns theology its place. A book by Kant is entitled *Religion within the Bounds of Pure Reason*. That tells the whole modern story. As we shall learn from Heidegger, philosophy needs to dim Enlightenment if it wants to approach the "divine God."

This inferiority of metaphors that is supposed to match the epistemological and even moral superiority of concepts is a common thread throughout metaphysics that only appears as arbitrary and unjustified in the critique of metaphysics. Nietzsche showed that this subordination is based on nothing, and Derrida went even further by showing that even the opposition is hardly valid. In this sense, the rapprochement between philosophy and theology lies beyond Hegel and his distinction and subordination of concepts and representations. Here we see a rather philosophical metaphor at work; there we notice a rather theological one. These turn out to be mutually intelligible without one having to rewrite the other in pure concepts or revelatory jargon and thus reduce it to itself.

This brings me to a final, important observation. Critique of metaphysics or continental philosophy is also referred to as differential thought.

Difference means that terms, words, and names can interact with each other without having to be accommodated in a structure that is established according to the principles of identity and opposition. Meaning does not belong to things or words, but hides in the way these differ from each other. Meaning also never "fills up"; there is always more coming in and always some leaking out. Here, meaning is not the product of a rigid logical system. A very interesting effect is that the other is also allowed to remain "other"—that is, truly different. That may sound strange, but not when you consider that "different" usually means different-from. This way, the other is again thought of as a function of a "self." This is how philosophy and theology used to treat each other, namely as the other-than-self, with that self as norm. Now their relationship is called "differential." That means they are not the same, nor are they opposites. There is no overarching or antecedent agency that controls or directs their relationship. There is no relationship in the classical sense, only a healthy tension and instructive caesura. They are . . . different.

Once again, I must insist on reminding the reader that this is a philosophical study, not a theological one. I intend to show that during the last century and a half, much has happened in philosophy that has unblocked the channels between philosophy and theology. I see this unblocking at work in the twelve philosophical apostles, even though most of them did not desire this unblocking—perhaps sometimes quite the contrary. That work has led to the futility of flat atheism and shows the need for a more philosophical version.

With great respect for other philosophies of life and interfaith dynamics, at least as long as not superficially lived or proclaimed in an exclusive register, this study is limited to Western philosophy and Christianity. I am of course aware of what both owe to other cultures and traditions, but again, that is not what this book is about. Of course, I am also not denying here the brave steps that great theologians have taken to rejoin philosophy, but that is again not what this book is about. Finally, I regret that the twelve apostles are all white males. This specific exclusiveness is, however, a pre-woke cultural-historical phenomenon for which I can hardly be held responsible.

This book does not aspire to convince; it only invites the reader to explore a perspective that I open enthusiastically—that means "visited by the divine." There are no logically-analytically compelling arguments for that perspective, fortunately. Nor does that perspective petrify into a system. My intent is more modest. Finally, to reassure the critical reader, all twelve chapters have been reviewed by experts in the respective fields.

"The purpose of philosophy of religion has changed. It is no longer an analysis of given statements of belief. It is a quest to elevate thought to a level that is divine."[7]

I would like to thank Ger Groot, Joeri Schrijvers, Herbert De Vriese, Roland Breeur, Walter Van Herck, Walter Weyns, Johan Taels, Jens De Vleminck, Wilfried Op 't Eynde, and Marc Meganck, whose pertinent comments on specific chapters have considerably increased the quality of this book. Thanks to Doug Donkel and James Peltz, editors. My students and pupils also remain invaluable. Their eyebrows alert me when I need to explain things more clearly.

I dedicate this book to my father Jacques⁺ and to my little son Ezra. They never leave my mind and, each in their own way, sat by me while writing this book.

1
Reflection
Feuerbach

You have to admire this fiery idealist's steadfastness of principle. He was vilified by many, spent the greater part of his life in relative poverty, and forfeited an academic career because of his views. Modernity had dragged religion before the tribunal of reason. Until then, reason had been entirely at the service of faith, as the maid of theology. Enlightenment turned the tables completely. Reason now acted as an umpire to measure how religion could fit within the scope of reason.

Of course, Feuerbach was not the first one in world history to be labeled "atheist." Xenophanes was already questioning the anthropomorphic features of the Homeric gods around 500 BC—and thus around 100 years before Socrates. He felt that their disposition and behavior were inconsistent with divine dignity. He is therefore wrongly introduced as the first atheist. The divine did exist for him, but it had a cosmic form, not a human form. He observed that African gods were black and European gods white. If horses pictured gods, they would look like horses. It is not possible for gods to have regional traits and for these just to happen to be exactly the same as those prevalent in that region. No, human is human (private, worldly) and divine is divine (universal, heavenly).

Feuerbach likewise denounced this representation of God as human, only he drew a very different conclusion from this than Xenophanes did 25 centuries earlier. The latter claims that the divine can be anything but human, whereas Feuerbach believes that the divine can be nothing but human. Not in a Homeric way, of course—no petty, jealous, greedy, bloodthirsty, horny, vile thugs and rascals. Feuerbach does share with Xenophanes the intuition that the divine, at least on a moral level, should be one step higher than the psychological norm in antiquity—or in modernity, for that matter. In both cases, this moral distance also and at the same time means a distance from the individual. The distance is therefore an abstraction, a move from the individual to the universal. But whereas the former denounced the human in the deity, the latter advocated the divine in humanity. For Feuerbach then, God needs to be *more* anthropomorphized.

Theology, Feuerbach argues, sees finite creation as the product of an infinite, absolute creator. But that is the reverse situation. It is actually from self-knowledge that humans come to the notions of absolute and infinite. This is not, to be clear, about a form of personal introspection. Theology is not psychology—although Feuerbach has sometimes been accused of turning the former into the latter—but rather a "stretched" anthropology. The self-knowledge of mankind leads to the idea of God and explains that idea. Only when man understands himself essentially will he also understand how the idea "God" works.

God is not the basis and origin of our being and knowing, but vice versa. Only, humanity seems to have stopped thinking halfway through the argument and installed a heteronomous God outside the world, set apart from humans. Indeed, God was not "first and foremost" but is the result of a double movement: projection and personification.[1] Projection includes everything that is not strictly personal. All that belongs to both human and non-human nature leads to God. All that we experience and determine as good in the world is attributed to a God in its purest and fullest form. Everywhere we see the hand of an infinitely powerful, wise, well-meaning agency, which we then "christened" God.

Feuerbach recognizes in that hand an authentic desire for God. The awareness of our own finitude stirs up a longing for an infinite, which we then situate outside ourselves. Everything is contained within it; everything originates from it: man, nature, history, everything. In this whole system, says Feuerbach, one unknown variable is still blank: our own, true being. Only and precisely *that* remains hidden from ourselves. Because we do not (yet) conceive of our true being, we trace all that we do think back to a God outside us, preceding us. However, it is precisely our own true being-human that makes us divine. Not that every individual is God; that is an entirely different school of thought. Each individual is a finite manifestation of infinite humanity, which in all its implementations—omnipotent, omnipresent, omniscient, all-good: the four classical categories of metaphysical deity[2]—qualifies as "divine" itself.

In religion that typically human desire, sprung from precisely human finitude, jumps out of its own being and beyond the divine identification of its being. Religion attributes infinity—infinite knowledge, goodness, etc.—to a superhuman entity without knowing that humanity itself possesses this very infinity. Religion maintains this "hiddenness"—namely, the fact that it outsources infinity to a non-existent entity—by placing a God "on High," apart from humanity. It is clear, says Feuerbach, that only by denying the infinity of humanity could God-on-High be appointed. Only by recognizing the essentially infinite nature of humanity, Feuerbach continues, can we proceed to true religion.

Projection

Feuerbach claims that God is a product of human imagination—and not the other way around, as in a dream of creation. Humans imagine an infinitely perfect being, free from all individual flaws due to their inescapable finitude. At first glance, this would seem to relieve humans of the need to work on those deficits; after all, we cannot all become godlike, can we? Wrong, says Feuerbach. No individual can become godlike, but Humanity—from here on with capital H because it concerns a Supreme Being—as such, in its totality, can. Humanity can be perfect: omniscient, spread all over the world, morally perfect and, on top of that, endlessly loving. In fact, that is its true vocation and its very essence. We should worship not an imagined God but real Humanity. Humanity itself is source and standard of truth, goodness, beauty, and meaning. God then becomes simply the name for all the good qualities of which each individual knows themself to be the limited, finite bearer. We would do better, Feuerbach concludes, to pay more attention to Humanity itself than to the creations of its imagination.

Feuerbach's projection is marked by ambiguity. Initially, he claims that God corresponds to an idea of perfection that every human being considers an ideal type. God then is actually the superman that everyone secretly wants to become. A desire for perfection, for omnipotence and omniscience, rooted in every human being, is thus responsible for that image of God in which every person, regardless of his private imperfection, can recognize himself. Later, Feuerbach becomes somewhat Freudian: he then sees God as the response to an innate longing for absolute security, for a God who, beyond the implacability of natural laws and the tragic nature of existence that is implied, cares about the welfare of every human being. Again, this is an illusion, since God's protection does not provide the same guarantee as the progress of Humanity—seen from a modern evolutionary (progressive, cumulative, growth . . .) perspective. Science and technology both offer guaranteed security, as Descartes promised those who will follow the scientific method.

Projection is an epistemological operation, a mind trick that is not worthy of a place in the relationship between man and God. For this reason alone, projection denies, even rejects, the very core of monotheism. This model states that no philosophical, logical, or scientific operation is capable of extracting knowledge concerning the divine from knowledge concerning things in and of the world. After all, monotheism is the contention that only God is divine. Nevertheless, philosophy enthusiastically—at least after a wobbly start—welcomed God into its midst and established a system that made reality derivable from God as Supreme Being—and vice versa. The history or system of those systems is called "Christian metaphysics" or "philosophical theism."[3] Even when God is removed or replaced from the position of Supreme Being, the theistic system can be preserved. Such is the case with Feuerbach, who replaces God with Humanity.

Then there is the notion of projection itself. This notion, of course, denies the prior existence of God, independent of Humanity. This was, at that time, a very serious matter: the whole idea of revelation wiped out in one sweep . . . We must, of course, remain philosophical, and with revelation we enter the theological department of thought, recognized by philosophy but not shared and only reluctantly entered, overwhelmed as we are by the grandeur of its edifice—barely aware of the same awe that theologians hold toward us philosophers.[4] Thanks to the reopened dialogue between philosophy and theology, I can say something meaningful about revelation here. Theology already teaches us that revelation is not a communication about God, not a proposition in the sense of "God is X" and "On top of that, God is also necessarily Y." Revelation is the manifestation of God himself; God is his own revelation. To be God is to reveal God. When philosophy thoroughly considers a revelation that precedes the world and humanity, it does not refer to an original Word, for example, in the sense of a grounding meaning, a primal ground or first principle that gives everything an intrinsic meaning forever that is revealed only to the initiated and passed on by them to the faithful.

Revelation in philosophy rather refers to a sense that enters and founds a world, to the ultimate possibility of meaning as such.[5] God then becomes a possible name for an opening in the world, an opening that once and for all avoids being recovered through a maneuver like projection—or through any other epistemological maneuver. God then becomes a philosophical name for the place where meaning is given and received, where meanings arise, where world is founded. God is a name for the gift of sense, for the unpredictable and uncontrollable event of meaning, an event that asks for thinking and thanking (in Heidegger's words).

Desire of God

This is indeed an old word that, curiously enough, still finds favor with Feuerbach—though not in the traditional theological sense. After all, Feuerbach's God is not dead but replaced, notably by Humanity. We must become aware that God is the effect of our natural desire for the absolute nature of a goodness that affects us personally. We ultimately desire a God who is so good that he surrenders himself totally to the world, serving each of us. In this way, Feuerbach reveals Humanity and not God as the ultimate goal of religion. Traditional religion is therefore not yet a lie, but rather a detour that humans take in order to finally take themselves seriously. "Finally" has to be taken literally here, meaning "at the end of history, which is modernity." Religion is only alienation as long as its anthropological finality is forgotten.

For Feuerbach, the successive images of religion throughout human history are as many steps on the way to self-knowledge. Christianity, the ultimate religion, insists on presenting to us the primacy of love, the most grandiose thing of which a human being is capable. Because love is the highest "existential" and because it is recognized as the most normative factor in human existence, it is at the same time a universal anthropological category, namely that to which every interpersonal relationship should mirror itself.

Desire is understood by Feuerbach to be the logical effect of finitude: the finite, out of dissatisfaction with a "deficit," will desire absolute perfection. After all, to lean on such perfection is to alleviate, even cancel out, the frustration of deficiency. In this sense Feuerbach's theology is a strong critique of Descartes's. After all, the latter agreed that the idea of perfection could never come from a finite, imperfect being. For Descartes, this is precisely the proof that God must exist. Thus, the idea of perfection can only exist independently of thought and "reveal" itself in thought.

Feuerbach's reasoning fully conforms to the Hegelian, dialectical schema. The experience of one's own finitude evokes in the individual the longing for an infinite goodness, which precipitates in the idea of a fatherly God. But this still appears to be marked by an externality, an illusory alienation, which Humanity must make its own. God is still sought "outside" Humanity. This alienation is resolved by referring God back to Humanity itself, as the absolute determination of the essence of every human being. The question then becomes whether religion represents a necessary step in human awareness. Why cannot individual reason conceive of the anthropological truth of religion from the very start? We must not forget that the nineteenth century could only think within the matrix of progress. Auguste Comte had just described how Humanity had evolved from primitive mythic-religious through ancient and medieval abstract-speculative thinking to concrete positive-scientific thinking that no longer reckons with religious or metaphysical ghosts but only with facts. You could argue here that Feuerbach's Humanity still belongs to the metaphysical register and that only Marx reduces that abstraction to its socioeconomic, scientific stature. But in any case, the religious phase is inescapable in Feuerbach's historical dialectic.

Religion *as such* is therefore not a bad thing altogether. On the contrary, it is an anthropological datum. Religiosity belongs to human existence. However, we must remember its proper place. It is not about a natural theology, about a God who exists absolutely and eternally and of whom we are a kind of derived product, a creature. To continue to adhere to this strange image, now that history has finally provided us with a different insight, would be backwardness—at least, that is how the nineteenth century came to think of religion. Theology poses no problem for Feuerbach, as long as it becomes an anthropology. He himself calls it "anthropotheism."

It is precisely against this that Marx and Freud will protest. According to them, Feuerbach underestimates the respective socioeconomic and neurotic elements in the explanation of the phenomenon of religion. They will therefore move away from the anthropological explanation and try to demonstrate the contingency of the phenomenon of religion. For them, unlike for Feuerbach, religion is a historical effect and not an "original" universal fact. Precisely because they do not accept religion as an anthropological constant, they must come up with a "collective" explanation. According to them, history itself gave birth to religion. To Feuerbach's mind, religion is as old as humanity itself, "at par" with human being. The latter means that it is not accidental that humanity and religion are the same age. For Marx and Freud, religion is an effect of the evolution of society, more specifically the effect of a well-defined transition of society from a "primitive" to a more complex stage—again, a typically modern schema. Whereas for Feuerbach religion is of all time and could only come to maturity in modern humanity, Marx and Freud consider religion to be a temporary phenomenon that once appeared and will disappear during modernity, precisely as a token of human maturity.[6]

Religious Atheism

Feuerbach, the father of modern atheism, called himself a religious person. This is not just because, unlike most committed atheists, he was very well versed in Christian theology and world religions. What is relevant here is that he shows us how an atheistic argument can be developed in a religious register. All in all, Feuerbach is certainly not an atheist in the common or flat sense. "God" is a conceptual detour, exists as an illusion, but seems an indispensable anthropological condition for a full knowledge of humans and their errors.

Actually, Feuerbach is an exemplary critical thinker who denounces a caricature of God. We will meet more like him in this book. Christian and other theologies can learn much from Feuerbach. They can redeem their images of God from idolatrous projections—that is, from superstition. After all, it is difficult to deny that the experience of God harbors an element of expectation. It is a sociological fact that in times of disaster and war, church attendance reaches full capacity. It is moreover a psychological fact that in times of adversity, people will more readily rely on prayer. Dietrich Bonhoeffer called that a "stopgap God," an authority that is invoked only when all worldly paths come to a dead end.

Is that a wrong or bad God? No, not necessarily. That is the God of hope. It becomes problematic, however, when he is considered to be the only God. That is what philosophy all too often tends to do, namely to reduce God to a well-defined image, to a specific function. This God appears in many well-known aphoristic clichés. Sentences like "God is nothing but . . ." betray what is called a "reductionist" approach. One selects a particular aspect of the divine experience and first declares it to be the only active, real aspect and then denounces that aspect as an illusion. We will encounter instances of socioeconomic (opium), psychological (father figure), and moral (liberty salvation) reduction in the following chapters. The curious thing about this approach is that in the illusion, a clearer and more comprehensible image of God is formulated than in theology or in faith. A God who remains hidden, inaccessible, silent, and mysterious to the believer and the right-minded theologian is suddenly given a ready-made definition by a philosopher.

Besides, something does not exist simply because we want it to exist—unless precisely as an illusion. The entrance of God into history as an effect of desire still sounds too naive, even to Marx. Of course, the reverse is also true: it is not because we desire something that its existence is by definition an illusion. The existence of God can be neither confirmed nor refuted by any reference to desire. To confine God within that desire would again come down to "reduction."

This reduction admittedly has on the one hand the advantage of clarity and explanation, but on the other hand the disadvantage of sterility, lack of nuance, and poverty of meaning. With a defenseless stubbornness, the name "God" continues to patiently withdraw from any reduction and explanation. By lack of a definitive explanation that can at once declare all reductions invalid, not even the label "illusion" sticks to that name. Then God suddenly becomes a "may-be" or a "perhaps," in the words of Richard Kearney and Jack Caputo.

The identification of the illusion "God" with the anthropological reality "Humanity" is, moreover, far-fetched. Humanity is too abstract a category, one that cannot simply be deduced from the "self-perception" of a concrete human being among others. Personalism, which is re-emerging today and hopefully will finally get the political recognition it deserves, does not accept the primacy of that category. It ignores the tension between individual and humanity—or other (sub)collections. The meaning of a person is not exhausted by its individuality nor by its belonging to a collective. These are liberal and social determinations, that each in itself and both together leave out something essential. If we look at modern politics, we see three great democratic families: the liberal, the social, and the Christian. Each of these represents the priority of one of the three pillars of modern politics: liberty, equality, and fraternity. The latter is conspicuously absent from contemporary political thought. The first article of the Universal Declaration of Human Rights reads, "All human beings *are* born free and equal in dignity and rights. They are endowed with reason and conscience and *should* act towards one another in a spirit of brotherhood" (my italics). Freedom and equality are determined as obvious, pre-given structures, as inscribed in the "natural law" of the modern democratic state. Fraternity, however, falls under the moral register of an appeal. Modern political philosophy, as we find it in the contemporary media, hinges entirely on the modern ideals of freedom and equality. Suspicion of religion, in this case Christianity, is apparently accompanied by the disparagement of fraternity. Without extracting argumentative potential from this, I therefore see a strong parallel between the political call for fraternity and the Christian call for charity. Of this call, every criticism toward the unilateral liberal and social determinations of society testifies.

The fraternity that our society needs so much is not found in the modern tension between finite and infinite, imperfect and perfect. It does not recognize infinite perfection in an abstraction like Humanity. Fraternity has nothing to do with infinity and perfection as such. The law of large numbers obliterates all individual deficits, but that does not affect the person. To a person, this perfection is nothing but an illusion that is not worthy of religious motivation.

In this sense Feuerbach's atheism, like the whole of modern metaphysics, leaps over Christianity. It ends up with a great system, held together by the grace of a Supreme Being, but that is not what Christianity is about. However apt his analysis of an otherworldly deity that is nothing more than a step on the road to humans' self-knowledge may be, the goal of Christianity is not the glorification of Humanity, as an abstraction. If the God of Christians demands anything of humans, it is precisely the "breaking" of such idols.

2

Opium

Marx

Marx, too, did not trade his convictions for an academic career. As with Feuerbach, friends—especially Friedrich Engels—and in-laws provided the bread on the table. One cannot accuse Marx of laziness; his productivity is legendary.

Marx is older than Nietzsche. He was thus unfamiliar with the radical critique of traditional philosophy or classical metaphysics that the latter instigated. Since we may assume that Marx was also unfamiliar with the work of his contemporary Kierkegaard, who will be discussed later, the latter's criticism of the great Hegel also remained unknown to him. What both Nietzsche and Kierkegaard do not accept, albeit for different reasons, is precisely what Marx takes over from Hegel, namely the idea that world history has a pre-given purpose.[1]

Along with Nietzsche and Freud, both of whom follow in this book, Marx was called a "master of suspicion" by Paul Ricoeur. This has to do with Marx's specific criticism of Hegel. For the latter, "spirit" was the substance of reality. Matter, material existence, is nothing but a function of that spirit. In human language: for philosophy, "matter" is a disembodied concept. Reason constitutes, truly and purely, the raw material of reality. Marx begs to disagree. Not speculative reason but concrete socioeconomic reality constitutes the true engine or motif of history. Ideas have a descriptive, explanatory, and even legitimizing function but hardly a motivating, edifying one. Marx turns Hegel upside down in this sense: he famously said that life is not determined by consciousness, life determines consciousness.

Thought, (socio-political) consciousness, and social selfhood are functions, effects of that reality. Philosophy is its effect and not its cause. This, then, is what Ricoeur means by "suspicion": along with Nietzsche and Freud, Marx denies the absolute autonomy of a pure reason—if this exists at all. They are not so naive as to deny the validity of reason. On the contrary, they use reason to suspect reason itself of being the product of something else. With Nietzsche that is the will to power, with Freud the unconscious, with Marx socioeconomic reality.

Marx hardly really wrote about religion as such. As far as he was concerned, Feuerbach had in principle definitively settled the question about religion by declaring it an illusion. Marx did not follow him when it came to the concrete settlement of this illusion. According to him, Feuerbach neglected the socioeconomic motif of the phenomenon of religion. His criticism therefore focused more on the world that "needs" religion than on religion itself.

Revolution

So Marx turned Hegel upside down. Ideas do not direct the world, but vice versa. That this reversal is not a purely theoretical matter is clear from his pithy eleventh "thesis on Feuerbach": "Philosophers have only interpreted the world differently; it comes down to changing it." To think is to act.

Giving meaning to the world is not a mental matter, is not a matter of idle speculation. In his rousing pamphlets, Marx breaks down all that he believes to stand in the way of humanity's true development. He calls this situation where human beings are kept away from fulfilling their true vocation "alienation." For Marx, atheistic communism was the only remedy for all human unhappiness, the true salvation, namely the abolition of this alienation. What makes a human being unhappy? Being alienated from what makes him human. What makes a human being a full human being? On this, however, Marx is not clear. In the preface to *The German Ideology*, he mentions someone who hunts in the morning, goes fishing in the afternoon, tends cattle in the evening, and writes reviews after evening meals without therefore being a hunter, fisherman, rancher, or critic. Like Feuerbach, Marx sees alienation as a necessary but transitory evil. They both, however, interpret the "medium" of that alienation differently. For Marx, alienation is not a spiritual or anthropological question, but a socioeconomic one. It concerns the "substructure" or socioeconomic reality.

The motive of Marx's thoughts is the indignation about the appalling injustice that early industrial society is inflicting on itself. An unprecedented gap between rich and poor gapes before everyone's eyes but no one does anything about it. On the contrary, everything and everyone seems to strive to preserve that gap. Examples are countless, but here are a few striking ones. Politicians, even Christian ones, refused to raise the minimum age for child labor in the mines; laws forbade any form of "medieval" corporation, which concretely meant a ban on trade unions and on strikes; scientific, e.g., capitalist, economic models justified massive investment in factories and machinery at the expense of workers' wages and other possible amenities because this sacrifice would bring prosperity to future generations while huge short-term profits were the only visible effect. Even art, according to Marx, was intended to preserve and even justify existing conditions. The problem is not that art in itself is evil, but it should, according to Marx, be created for a good cause—more specifically, for socialism. And, of course, there is religion, this famous opium of the people, picturing an afterlife of eternal bliss to a proletariat that is succumbing to misery.

Conditions were so wretched that the average life expectancy in Marx's days hovered below forty. Children slept in coal mines from the age of five because it was not worthwhile to go home between working hours—if there even was such a thing as a house and home for them. There was no education, no vacation, no health insurance, no unemployment compensation, no money, no food, nothing. Work meant survival, no work meant death.

Marx attributes this to what he calls the "superstructure." Sometimes this is misunderstood as the establishment, the rich. However, superstructure stands for the whole system of politics, law, science, and church that makes that welfare gap, this exorbitant injustice, seem "normal" and acceptable in the eyes of both the rich and the poor—almost like a natural law, the will of God. Marx does not agree with the questionable caricature of politicians, entrepreneurs, economists, and church leaders all conspiring to exploit a working class. Capitalism is not a gutsy strategy but an inescapable historical phase—in a Hegelian dialectics. People then truly believed that society behaved the way it should do, whether they benefited from it—the owners of the means of production—or lost everything to it—the people who, along with the machines, were reduced to mere means of production. That was what Marx saw as his mission: to make all people, society as a whole, rich and poor, aware of how that superstructure works. This awareness, in turn, would mean nothing less than the abolition of alienation. Alienation takes place in a world where people are not "at home." The superstructure at that time appears incapable of bringing peace and quiet, let alone justice, to early industrial society.

With Marx, the "revolution" that seems so inherent to Marxism is not a matter of bashing the heads of the rich and taking over all factories. Nor is it a matter of drawing out an abstract blueprint and then implementing it *manu militari*. These last two (wrong) interpretations did support certain fascist regimes. Such regimes were certainly not what Marx had in mind.

However, Marx was convinced that history cannot or should not be stopped. Hence, he was not even really against capitalism, as long as it did not represent a culmination point, as in some liberal models. Capitalism was a necessary stage on the way to a world freed from every illusion and flight. This is why Marx wants to show his contemporaries how history works and even liberates—i.e., from alienation and misery. He wants to make everyone aware of this but since there exist a happy few who benefit largely from the status quo, it will be up to the proletariat, as a historical instrument, to break out of this numbing alienation and lead humanity to a better future. This liberation or redemption does not take place in or through thought or through the detour of religion, but in the world itself.

Marx's analyses of historical processes and transitional situations are based on the idea that in reality an interaction, a tension or contradiction even, seeks a new balance through and out of that tension. This is called dialectics. Any equilibrium is the temporary reconciliation between two opposing poles that in its turn causes a reaction, a tension, and so on. Since those poles can be valued as good and evil, it turns out that any evil can still be turned into good by carrying it to the next equilibrium state. Thus Marx understands injustice in society in terms of disequilibrium, of tension, especially between the lower and upper classes.

Marx explains history from the tension between old and new relations of production, between possessors (private property, basic element of bourgeois capitalism) and those who possess nothing (proletariat), between all "antitheses," as they are called in modern dialectics. These are the necessary poles that are not installed by something or someone, out of free will or desire or some form of insight. These poles call each other into being. History takes shape as a thesis that repeatedly provokes an antithesis, causing a tension that "dissolves" itself into a synthesis that itself functions as a thesis that in its turn provokes an antithesis, and so on.

Capitalist superstructure does not come falling out of the blue as an idea or theory but emerges, as it were, from the socioeconomic substructure. Nor is it the result of a critical evaluation of the feudal structure of society.

Superstructure does not work as autonomously as, for example, young (and left) Hegelian Feuerbach still assumed.

This capitalism consisted of the bourgeoisie taking over everything and leaving nothing for the workers. This created a possessing class as opposed to a non-possessing class. This was legitimized in the superstructure by, among other things, a new economy that emerged from industrial production. The proletariat does not recognize itself in this model and finds itself not at all represented by this superstructure. This means total alienation. The proletariat can reclaim its material existence only by abolishing private property and thus dismantling capitalism. That is the socialist revolution, nationalization (as the antithesis of privatization), which in turn will necessarily culminate in communism, the classless society, the ultimate synthesis. Since classes are the ingredients of tension and alienation, which must seek new equilibrium states over and over again, the classless society will be without tension and therefore eternal. This is heaven on earth, actually, the synthesis that no longer provokes any antithesis.

So for Marx, history always starts with raw material, the substructure, the production forces and how they are historically organized. This is translated into institutions and structures, economic theories and political models, arts and sciences, theology and church. In the feudal era, the whole social structure looks considerably different from the one that governs the industrial one. It is not that concrete agriculture and manual labor were the implementation of a feudal ideology; no, it works the other way around. Agriculture (large landholdings) and manual labor (crafts) befit a feudal culture. Factory labor (urbanization and machinery) befits capitalism and liberalism. Human labor, free from alienation, befits communism. Again, true transition, according to Marx, takes place on the substructural plane.

Marx himself plays a key role in that history, which is liberation through awareness, the tilt between theory and praxis, between illusion and reality. In his own words, at the end of his introduction to *A Contribution to the Critique of Hegel's Philosophy of Right*, "As philosophy finds its material weapon in the proletariat, so the proletariat finds its *spiritual* weapon in philosophy. . . . Philosophy cannot realize itself without the transcendence [*Aufhebung*] of the proletariat, and the proletariat cannot transcend itself without the realization [*Verwirklichung*] of philosophy."[2] Here, Marx himself impersonates philosophy. In his razor-sharp scientific (i.e., not utopian, idealistic, swarthy) analysis of history, it/he discerns the dialectics of redemption.[3]

Marx is never clear about what that future paradise—communism—should look like, which in fact makes him a prophet rather than a scientist. This has proven dangerous, given the way Marxism took shape in some regimes, as mentioned above. Not all politicians turn out to be great thinkers . . .

Opium and Ideology

In a communist regime, no one would need opium, and that is what we are concerned with here. In communism, where everyone would know happiness during life here and now, a hallucination about happiness after this life—religion—is meaningless. The "opium" of which Marx speaks is somewhat ambiguous, and Marx himself understood this only too well. As a medicine, opium is a sign that a problem has arisen, that a (social) illness has presented itself, and at the same time an attempt to overcome that problem. Opium then counts as both symptom and cure at the same time. Of course Marx knew very well that religion offers solace. He even called religion "the heart of a heartless world." In his view, it was necessary to remove the (substructural) causes of social injustice and misery rather than to fight the (superstructural, in this case religious) effects or symptoms. He wanted to resolve the ambivalence inherent in the opium metaphor by a correct diagnosis of the problem. Marx's historical optimism then teaches that this diagnosis itself opens the way to the remedy so that a cure becomes superfluous.

For a proper understanding of the following argumentation: this is about opium *of* the people, not *for* the people—the latter version was coined by Lenin. Marx does not suspect religion of deliberately, strategically spreading an illusion among the workers, fully aware that it is nothing more or else than one massive deception. But well-intended or not, it is and remains an illusion, and that can produce bad consequences. Look what damage religion did during the industrial revolution, cries Marx. The proletariat is mercilessly exploited. The whole culture—the superstructure—is mobilized to perpetuate that unjust state of affairs. And then religion made it even worse. The church made the poor workers believe that it was good to lead a miserable life because it would be compensated all the more in the life hereafter.

Marx claims it is wrong for religion to be necessary because of this misery. Whether religion should be possible then, depending on free choice or conversion, seems barely relevant to him. Marx did not see much religion apart from political abuse of Christianity. That someone really professes a

God who provides solace in hopeless situations, such as working-class life in Western Europe at the time, without therefore legitimizing an economic system, remained below his analytic radar. For him, religion could only mean one thing: to take one's eye off the only reality that matters, namely the economic and social world—substructure.

This, however, did not eliminate the problem. For why do people want opium in the first place? Well, because opium paralyzes consciousness, and thus temporarily "solves" any misery. But a temporary solution is not a historical one. There is no point in fighting the opium itself. Self-deception cannot be reasoned away. It does not seem a good idea to argue with people who are dying of misery about the truth claims of Christianity, their only solace. It is precisely the cause of the misery that must be addressed.

Fighting superstructure, by the way, would also be of no avail. After all, that would mean attacking politics, economics, law, religion, and art with political, economic, legal, religious, and aesthetic arguments. This was precisely what Marx accused the utopian socialists of, namely of moving exclusively in the field of ideas, programs, blueprints, ideologies, and good or bad intentions. The whole, well, "common" thread throughout Marx's discourse is precisely that the conceptual determination of reality is inferior to the material. It is not ideas that change the world. In his philosophy, therefore, Marx does not so much provide new or his own ideas, he opens everyone's eyes to reality.

Suddenly he discerns the messianic role of the proletariat. This is the result not of a political or socioeconomic analysis, but of a strictly philosophical derivation. The proletariat consists of people who own absolutely nothing but their humanity. That makes them one class: the naked human being.[4] As already mentioned, at that point the proletariat no longer recognizes itself in the current superstructure, in any way. Conversely, the rich no longer have any contact with the proletariat either.[5] Therefore the latter is the chosen historical material element in which the revolution can take place and in which new relations of production can be established, after which the superstructure will adapt itself according to the same laws that determine history as a whole.

So what exactly happens to the superstructure, the opium kit? On the one hand, Marx shows consistency here by not making any predictions in this area. After all, superstructure is always an effect, namely of concrete historical socioeconomic dynamics. There is no way to conceptually derive future superstructures directly from the current one. Once Marx has predicted the historically necessary revolution in—at least according to him—a strictly scientific way, he lets go of science and becomes a prophet. Remember his analogy about the man who hunts and fishes.

Marx does suggest that in communism all the distinctions and tensions that represent alienation will disappear. For example, the political structure of the modern nation-state will disappear (for the most part). This structure is supposed to align the self-interest of the citizen with the common good, but when these coincide in communism, such political mechanics become superfluous. In the end, not only the tension between a person and society, but also between a person and nature, history, the other, etc., disappears.

It is therefore sometimes suggested that in communism, there would or even should be no superstructure at all. An administration that is in no way embedded in political, legal, academic, or religious institutions would automatically apply a just distribution key that divides work and income among everyone without requiring (other than historical) legitimation, such as a political decision or a divine decree. People sometimes refer to the principle "work according to everyone's ability, wages according to everyone's needs," but Marx himself uses this quote only once. Political decisions and ecclesiastical ordinances thus become superfluous. Law also becomes superfluous because no one takes to crime anymore—who would go out stealing when they have what they need (a reasonable albeit ascetic point of view on human beings as rational consumers). Science becomes redundant because there are no abuses that require academic condoning. Even art becomes redundant because any flight from reality is rendered pointless. Whoever wants to be artistic will spontaneously take paradise itself as favorite theme. When science and art are detached from the superstructure and relinquish their legitimizing character, they acquire their own finality, which consists of creativity in function of social justice—and not submitted to totalitarian imperative. Churches are obviously empty because everyone finds happiness here on earth and does no longer need an outerworldly institute to demand compensation for innerworldly misery. In any case, this could all be true as long as no one ever wants to do anything else but hunt, fish, farm, and write reviews, and if all political, scientific, aesthetic, and religious motives remain pure functions of a healthy socioeconomic constitution.

This is perhaps a naive representation and an all-too-eager misunderstanding of Marx's own prophetic vagueness on this point. After all, the illusory, conservative, privileging effect of the superstructure does not exhaust its meaning and function. Indeed, this element also articulates social imagination or ideology. Superstructure contains the self-image of a society. A false self-image, psychology teaches us, is counterproductive.[6] Seen this way, according to Marx, the early industrial superstructure is evil not because it concerns the domain of ideology, but because it installs a perverse ideology. In communism, too, the superstructure affirms the prevailing conditions, but because the condition itself is healthy, free from alienation and thus from history, the operation of the superstructure is now also declared healthy.

This raises the fascinating question: which role does religion play in the socio-political self-image of a society? Does history show a positive impact of Christianity on the organization of society, for example, organizing education, fighting poverty, and caring for the sick? Is not the fact that a term like "political theology" is making headway these days an indication that this role is at least not imaginary?[7]

And yet another fascinating question: did not communism itself turn into something of an institutional religion? Once the intuitions and prophecies of Marx have been cast into a dogmatic system, with a strict central political institute and its inexorable mechanics of censorship, excommunication, and even execution, this communism suddenly resembles the Catholic church during the Inquisition rather than a liberating philosophy.

To find an answer to those questions, we need to return to the opium kit. The role Marx attributes to the church is not necessarily the only one or even the most accurate one. Rather, it involves a pernicious distortion in society's self-image. To Marx, the church is an institution that colludes with property and that belongs to a system that means to concentrate and conserve property and power—i.e., a superstructure. Anyone who claims that no member or segment of the church has ever been tempted to do so shows ample ignorance regarding church history. There are, of course, the rather naive reservations about the wealth of the church. Some people claim that the Vatican should sell all its art. With the profits we could then distribute a thimbleful of rice to every hungry person in the world, and that's it. Then hunger returns and there would be no more Vatican museums.

Throughout the history of the world, every religion has always used the noblest materials for worship. This indeed may or may not be expensive. This nobility is supposed to attest to the special, sacred nature of the event in which those objects are used, such as a divine celebration. In the Bible there is something about melting swords into plowshares. During the French Revolution, chalices and the like were melted down into swords. Magnificent paintings of religious scenes were torn from their frames to rub horses warm and dry. Ammunition was piled up in churches. This happened during the first modern revolution, that of 1789. During the last one, that of 1968, imagination ruled. Priests then came up with the idea of doling out the host from a plastic coffee cup in jeans at the kitchen table. It takes a lot of imagination indeed to see the sacred in such a version of the sacrament.

On the other hand, the church has been accused of keeping attention away from the pathogenic nature of society by distributing soup and socks to the poor on Sundays. These good works tend to hide her own wealth on the one hand and poverty in the "real" world on the other. This form of material charity would thus help to cover up injustice and delay the socialist action that was nonetheless historically necessary (according to Marx's dialectical schema). When nobody would show any charity, only then would the scales fall from everyone's eyes.

Liberation theology, once a hype in the West, still remains a significant movement in South America. It is still a theme that divides the church, especially now that a bishop from South America has become pope and obviously wants to leave his mark on the organization of the world church. In any case, it involves two divergent visions on the church, to a great extent irreconcilable self-images. In the one case, the church does not consider itself competent in worldly affairs and guards the tradition of liturgy and almsgiving, thus siding de facto, in socio-political terms, with the big landowners, while insisting that it has nothing to do with them. In the other case, the church reads in the gospel a call to an unconditional option for siding with the poor, and insofar as this entails armed defense or armed action, so be it. An intermediate position can be seen in the figure of Oscar Romero, a representative of the South American Church who changed position and turned away from the landowners to side with the poor. This archbishop, although considered a father of liberation theology, distanced himself from the militant-political guise of this movement. He sided with the poor out of evangelical concern but did not want to overthrow a political regime or social institution (such as landownership), following Paul here. His position was rather that of passive resistance, of working behind the scenes. Romero was assassinated by a death squad while celebrating mass before a full church.

Of course the church, especially since *Rerum novarum*, has been concerned with the world, though not always in a way that the world considers useful. This may change with, again, the current pope. In any case, his encyclical *Laudato si'* is taken very seriously and is widely read, also outside the church community. Bruno Latour estimates the impact of this encyclical of the order of *The Communist Manifesto* (see also chapter 11, note 23). This indicates that the social teaching of the church claims a voice in the social debate, if only because it represents one vision in the midst of a world that has been analyzed to pieces and where science has to admit that it does not really know anymore either.[8] But it would be unfair to conclude from this that the gravitational center of faith and the church must lie within the world. It has always been the task of the church, since the age of the prophets, to maintain a critical distance from the world without wanting to change it, because the world does not really need a church for that.[9] To conclude from this that the center of gravity of the church should lie outside the world is again a bridge too far in the other direction. The church does not dwell in the other *than*, but in the other *of* the world—an alterity that has been explored by Nancy in his deconstruction of Christianity. This is implied in the aforementioned social doctrine of the church. Marx, however, saw no church apart from the political and recognized no history apart from the socioeconomic.

Religion

It is often suggested that Marx's teaching is nothing more or less than a secularized version of Christianity. We owe this suggestion to Karl Löwith, who understood modernity in this way—see his famous *Meaning in History: The Theological Implications of the Philosophy of History* (1949). In his view, modern philosophy professes a horizontal or secular Christianity. In Marx's case, I recognize salvation from the original sin of ongoing class struggle, with communism as the eschatological end and completion of that history. The world will then be entirely free of tension and discontent. In that completion, final judgment suddenly takes place, the ultimate synthesis against which no appeal, no antithesis, is possible and which thus sets off eternity. The proletariat plays a messianic role in this salvific event; there has been talk of its "crucifixion." The capitalist is Judas, evil incarnate, but nevertheless a necessary link in the dynamics of salvation.

Very striking in this context is also the way Marx sometimes writes about money. Take some paragraphs from well-defined texts and replace "money" with "God," and you get an exemplary theological treatise. Marx's monetary theology is very illuminating. He prophesies that in modern capitalism money becomes the only universal "signifier," that the value of every creature can only be expressed in money, that money deprives things of their real, true, intrinsic value and meaning. Here we have the ultimate alienation, the deification of money, the universal "monovalence," the economic version of what is commonly but wrongly understood by monotheism (see chapter 11, note 16).

Michel Henry called Marx one of the most important Christian thinkers in Western philosophy. This sounds rather provocative, but then again this claim is not without reason. The key word here is again "alienation." For Henry, Christ is in a sense Life itself. Christ's message reads: the meaning and significance of life cannot be found outside of life itself. Any attempt to "objectify" life and to grasp it in concepts that are alien to life, thus to give it an abstract (scientific, political, etc.) meaning that resides outside the experience of life itself, is a form of alienation. Ultimately, Henry also recognized this message in Marx's philosophical writings, such as *The German Ideology*. Here, Marx explains how the meaning of labor, the basis of human existence, cannot be outsourced with impunity to a superstructure, to politics, law, or science. Those who hunt must then become hunters. But, says Marx, in labor itself man must recover precisely the meaning, the value of his life.

This value is acquired not in heaven but on earth, at least if earth is incorporated into a communist world. Otherwise, all worldly value, in the form of money, belongs only to those who possess it. In this, too, I see a typically Christian characteristic: Marxism concerns everyone, the whole world, and not just a "chosen section" as, for example, in nationalist politics. This universalism is credited to Paul. This is one of the reasons why Marx situates salvation in the proletariat: because the proletariat has lost everything but its humanity, it suddenly also appears as the most universal category. If the proletariat is saved, then by definition the whole of humanity is saved because in the proletariat there is nothing to save but humanity.

Marx's thinking was perhaps best known through the witticism of the socially critical playwright Bertolt Brecht, "Erst kommt das Fressen, und dann kommt die Moral" (First comes food, then comes morality), from *The Threepenny Opera* (*Die Dreigroschenoper*, 1928). There is no point in spoon-feeding people a lofty morality when they do not even possess the most basic means of existence. Is this merely inflammatory talk from socialists on the loose? Another insight runs parallel to this. An ancient Roman wisdom reads, "Primum vivere, deinde philosophari" (First live, then philosophize). This may mean that one must first have the necessary means of existence before being able to afford the luxury of reflection. In Greek, *scholé*, from which our word "school" is derived, means "leisure," the time that did not have to be spent in function of survival. Philosophy arises in the transition from surviving to living—more specifically, living together. However, it can also mean that philosophizing is a pointless activity if it does not concern itself with life, if it ignores concrete existence. It can then count as a warning not to allow thought to jump past life at the aforementioned transition, only to arrive in philosophy completely alienated. This way, Marx keeps us on our toes.

However, by only paying attention to the way in which religion arises out of socioeconomic reality as an illusory solution to a real problem, Marx completely misses the critical function of religion. The concrete needs that the church has encountered through her critical function and her mission (*kerygma, diaconia, caritas*, etc.), by developing a whole system of care and education with its own resources, are ignored in Marx's analysis. The role that the Franciscans have played in the development of the modern market and capitalism is also left out of Marx's analysis. However, he did accept a "feedback" from superstructure to substructure, an interaction that most of his followers rejected. They preferred a simple one-sided determination of superstructure by substructure—so much so that some Marxists simply wanted to abolish this superstructure. Incidentally, it has not been universally shown that socioeconomic improvement brings about a proportional decline in religiosity. However, an ascertainable effect does not absolve religion from the accusation of being an illusion.

Actually, Marx and Christianity are indeed pulling the same string. They both, as Henry observed, denounce alienation. Christianity does this subtly, by always remaining "alien" to the world, by never becoming completely absorbed in the world and its discourses—political, scientific, theological, and so on. What Christianity proposes is actually what is contained in the "other *of* the world." This irreducible alterity resists the possibility of ever arriving at a "total social self." Never will a worldly prescription by itself install the Kingdom of God,[10] not even Marx's paradise. That is why communists do not like Christianity, even though the word "communism" comes from monastic tradition. What remains is modesty à la Romero, who wanted to improve the lives of all people without launching a political revolution. This sounds essentially biblical. Christ himself declares that he has no intention of changing the Law, basis of Jewish society, but in the meantime preaches an unprecedented commandment of love that "overturns" the whole Law and thus radically redraws the meaning of the world (Mt 5:17–18 and then all the way to 48).

The question then remains whether the tension between humanity and society, humanity and nature, humanity and history, me and the other . . . is historical or rather inherent. In the latter case, communism becomes a new heaven, against all nature, history, and alterity. Then we will never experience communism, as Marx dreamed it, during this earthly existence. Instead of dreaming of a tension-free existence, we must then look for the optimal way to live together within the given tensions, to lend those tensions the most societal form. Here Christianity shows itself to be more realistic than Marxism because it tolerates this tension almost on principle, without therefore passively accepting it or even condoning it. Permanent vigilance remains necessary to sit out and live down those tensions. It is then up to politics to arrange those tensions into an (always temporary) equilibrium. To the extent that politics recognizes its own Christian heritage, it wants to question those balances each time they are established. No worldly state of equilibrium is eternal.

In the first, historical case, things get a little more complex. To begin with, the socialist recipe for tension reduction is not necessarily singular. Liberalism had also formulated a recipe before, namely the "invisible hand" (which, by the way, appears only once in Adam Smith's work). But apart from that, and this is much more relevant here, history may not be at its completion but rather at its dissolution. Perhaps, as postmodern thought suspects, there is no linear progression, no dialectic, no rational historical dynamics, no History that conforms to one underlying law as Hegel and Marx deemed evident. Perhaps actuality is rather the provisional result of intersecting processes, each with its own impact. Should this be the case, then the aforementioned tensions gradually lose their rigidity and even validity. Also the idea of a teleology in world history would be completely abandoned. Most remarkable is that precisely in this time of dissolution, of "crisis," philosophy observes that (in the words of Marcel Gauchet) the religious is "returning," albeit not in its traditional form, so that this return at the same time implies an exodus from (institutional) religion. In the absence of a social or liberal completion of history, in the case of the "end" of historical political programs, we should perhaps fall back on political theology which, in Christian terms, without of course becoming religion or turning society into church, is prepared and able to dust off that third pillar of modern politics: again, fraternity.[11]

When he noticed the way his thinking was received among his disciples, Marx must have sighed, toward the end of his life, "One thing I know for sure, that I am not a Marxist." Raymond Aron called Marxism "the opium of the intellectuals." However, he referred to midcentury Parisian Marxists, not to Marx himself. After World War II, to be leftist became fashionable among French thinkers. Sartre and Louis Althusser are eloquent (and authoritative) examples of this rather blind complicity with communism. Jan Assman, meanwhile, records that religion has evolved from opium to dynamite of the people. Where previously religion kept the poorest from revolution, it gradually became the engine of revolution—albeit in a different tone.

Marx died neither from opium nor from dynamite. He never recovered from the death of his daughter Jenny. Twelve men walked behind his coffin—not even apostles.

3

Leap

Kierkegaard

For a long time no one really knew how to classify Kierkegaard. He was thought to be a spoiled nag, a moralist, an incorrigible romantic, a local troublemaker, a schizophrenic writer, and a religious fanatic. It took some time before philosophy recognized him as an authentic and rich thinker. This recognition pretty much coincides with the existentialist critique of the great systems such as Hegel's, perhaps the most systematic in the history of philosophy.

From the beginning, every form of existentialism has always resisted the idea that concrete existence would be completely open to a theoretical approach. Emmanuel Mounier understood existentialism to be a philosophy of "person" in reaction against the excesses of the philosophies of ideas and those of things, that is, of the great idealist (Hegel) and materialist (Marx) systems of thought.[1] Kierkegaard does not accept any form of total determination of human essence that is theoretically accessible even before existence has unlocked or disclosed its meaning for that person itself.

Consequently, he never drew up a systematic philosophy—nor even a systematic theology, for that matter. This has everything to do with his "baseline," the line that runs through his entire work, namely, that philosophy and faith should not just think *about* life but should make up life itself. Actually, as such he was the first and also the most radical "full" existentialist. This is, however, a religious, a distinctly Christian existentialism and not an immanentist, atheistic humanism as, for example, would be rolled out by Sartre—who, by the way, along with Simone de Beauvoir, greatly admired Kierkegaard. For Kierkegaard, the full meaning of existence lies in Christ, with God.

In the eyes of many, this makes Kierkegaard not a philosopher, but an astute and tormented religious fanatic and church critic. Wittgenstein, on the other hand, who is discussed in chapter 7, can be said to be an astute and tormented language fanatic and academy critic. This does not discredit his philosophical value in any way. Both thinkers agreed on this: as long as philosophy does not concern life and vice versa, it remains meaningless. What else could Wittgenstein have meant when he called Kierkegaard the most profound writer of the nineteenth century, yes, even a saint?

Trying to distill from Kierkegaard's "pseudonymous" writings one clear and fixed point of view does not seem to work either. It appears to have been Kierkegaard's intention, precisely through the use of pseudonyms, to avoid being pinned down to one philosophical, ethical, or socio-political position. When it comes to his deepest convictions, however, he suddenly becomes very unambiguous, especially in his "religious" writings—which he publishes under his own name. There he unfolds what he fully stands for. The pseudonyms occupy positions that Kierkegaard had previously denounced, positions that he himself may have taken and that he then saw to be inadequate. After all, he once *was* a dandy, an intellectual, an exemplary fiancé, a careerist, a moralist, and a do-gooder.

Perhaps, then, Kierkegaard's most important thesis is that the full meaning of life cannot be exhausted in a theory, in an abstract model, in a rational (scientific) system. Hence his criticism of Hegel, who wanted to subject reality to the system. When someone pointed out to Hegel that reality did not always behave according to the laws of his system and should therefore remain incomprehensible, he replied laconically, "That's too bad for reality." Hegel's system was meant to reconstruct all of world history as a steadily advancing insight that comes to completion in his own thinking. And this is not accidental but historically necessary, inescapable.

It's not that Kierkegaard wanted to think against time, against the course of history. He was a modern thinker, but with a keen eye for the excesses of modernity. The rational, instrumental, objective, and systematic nature of modern thought was, in his view, inadequate, lacking a certain dimension. It is this dimension that he will explore. That makes him a true philosopher: he does not start to think from the answer, viz. God or the Bible. His search is even risky, because he leaves out typically modern legitimations. He does not legitimize the religious from ethics but rather the other way around. Not that Kierkegaard would be a fundamentalist; with him, ethics cannot be derived from a dogma. But in faith, a call resonates that is of a different, higher register than the rules of any culturally and historically determined moral system.[2]

Perhaps Kierkegaard's best-known statement is that while life can be understood backwards, it can only be lived forwards. Hegel's theoretical reconstruction is at odds with life and is therefore a sterile treatise on alienation that itself installs the supreme form of alienation. This is reminiscent of an existentialist paraphrase of Marx's already quoted eleventh thesis on Feuerbach: "Philosophers have only interpreted the world differently; it comes down to changing it." A person is not born a Christian and therefore does not get there by looking back. The conversion, the turning to Christ, requires a leap forward. This leap will become a central term in Kierkegaard's thinking.

Existence and Subjectivity

In all the manuals we find Kierkegaard's well-known three stages of life: the aesthetic, the ethical, and the religious. Here the last stage is particularly important, but to get to it we must also discuss the first two. I will not—and simply cannot—turn Kierkegaard into a pure ethicist, though it has been done. Kierkegaard's ideas about both first stages are fairly complex because, as mentioned, he writes from different positions, under multiple pseudonyms.

A person is not born a devout Christian. This insight alone allows Kierkegaard to be classified as an existentialist. The full meaning of existence does not precede that existence as an essence, as an abstract truth, as an ahistorical cause, as an original blueprint or definition. As with Kant, nature is the terrain of necessity and causality. Man is born into the immediacy of things, but this does not yet determine his whole existence, as with animals. The latter are equipped with instinct, an unfailing device that meticulously determines that immediacy. Without any reflection, a puma knows perfectly what to do with a deer, a fly how to react to movement, an arboreal bird how to seduce a female with a dance and some colorful fluff. No lion in the history of nature has ever had the idea of building a colorful entrance for a female, or, perhaps inspired by a befriended giraffe, of trying a diet of succulent tree leaves. The relationship to the environment, to the biotope, is completely fixed. Instinct leaves nothing open to evaluation, negotiation, or interpretation. In the wild, to interpret means to get killed. Even if no evidence of this exists, it seems to me extremely unlikely that this same lion, or by extension any animal, has ever pondered the meaning of existence.

An animal that is devoted to such questions is not likely to live a long and healthy life in the wild.

Initially, it is the same with humans. At birth, an infant is only concerned with what presents itself and it classifies these stimuli as either pleasurable or unpleasant, according to Freud's pleasure principle. This thoughtlessness is not a mere developmental psychological stage that a human being necessarily works through. In a philosophical sense, it is an existential stance that can be held for life. Kierkegaard calls this the aesthetic stage in existence. Most people never leave this stage. And it remains a moot question whether it is possible to abandon this stage completely.

At this stage, life cannot be lived beyond the self and beyond attachment to ephemeral things, to the world. This life is lived in an atmosphere of fleeting enjoyment. Not that there is anything wrong with enjoyment, but if this enjoyable existence only has the self, the *ego*, as its goal, if one only uses enjoyment for oneself, then even the greatest aesthete cannot escape boredom and despair. This is a philosophical interpretation of boredom, of a superficiality that never escapes itself, never transcends itself. This stage revolves around an externality without inwardness, without distance that allows for reflection and evaluation, where the self can only be experienced as emptiness. The self does not even have a "self," for that already presupposes an essential relationship, which is not present at this stage, neither with itself, nor with the other, nor with the world. There is nothing that mediates between the self and the non-self; the self exists purely in immediateness. At this stage, a person continues to search relentlessly, but also pointlessly, for an illusory filling of the void.

Note that this has nothing to do with intelligence or culture. The greatest intellectual, be it an academic, a man of letters, or a visual artist, can remain stuck in the aesthetic stage. It is perfectly possible to focus scientific research or art only on yourself, on your *ego*. It is by no means a trivial matter to deal with that *ego*. From superficial pseudo-spiritual do-books on "Ego-Dropping in 3 Steps" to the most authentic mystical attempts to leave the "I" behind, a first step in any case is to confront oneself in the paradoxical emptiness of a full ego.

This confrontation can—need not—lead to a first movement of conversion or repentance. This is a matter of recognizing despair, of no longer masking the emptiness behind yet another attempt to find a self in enjoyment—which is something else than to enjoy something as a self. This repentance, which actually already has the structure of a leap, leads a person into what Kierkegaard calls the ethical stage. Here the self assumes itself *as* a self. It relates to a past and a future in a more substantial way than surfing from one superficial satisfaction to another—that is, the passage of time without this ever becoming personal history. Any responsibility only becomes possible in a personal history, the history of a self that vouches for that self.

Kierkegaard finds further transcendence of the purely aesthetic in the common good, in the prevailing mores and customs, in what "belongs" within society and which norms apply, implicitly or otherwise, in society. This still does not guarantee "the good." Human sacrifice can hardly be validated as morally good and yet this is also a social form in which self-interest is subordinated to the "common good." Kierkegaard gives the example of Agamemnon sacrificing his daughter Iphigenia to Artemis so that the latter would allow his war fleet to sail out under a favorable wind. Agamemnon's troops would not accept any sentimentalism to interfere with war, so a father has no choice but to sacrifice his daughter to the gods, on behalf of politics.

The ethical stage is still not quite adequate for several reasons. People may do the right thing for sentimental reasons or under external pressure. Someone sees a picture in the media, photoshopped or not, of a hungry child and immediately (the term "immediately" seeks to connect the ethical stage to the aesthetic) donates $10. Peer pressure makes a student decide to "do charity"—or worse: he or she gets school credits for it. Someone reads a rather smoothly written manifesto on solidarity, does not immediately (that term, again) find a valid counter-argument, and owes it to his own demand of consistency to "do something" in order not to end up in moral-cognitive dissonance. And so on. Kierkegaard makes it hard to find a respectable moral motive. Not that he has anything against what afterwards has come to be called a "person of good will."[3] The ethical stage is the stage in which the other enters my existence in a more or less coercive manner. Yet the relationship between the other and myself is not yet "pure." From whatever motive someone acts, the self still remains the starting point of that action. Any action is still the result of "calculation." The good is weighed up, the "goodness" of the relationship between me and the other is still conditional. An explanation can still be provided for every good deed. A good deed can still be justified by means of (psychological, sociological, economic, political, etc.) arguments. We will see further on how Levinas brings ethics and religion closer together.

The ethical stage is already marked by a certain decentration of the self but the focus is not yet completely on the Other—it remains stuck halfway, you could say. The relationship, in all its manageability, remains normative at this stage. The good has something contractual here. The word "contract" has the same Latin root as "contraction." Two parties are *brought together* and articulate to each other their respective moral supply and demand. Then a balance is articulated whereby both positions are drawn together into one shared moral position that then becomes the "good."

But what about Father Damien? Or Mother Teresa? What they did is beyond any scientific or even broadly rational explanation. A Dutch researcher who nevertheless attempted to find such an explanation came to the conclusion that what drives these people is ultimately nothing more than a strategy to come to terms with themselves and to cope with their own traumas. That strategy was then disrespectfully christened "Mother Teresa Syndrome." This can at least be called an example of "scientific reductionism."[4] It shows an unwillingness to accept as meaningful something that lies beyond the limited reach of human science.

The moral accountancy of these saints contains a vanishing point that cannot be closed off. Nothing returns from where it is received; it disappears into the social invisible. What human category are we talking about here? Kierkegaard will not blame me if I interpret those invisibles biblically. They are the poor—not necessarily or only in an economic sense. They are the almost-nothing in an "ontological" sense, those who barely and merely exist but do not "possess" any category of their own. They can indeed be united in terms such as "extremely poor," "leprous," and the like, but these are exclusive terms, terms that serve to justify social exclusion. They are not positive categories as, for example, "servant" versus "worker" or "self-employed" versus "employee." An employee and a self-employed person have a status and as such enjoy administrative recognition; they are married or not, are resident and insured, are paid and taxed, carry one or more nationalities, etc. Whether the "almost-nothing" is married or not, lives in a box or not, is irrelevant. Today we do not have to look far either. The homeless refugee now takes this place. I will elaborate on this with Levinas and Derrida, who have specifically addressed the otherness of the other.

Now let us go back to the ethical stage. Initially, Kierkegaard is sympathetic to Kant where the latter placed God beyond the reach of theoretical, scientific reason. However, he no longer follows Kant where the latter recuperates God along moral lines. For in this way ethics and not faith is placed at the center, which again threatens to place theory above praxis. Faith is then inserted into pure practical, moral reason rather than into pure theoretical, scientific reason.

For Kierkegaard, the full sense of existence lies beyond any scientific and moral (in the narrow sense) reach. In the end, (psycho-)social givenness is not the only or even highest criterion for ethics; God is. This is what I understand from Christ's gruff response to the "rich young man" (see note 3). A sympathetic fellow comes to ask him what "good" he must do to bring heaven on earth. Christ grumbles, "Why do you ask me about what is good? There is one alone who is good." This is pure genius. No ethics, no moral standard or law exhausts "good." No worldly law—political, moral, economic . . .—can be identified as ultimately and wholly good. Hence Kierkegaard gives the good a "divine" status—as both Plato and Kant did, though each in their own way. After all, in the monotheistic tradition, "divine" means perhaps *in*, but certainly not *of* the world.[5]

Kierkegaard draws an original comparison with the sacrifice of Isaac by his father Abraham (Gen 22:1–13). Here the father does not bend to the demands of the community, like Agamemnon, but obeys God. More seriously: what he does goes against community ethics. Such a deed can in no way be legitimized on the basis of common shared norms and values. YHWH asks Abraham, by way of a test, to show that he realizes to whom he owes his happiness in the shape of a descendant. Is Abraham willing to return the gift to its giver and rightful owner? Or does Abraham feel that Isaac belongs to him as property, recognized by the community and its laws as his son? Just as Agamemnon knows that he cannot ignore prevailing morality, so Abraham realizes that he cannot ignore YHWH.[6]

We are not dealing with religious fanatics here. Kierkegaard tries to identify the ultimate motive of morality: either the singularity that goes by the name "God," or community. For Kierkegaard it is God, no doubt about it. Only, as the example shows, God is by no means an extension of community. God is not a sociologically (and therefore theoretically) derivable concept. There is no moral continuum that leads from community to God. What is needed here, says Kierkegaard, is a "leap." Not a leap out of ethics but the risky adventure of an ethical consideration that is not entirely determined by any prevailing ethical norm. Kierkegaard calls it a leap because no rational-argumentative continuity can be invoked. There is no reasoning that leads from ethics to religion—at least not to "full," authentic religion (see below). As it is, reasoning rather stands in the way of the leap.

This leap is a highly subjective choice that does not result in another objective state but leaves the opposition between subject and object behind and surrenders to the imitation of Christ. Kierkegaard mistrusts objectivity—a bit like Levinas, as we shall see. For Kierkegaard, the leap is the only authentic act through which a person takes on full life in full responsibility for the self and the world, free of alienation.

Here is this alienation again. It lives on in Heidegger's "das Man" and in Sartre's "mauvaise foi." With Kierkegaard, the point is that every person always has the choice between either claiming their own subjectivity or surrendering to objectivity. The alienated person joins an impersonal discourse that they share with many, without any risk.[7] Kierkegaard called this the main immorality of his time. He blamed it on the rise of great systems like Hegel's and powerful institutions like the modern church and ditto state. These systems and institutions represent objectivity—which for Kierkegaard has little to do with the truth claims of science. Not that science goes unstained with Kierkegaard. Take even theology: there too, faith has become a matter of knowledge and precepts, of theory and morality, which can be blindly applied. True life, however, is a matter not of information, but of transformation. Transformation is the work of faith.

Leap of Faith

People should actually take a careful step back—I borrow this term from Heidegger—before diving headlong forward into a social dogmatism that directs their morality, their lives, and their faith. They should guard against the trap, against the illusion, against the aptly veiled ruse of objectivity. This is precisely why Kierkegaard does not elaborate a system that he then imposes on the world, but rather advocates the most unsystematic, subjective maneuver: a leap.

Reculer pour mieux sauter. The step back, as a prelude to the leap, confronts a person with their own existence, with their deepest motivation where speculation and doctrine, fashion and peer pressure, rashness and docility cannot reach. This is about opening your "own" stance where logic has nothing to declare. Such a subjective position can be neither confirmed nor refuted by reason or cognition. Furthermore, this belief has neither aesthetic nor moral legitimacy.

This leap is, again, very Biblical. The famous Sermon on the Mount begins: Jesus takes some disciples up the mountain with him. This is not a tourist venture. It literally means taking on another point of view, opening up another world that is not translatable into or derivable from the "ordinary" world of the plain. So there is indeed a discontinuity, aptly represented by the notion of the "leap." The leap does not allow for a gradual transition between superficiality and profundity.

Some, such as "weak thinkers" John Caputo, Richard Rorty, and Gianni Vattimo, discern a dangerous element in the leap, as if it were a leap out of this world into another one to which only the initiated, those who are already familiar with the stakes of the leap, have access. In that other world everyone is saved and purified from the laws and ways of the world. However, this is a blatant misunderstanding. For Kierkegaard it is not a leap out of the world but a leap away from the complacency and self-explanation of the world into a perspective of and on the world that cannot be derived from that. The misinterpretation still hinges on a philosophy that "weak thought" wants to leave behind. That philosophy still sees the world from a Cartesian perspective, as a thing alongside which we can conceive of a second thing with the possibility of communication between these two.

Vattimo fears that the leap represents a desire to deny or escape the radical finitude of existence, of the world, of humanity, and of history. But for Kierkegaard, the leap means precisely the recognition of that finitude, a finitude that is not even redeemed from its tragedy by an absurd invasion of infinity. This is, of course, an overt criticism of Hegelian Feuerbach. The leap is the reasonless, groundless acceptance of that finitude and not the realization of the infinity of humanity.

The leap has a salutary effect, but not through any superficial causality or any form of white magic. Indeed, the leap only appears as meaningful at the moment that man is seized by fear. This fear, which is also penetratingly described by philosophers such as Heidegger and Sartre, arises from the awareness of the inadequacy of an aesthetic and ethical existence. You can remain stuck in fear, once you are being confronted with it, and keep falling back on aesthetic and ethical recipes. However, this dynamic is at most capable of pushing fear forward and temporarily suspending it. You can prefer to wait for *kairos*—a term in Paul's narrowest sense meaning: the right moment. That moment is the leap where finitude and infinity intersect without canceling each other out. *Kairos* here means nothing more than that the leap does not involve a plan, as in "Monday at 8 AM, I'm going to jump into faith."

I would read the leap, as a discontinuity, in a different register. I prefer to recognize it in the spirit of Christ's statement in the Sermon on the Mount in which he claims not to change the prevailing Law, not even by removing a jot, but to redirect its whole meaning (Mt 5:17). The leap, then, is not between two worlds as things, but between two worlds as perspectives. After all, the Law is Hebrew actuality, the world of Judah. Christianity is the world of charity, the possibility of a heaven. In both worlds, things mean something different each time.[8]

Yet philosophically there is a sting to this leap. After all, does not the leap into faith itself testify to an already existing faith? When God instructed Abraham to leave all his goods and chattels behind to make his way with his family and household into the desert to a land God had promised him, did Abraham ask God for a guarantee, a travel brochure perhaps? No, he went. When the angel visited Mary, the second great paradigm of faith, and announced that she would give birth to God's son, did she first ask for a report by a gynecologist? No, she said "yes," *fiat*. That trust, that surrender, is that not itself already a form of faith?

Perhaps that is why Kierkegaard distinguishes two forms of religiosity. A first form has something of the experience of an inadequacy, a confrontation with an infinity, an eternity, an absoluteness that cannot be extracted from the world or from my own existence in itself. This existential experience is marked by anxiety (or *angst*) and guilt—an objectless, metaphysical anxiety and an irredeemable guilt that is only bearable through God's forgiveness. As for the former, anxiety is different from fear, which is always fear-of. There is a reasonable and an unreasonable form of fear. Fear of lightning during a thunderstorm in an open field is a reasonable fear. Fear of spiders is unreasonable (except in areas with venomous spiders) and belongs in the mildly psychopathological register. Anxiety has no object and therefore cannot be divided into reasonable or unreasonable. Further, regarding the latter, only God can forgive me the guilt, no one else. This is not surprising, since all other potential forgivers are themselves always in debt.

This form of religiosity has not yet taken the leap. That form is still totally attached to the world, albeit as a flip side. The experience of inadequacy mirrors the experience of emptiness that haunts the aesthetic and ethical stage. This religiosity is still an extension of ethics, and can still be justified by deeds, thus from human initiative. For the second form this legitimation no longer applies. This form is the "true" religiosity, with all its absurdity.[9] Only here, at this stage, does Christianity become completely free of mediation. It is not (any longer) represented in a doctrine, a teaching, a theory, a moral recipe, or a political system, but in praxis, in life, and in a moral existence.

Here we also find another reason why the option for God cannot be an extension of the option for the community: the latter presupposes identification with that community, an attunement to the "general will" and to the prevailing morals and customs, to an observance of the customs, written or otherwise. The option for God, on the other hand, is a highly personal, subjective one—and for that reason alone more valuable in Kierkegaard's eyes, those of the right-minded existentialist. Here we stumble upon Kierkegaard's whole religious knot. Without abolishing prevailing ethics, he argues that the relationship with God should be the ultimate moral reference point, and not the other way around. We should not measure or motivate our religious experience by moral criteria, but again the other way around. We should let Christ motivate our moral actions. This paradox is also what the church comes up against. For the church is also a community, a community that according to Kierkegaard threatens to stand in the way of a personal relationship with God.[10]

This shows the philosophical rather than theological character of Kierkegaard's thinking. After all, it is not at all alien to the Lutheran thinking in which Kierkegaard was raised to receive the truth of personal faith in terms of grace and in the meantime to engage oneself into a local congregation on all levels. Kierkegaard almost turns the whole thing upside down by denouncing the structure and praxis of the congregation and making faith a matter of personal choice.

Even as a philosopher, Kierkegaard remains true to at least three *solas*.[11] Protestantism teaches that salvation is achieved only by faith, grace, and the Bible. It is not through immersion in the world, to the point of politics, art, and science, that one may expect any salvation (the aesthetic stage); that comes only from God-given grace. Only grace can calm the hunting and raving of the world. Desire will never have enough of the world. Nor can one obtain that grace by doing good works in the community (the ethical stage). Kierkegaard criticizes the church (in Copenhagen, throughout Denmark) for falling back too easily on both stages. The church only seeks to preserve power and wealth (aesthetic), and preaches charity without practicing it herself (ethical). The church became too much of a substantial entity and declared itself indispensable to the mechanics of salvation. It had become, in Kierkegaard's eyes, Protestantism in a chasuble.

Further criticism states that faith, or at least the question of faith, had become too theoretical. Academics increasingly tried to rationalize faith, which completely coincided with its moralization—this is what Nietzsche holds against Christianity. Augustine and even Paul spoke of Christianity as a "stumbling block" (*skandalon* in Greek) and not a smoothly reasoned discourse with a transparent and conclusive salvation economy. According to Kierkegaard, faith does not tolerate rational, logical explanation. This is still something quite different from the blunt identification of faith with irrationality. Faith is not unreasonable; it merely leaves behind aesthetic and ethical logic without condemning and rejecting pleasure and the good.

The Bible contains a logic that is not the logic of the world. Not that we encounter koans there, but some of Christ's words nevertheless sometimes raise eyebrows, and not just in indignation. Their logic is that of inspiration without rational justification. It is impossible to theorize the Bible, to present the Good Message as a theory.[12] Nor does that message need any other message beside it to work.

Personalism

Does the leap still have the same radical meaning in a postmodern world where the systems to leap away from are gradually becoming exhausted? The liberal and social determinations of society today are losing their stringent and clear ideological impact. We should turn to personalism, which we encountered briefly with Feuerbach. In his case I referred to personalism in connection with the modern neglect of fraternity. Here we are concerned with another aspect of it, namely the recognition of the undeniable philosophical (religious?) nature of the person, and therefore necessarily also of society. Political neutrality is not an option here. Every person is essentially philosophical and this determines where this person stands on social issues.

Kierkegaard would be ambivalent about this. He would certainly not entrust the philosophical direction of society to politics or to the church. Philosophy of life is and remains a subjective choice, a personal conversion. Once that choice is made, the person involved would consider it unjust if the effect of this conversion did not filter through to the concrete society. Kierkegaard was not a desert father.

The immersion of the church in the world was a thorn in Kierkegaard's side. In this sense, he would be sympathetic to secularization, at least according to the interpretation in which everyday life detaches itself from the impact of the church as a social and political institution. Again, Kierkegaard's philosophical interest lies, among other things, in his relentless criticism of any (academic, social, religious . . .) complacency, which makes his existentialism difficult to reconcile with that of Sartre—whom we will meet later on in this book.

If true existence must be a reflection of Christ and image of God instead of a theory, what about all those books Kierkegaard wrote? After all, surely the life of faith cannot be arranged from books—unless it were the Bible: *sola Scriptura*, remember. Yet every true Christian is under the obligation to, among other things and in accordance with the spiritual works of mercy, instruct the ignorant, counsel the doubtful, and admonish the sinners.

This Kierkegaard did without any compromise. Until after his death, he caused theological controversy within the Church. He refused his brother Peter, a bishop, at his deathbed and he resolutely threw out the pastor who brought him bread and wine. As Kierkegaard told his family, there is no correct solution to the question of whether he should be buried inside or outside the church.

4

Dead

Nietzsche

You will barely believe this, but I introduce Nietzsche, the author of *The Antichrist*, as the son of a preacher. He even took up the study of theology, as well as classical philology, but then left the former along with the Christian faith that used to go with it. In barely twenty years, he composed an oeuvre that irreversibly recalibrated Western thought. He paid for it with his mental faculties.

He retired at the age of thirty-five because of his poor health. He traded a cloudy and misty Basel for southern, warmer, drier places where he walked, thought, and wrote. To Nietzsche, walking was thinking; he managed to write down his thoughts only between periods of physical discomfort. His literary productivity soared and it began to rain revolutionary insights. His Zarathustra descended from the mountains, bringing with it overman, will to power, and eternal return of the same. And, of course, the madman who accuses us, modern atheists, of having killed God. Then Nietzsche sank into an enigmatic state of confusion, howling and dancing between periods of absolute silence, for more than eleven years, and then died.

Few philosophical formulas have been so often quoted and at the same time so persistently misunderstood as "God is dead." Nietzsche seemingly hesitates himself to take such a weighty announcement into his own mouth; he quotes a "madman." In a frankly brilliant philosophical as well as beautiful literary fragment (§125 from *The Gay Science*) Nietzsche introduces us to this madman with his mind-blowing message. The text itself is too wonderful not to be included here.[1] It is bursting with the most powerful metaphors in the history of thought.

Have you not heard of that madman who lit a lantern in the bright morning hours, ran to the market place, and cried incessantly: "I seek God! I seek God!"—As many of those who did not believe in God were standing around just then, he provoked much laughter. "Has he got lost?" asked one. "Did he lose his way like a child?" asked another. "Or is he hiding? Is he afraid of us? Has he gone on a voyage? emigrated?"—Thus they yelled and laughed.

The madman jumped into their midst and pierced them with his eyes. "Whither is God?" he cried; "I will tell you. *We have killed him*—you and I. All of us are his murderers. But how did we do this? How could we drink up the sea? Who gave us the sponge to wipe away the entire horizon? What were we doing when we unchained this earth from its sun? Whither is it moving now? Whither are we moving? Away from all suns? Are we not plunging continually? Backward, sideward, forward, in all directions? Is there still any up or down? Are we not straying, as through an infinite nothing? Do we not feel the breath of empty space? Has it not become colder? Is not night continually closing in on us? Do we not need to light lanterns in the morning? Do we hear nothing as yet of the noise of the gravediggers who are burying God? Do we smell nothing as yet of the divine decomposition? Gods, too, decompose. God is dead. God remains dead. And we have killed him."

"How shall we comfort ourselves, the murderers of all murderers? What was holiest and mightiest of all that the world has yet owned has bled to death under our knives: who will wipe this blood off us? What water is there for us to clean ourselves? What festivals of atonement, what sacred games shall we have to invent? Is not the greatness of this deed too great for us? Must we ourselves not become gods simply to appear worthy of it? There has never been a greater deed; and whoever is born after us—for the sake of this deed he will belong to a higher history than all history hitherto."

Here the madman fell silent and looked again at his listeners; and they, too, were silent and stared at him in astonishment. At last he threw his lantern on the ground, and it broke into pieces and went out. "I have come too early," he said then; "my time is not yet. This tremendous event is still on its way, still wandering; it has not yet reached the ears of men. Lightning and thunder require time; the light of the stars requires time; deeds, though done, still require time to be seen and heard. This deed is still more distant from them than most distant stars—*and yet they have done it themselves.*"

It has been related further that on the same day the madman forced his way into several churches and there struck up his *requiem aeternam deo*. Led out and called to account, he is said always to have replied nothing but: "What after all are these churches now if they are not the tombs and sepulchers of God?"[2]

God is dead and we killed him. What does Nietzsche mean? Which God is dead? How did we kill him? Why? Why exactly must a madman explain to non-believers that God is dead? And why do these stand around laughing at him rather foolishly? Apparently the modern non-believers, the self-proclaimed atheists, have not understood what is going on.

An exegesis of Nietzsche's writings is not easy. Like Kierkegaard, he uses pseudonyms and characters to make a point. There is the madman from the aforementioned fragment; there is Zarathustra from the famous *Also sprach Zarathustra*; and one of his very last texts, a letter, he signed as "Dionysos versus the Crucified." If Nietzsche knew how many hours of study and discussion, how many pages have been spent on this signature . . .[3]

He also uses different styles. Until then, German philosophy had confined itself to a bone dry form of argumentation, with unwavering logical consistency and merciless conceptual transparency. Nietzsche was firmly convinced that, however brilliant, this style did not fit actuality, thought, and truth. These are not logical and are anything but transparent.

Initially, as is often the case with great and original thinkers, philosophy found it difficult to place Nietzsche. He was classified as a poet, classicist, rebel, devil, proto-Nazi, psychopath, artist . . . although most knew him only by his iconic mustache. It was not until shortly after his death that he was recognized, especially by Heidegger, as a philosopher in his own right.

Nietzsche was a prophet. He foresaw a crisis of Western Christian culture—a prediction that came true a century later. What we now call the postmodern experience of life belongs to the experience of the death of God. The postmodern, somewhat noncommittal "swooning" is aptly expressed by Nietzsche above. Anyone who "shares" the postmodern sense of things is burdened by the death of God and at the same time indebted to the death of God. Faithful or faithless, Christian or atheist, all this has hardly anything to do with this experience.

With his most famous statement, Nietzsche incurred the wrath of all faithful and of the entire church. However, there was little reason to do so. To begin with, the statement "God is dead" is not new. Luther and Hegel, among others, had already proclaimed this event in their own name. Furthermore, it remains to be seen which God is actually the subject of this philosophical autopsy. Over and over again Nietzsche denounces the way in which Western thought keeps referring to an "external reference." Over and over again philosophy tumbles into the trap of installing an anchorage outside thought, outside the world, with which philosophy can dock itself without any "risk." Since that anchorage lies outside thought, it cannot be refuted. Nietzsche repeatedly lifts those anchors to set thinking free. The heaviest anchor of all is called "God."

Hammer

Nietzsche called himself "the philosopher with the hammer." He just went on tapping every solid concept, like a physician. None of these certainties remained unscathed. Not because Nietzsche smashed them to pieces, no, because they were so hollow that he only had to tap them once and they fell apart. The hammer did not serve to destroy everything, as people who love certainties accuse Nietzsche. It was a tool to diagnose culture, philosophy, morals, religion.

Nietzsche's nihilism has nothing to do with "an-nihil-ation." After all, any destruction on human initiative always happens in the name of something "other," of yet another "external reference," of yet another god that then overrules all previous ones. He wanted to show that the systems that modernity had erected mainly consist of "thin air." The loud terms that are brandished in politics, in ethics, in science, in metaphysics . . . they are all hollow, empty—no matter how grandiose. No matter how they are presented as full of meaning and even irrefutably true, in the end they always turn out to be constructions that must serve some interest. Here we already touch the question concerning the will to power.

Take the Christian love of truth. Christian—and for that matter, ancient Greek—metaphysics placed this "truth drive" at the top of the list of passions. It became the most valuable, worthy, true passion of all. The other drives were called sensual drives and as such were considered inferior, less reliable in the light of the plan of creation in which reason was inscribed as exclusively human. But this passion for truth eventually culminated in science—psychology, for example—which reveals the "truth *about* drives" and saw no reason for the promotion of the "truth drive" or reason. Drifts are drifts, period. Their Christian-metaphysical indexation is arbitrary, just one of many possible options. There is no objective universal order, no external reference that legitimizes this particular one—or any other—option. That this option for a "monopoly of reason" presents itself as obvious, as a natural law, and therefore by no means negotiable, is what Nietzsche reproaches Christian morality. It pretends that this arrangement is valid simply because God wanted it that way. Ultimately this is only due to the Christian urge to install a "true" moral system, a hierarchy of values to the benefit of the weak. I shall deploy this "slave morality" below.

Nietzsche had no intention to develop a new morality, to invent new values. He wanted to dismantle its sacred order, this "hierarchy."[4] He wanted to "revalue" the values. After all, there is no pre-given order. Will to power, that is what it is all about.[5] Truth, Nietzsche said, is only true when we want it to be true. We pretend to collect truth from a reliable source, preferably an external reference, but this is just a rhetorical trick. Nietzsche called Christianity "Platonism of the people." In fact, he read Plato through a Christian lens. Christian metaphysics redirected Plato as thinker of the "upper world." If Nietzsche can blame Christianity for anything, it is turning Plato into a dualist. What a commotion there would be if Plato could make use of his "Right of Reply" to both Christianity and Nietzsche.

Heaven

Everyone is familiar with that painting by Raphael, *The School of Athens*. At the very center of that gathering of figures who represent just about the entire ancient intellectual world, Plato and Aristotle stand fraternally side by side. Plato points upward, to the Forms, and Aristotle downward, to the Things, as if they have lost their way philosophically, like a bickering couple at a crossroad. In fact, those two fingers opened the whole philosophical field for the following 2,500 years, the whole debate concerning truth as the relation between thought and being—in short, metaphysics.

Yet the painting offers a somewhat unsubtle picture. Aristotle admittedly was a philosopher with a keen interest in science and logic, but in his forwardness he installs at the core of his thinking that infamous Unmoved

Mover. This is a principle so unaffected and lofty that he would have to lift his arm out of the socket to point at it. It is that for the sake of which everything exists. Plato, on the other hand, is allowed to lower his arm a little. This world of Forms, a metaphor like any other, should not be taken too literally. The grateful amazement with which Plato contemplates the experience of understanding does not lead to the discovery of an entirely different world. It is true that Plato did not want to "lock" this insight up inside things, which is what Aristotle did try to do. According to Plato, the fact that things can be understood cannot be attributed to the things themselves. After all, we are not thinking "in" those things. It is as if their intelligibility hovers "above the things," so that we can reach them with our thinking. When we think, we do not have direct access to things, but we do have access to their intelligibility, to their understanding. This intelligibility does not belong entirely to things themselves, nor is it entirely separate from them. But to read in Plato another world alongside, even above, this one, on the basis of this, is going too far.[6]

Nietzsche settled with this dualistic reading of Christian metaphysics in another brilliant fragment, particularly the fourth chapter of his *Twilight of the Idols*. Here he races through Western philosophy in six stages.

> 1. The true world, attainable for the wise, the devout, the virtuous—they live in it, *they are it.*
>
> (Oldest form of the idea, relatively clever, simple, convincing. Paraphrase of the assertion, "I, Plato, *am* the truth.")
>
> 2. The true world, unattainable for now, but promised to the wise, the devout, the virtuous ("to the sinner who does penance").
>
> (Progress of the idea: it becomes more refined, more devious, more mystifying—*it becomes woman*, it becomes Christian . . .)
>
> 3. The true world, unattainable, unprovable, unpromisable, but a consolation, an obligation, an imperative, merely by virtue of being thought.
>
> (The old sun basically, but glimpsed through fog and skepticism; the idea become sublime, pallid, Nordic, Königsbergian.)

4. The true world—unattainable? In any case, unattained. And if it is unattained, it is also *unknown*. And hence it is not consoling, redeeming, or obligating either; to what could something unknown obligate us? . . .

(Gray dawn. First yawnings of reason. Rooster's crow of positivism.)

5. The "true world"—an idea with no use anymore, no longer even obligating—an idea become useless, superfluous, *hence* a refuted idea: let's do away with it!

(Bright day; breakfast; return of *bon sens* [good sense] and cheerfulness; Plato blushes; pandemonium of all free spirits.)

6. We have done away with the true world: what world is left over? The apparent one, maybe? . . . But no! *Along with the true world, we have also done away with the apparent!*

(Midday; moment of the shortest shadow; end of the longest error; high point of humanity; INCIPIT ZARATHUSTRA.)[7]

Nietzsche follows the erosion or decay of the Platonic, dualistic inheritance in philosophy and turns it completely upside down. It is not about the God himself, who is dead, but about his appropriate abode, heaven, that "other" world that is more true than this one, from which this world can extract its true meaning. The title of this clenched text reads: "Why the 'True World' Finally Became a Fiction." The idea of a "true" world, as opposed to a make-believe world, has been discarded, along with the idea of God. There is no longer a true world on the one hand and an untrue world on the other; there is only world.

In order for this world—or any other—to be declared "true," a guarantee outside this world, an "external reference," is needed. So even the promotion of "this" world to "true" world brings in that "other, even more true" world again through the back door. This has always been the great paradox of any model of immanence: the guarantee of that immanence always seems to be outsourced to an agency outside this world. Relativism, for example, presupposes a position outside thought that establishes and imposes equivalence on every thought, theory, model, etc. But that position has now been vacated, eliminated. The position outside thought remains empty, abandoned. God in heaven is dead, the Supreme Being in the Other World has left the metaphysical building.

We must take great care not to fall into the trap of calling this world the "true" one anymore. This is what science does. According to Auguste Comte, history, i.e., progress, has evacuated thinking step by step from that "higher" world full of gods and principles, in order to be able to devote itself at last to the world of facts, this world. But—and here science fanatics start yowling—Nietzsche distrusts even the facts. A famous excerpt from his *Posthumous Fragments* reads, "There are no facts, only interpretations . . ." Usually, however, the sequel is omitted: ". . . and this too is an interpretation."[8] The latter shows how meticulous and consistent Nietzsche is. A proposition like, for example, "Science is the best, even the only access to truth" is itself not scientific. It is an article of faith. Nietzsche doesn't make that mistake to confuse faith with fact. To bluntly contend that there are no facts, only interpretations, would in turn be a statement of fact based on an act of faith. It would amount to claiming that the hermeneutic world is the only true one. The death of God, the "end" of the "true" world, overman and the like, do not belong to the register of fact, but to that of interpretation. This is a philosophical experience, an intuition that does not provide access to a super-worldly and super-temporal truth, but that grasps actuality, history as happening.

This is, of course, a very complex idea. Is there anything more difficult than grasping "our own time"? Where must I stand to measure (from outside?) actuality, to which I belong? Nietzsche perceives the world from within. In his own words: in him something has become conscious that marks the very essence of his time. Of course, he must then renounce any objectivity. For the one philosopher this is an unconditional requirement, for yet another it is a dangerous illusion.

The Death of God, Then

In the Middle Ages, the jester assumed an important social role. He had to present the truth to the king, but in such a way that it seemed as if the king had discovered this truth himself. Preferably with a quip that only the knowledgeable bystander could grasp. The oldest known jester is perhaps Diogenes of Sinope (yes, the one who slept in an amphora), who, against all cultural conventions, went to the marketplace bare-chested in search of "a human being," just as Nietzsche's madman goes in search of God. A message like "God is dead" cannot be pronounced by a recognized intellectual who owes his social status to the system he declares obsolete. Indeed, such a message can only come from a barrel outside the city walls, or from a madman who lights lamps in broad daylight because the sun is unable to make people see clearly what is going on.

The God who has died is not a God who does not exist, but a God who had once, as it were, "lived"—not in its biological sense but as in "lively imagination." It must therefore be a God who held a function, a distinct position in the order of the world. In God, humanity once found the meaning of things, the explanation of why they are as they are, and above all the unshakable prescriptions on what we should do and must not do. Nietzsche observes that this reference, against which there is no appeal, has become obsolete. Again, it is still not about a god who once actually existed, whose life was a plain fact, but about a being who was promoted to the top of creation and who derived from that position a well-defined function in thought. And now, this idea has lost its potency.

The world is losing its central coordination at every level: moral, political, historical, cognitive, etc. It is falling apart. The old grounds on which firm institutes can rest have become abysses. This is not the work of human beings; it is not as if a cultural-historical (political, scientific . . .) delegation has decided to withdraw its confidence in the CEO of World History. Modernity has analyzed the concept of God until nothing remained; it has used it all up and exhausted its possibilities. I refer to the Christian love of truth above, which led to scientific reason. It is that reason that unmasked God as a construct.[9]

The crumbling of the ground, to stay with that imagery, is only frustrating for those who cling to the ground, for those who cling to certainties—however hollow. For those who want to fly, the abyss is just the point of letting go of the ground and therefore offers liberation.[10] To formulate this a bit more philosophically: the abyss is not where meaning, certainty, and truth disappear, but where new meaning can appear. Nietzsche experiences this transition from loss to liberation as a promise, as a cure. Sick nihilism is the culture that grieves for what was lost; healthy nihilism, overman, is the culture that discerns an opportunity, a challenge without any guarantee but with a free gluttony for a future. Nietzsche does not offer new certainty or new footing. He does not replace God with Humanity or Reason or anything else. The series of substitutions ends here. The succession is concluded, the dynasty of Supreme Beings has come to an end. Those who cannot live with that end are not even wrong—for what does it matter anymore—but just plain unlucky.

Incidentally, one of the most fascinating contemporary implications of the death of God is that we no longer have good reasons to be radical atheists. The experience of the death of God does not answer the question of whether God actually exists or not, but declares such answers invalid and the question meaningless. Whoever claims that God does not exist has not heard the death of God. Neither has anyone who claims that he does exist.

Statements like "God exists" and "God does not exist" are stripped of their factuality and remain, at best, interpretations. Yes, it is precisely this theism as well as its "godless" version, atheism, that Nietzsche has declared invalid. He is not so much aiming his gun at God "himself," at the "holiest and most powerful thing the world has possessed so far." Nietzsche observes that the promotion, any elevation to "holiest and most powerful," has come to an end. The system, any system, that establishes a well-defined being as the One Supreme Being loses its truth claim. It does not matter whether that Supreme Being is called "God," or "Man," or "Reason," or "Will," or whatever. It is, taking up the metaphors in the text above, about every sea we sail, about every sun to which the earth is chained, about every horizon where we flee the empty, cold, and dark night—about every external reference.

So is this the God of faith? Yes and no. Such ambiguity is not unfamiliar to Nietzsche; on the contrary, it characterizes his thinking, trying to move away from the mechanics that sets one truth apart from all irredeemably false opinions. While Nietzsche regularly denigrates Christianity, charity, and the figure of Jesus, elsewhere he extols Christ in words of unmitigated praise. Nietzsche appreciated the way Christ went completely his own way, against all prevailing norms, paying for his conviction with his life. Nietzsche declared that the "God" who stands in the way of faith is dead. Dead is only the God who served the world, as Idea, Norm, and Principle.

Is Nietzsche an agnostic, then, when he denies the truth claim of all statements about the existence or non-existence of God? No. We would love nothing more than to know about God, but we have no access to God. If God exists at all, God deliberately outruns the reach of our reason; God conveniently avoids our thinking. To the exact extent that we have tried to bring God within that reach, we have killed him. So was that the true god or a false god? Again, wrong question, for what supreme god could decide on this? Here, Nietzsche appears as the liberator of true Christianity, and as the thinker who caught the West abusing the name (of) God.

Overman

The death of God gives birth to overman. Initially, out of the mouth of Zarathustra, overman was a figure, but this seems difficult to sustain. Overman is an epoch, a messianic future, an advent, not a psychological type or socio-political status. Overman is not a typology, nor a superman or Aryan or the richest or the strongest or the fastest. It is civilization, thinking beyond the primacy of humanity, beyond humanism. Humans may be the only thinking beings but they are not what it is all about. "Human" must not sound like a supreme category. A philosophy that starts from and ends with the human phenomenon runs aground. Thinking must start from the events of the world—of which humanity, by the way, is only an effect.

The greatness of overman lies in leaving behind all definitions that set the human phenomenon apart from all other things and on the grounds of which humans claim a special place in the world for themselves. A human being is indeed not a thing like any other being, but the difference between them is more subtle. Humanity, as the subject of the world, is a modern invention that sided with the birth of human sciences and is valid only within the realm of those sciences. In his famous speech *Words and Things*, Michel Foucault concluded that one day "human" will disappear as normative category.[11]

Any idea what overman looks like? A famous song from *Thus Spoke Zarathustra* may give us a key. Overman is like . . . a child. A child carries no historical, cultural, or moral ballast; it has not yet conformed to anything except its own pleasure; it experiences the whole world as a game, a challenge, an opportunity, an exploration field, an experimental laboratory. The child is, so to speak, the antithesis of the camel who continues to carry the burden of history and culture—Christianity and its morality, at which Nietzsche is so eager to aim his guns. When the lion comes, the first nihilism, the ballast is thrown off. The lions are those well-known demolishers: d'Holbach, Voltaire, Diderot, de La Mettrie, Laplace, Jean Paul (Richter) . . . They spare nothing, nothing remains the same. Precisely for this reason the child can appear in a new, bare world. It is useless to suspect any kind of dialectic behind this, a three-stage process. It is not about logically indexed periods or theories but about a puncturing or unmasking, even of the unmasking itself. For a child it does not matter much, whether mask or not; it is all play.

By no means does childlike overman constitute a culmination of history, like Hegel, Napoleon, and Beethoven all in one. No, overman appears on the world stage where and when all certainties have melted away and all truth has evaporated, where God is dead and the mourning period is over. That is ultimate and healthy nihilism. Man picks up his existence, without rancor or regret—what could a child regret? And does not Christ say that it is the spirit (as) of a child that receives and enters heaven? (Mk 13:15)

Those who are still acting out the lion after Nietzsche, like Richard Dawkins and all other apocalyptic horsemen, are actually stuffed lion heads on a nail in the wall. They even continue the dynasty of the camels, but in lion's clothing. Instead of accepting the death of God, they provide a substitute. Reason takes the place previously reserved for God.

Postmodern Antichrist and the Theological Virtues

Slavoj Žižek, the roaring *divo* of contemporary philosophy, as a rabid anti-Catholic, has nevertheless shown the intellectual courage to go in search of the added value of Christian heritage for Western culture.[12] The two reasons he cites for never forgetting Christianity are also the reasons why Nietzsche has such a problem with it. By concealing the antique, tragic sense of life behind a loveliness within which the weak, the moral plebs, the insipid, and the colorless can "flourish," Christianity has deprived the world of its grandeur in Nietzsche's eyes. To Žižek, Christianity has freed the world from a crushing fate and a stifling hierarchy. Indeed, Christianity has installed in the world—then the ruins of the Roman empire—two original points of view, namely one from which everyone can always shed the past and start anew (resurrection) and another from which everyone is fundamentally equal, regardless of their social, economic, political, academic, etc. status. In the midst of all possible, compelling positions in the ancient world, Christianity inserts these two redeeming zero points.

Nietzsche has nothing to do with these zero points. Equality, as an imposed system, is an abomination to him. An even greater abomination is the flight from time, from the world as becoming. He himself called this insight his deepest mystical experience. We came to know this as the "eternal return of the same." Nietzsche preaches the acceptance without regret that there is no purpose in history, no progress, no meaning. Life has no privileged moments in the sense of those Christian zero points. There may be happy and sad, ecstatic and serene episodes, but no points at which the meaning of life can be fundamentally overturned by setting the counter back to zero. No one escapes time, as the earliest and oldest law.

In this sense, one can call Nietzsche pre-Christian, an "ante-Christ." He has more appreciation for the tragic and heroic world of antiquity in which the strong—and this has nothing to do with eugenics here, just to be clear—accept their fate without complaint or regret and even take it up in order to build their lives on it. That, for him, is the true "religion." If *re-ligare* means (re)connecting, then for Nietzsche it is about the affirmation of one's fate. Christianity, in turn, opposes this attitude, as if it were an anti-religion.

The core of the anti-religious message of Christianity is found in the account of the so-called temple cleansing, the only place in the Gospel where Christ becomes truly enraged.[13] What infuriates Christ is the notion that a human being can make a deal with God through sacrifice. In the temple, people could change money into sacrificial money to buy sacrificial animals and then slaughter and sacrifice them there. With that sacrifice they were buying off specific favors from God. This is a salvation economy whose accounts are supposed to balance. Christ, however, proclaims a mercy that inflates all accountancy. The whole Passion must testify to a reasonless, incomprehensible, unconditional, unquantifiable, abundant love. Anyone who reads the Passion as an investment with eternal salvation as a dividend has not understood the Christian notion of salvation at all. In this sense, the death of the cross must be understood as a sacrifice in a real, non-religious sense, because nothing is asked for in return. The death on the cross is not the price to pay for a chair at the right hand of the Father.

Whereas Nietzsche sacrifices love to the world, Christianity, he says, does the opposite. He recognizes one great form of love and that is not charity, but *amor fati*. Embrace whatever happens to you. Make fate your friend. It befits one not to count on another, or the Other, to protect oneself against fate, against becoming and the mercilessness of time. In truthfulness, we stand face to face with our own history. Bear this history with dignity. According to Nietzsche, Christianity strives for a devaluation of that dignity. He expresses this in the transition from master morality to slave morality. Christianity is then the affirmation, not the cause, of the rise of slave morality. In fact, according to Nietzsche, ancient morality had already been deteriorating since Socrates and Euripides. In master morality, the noble, the heroic, and the courageous are the norm. Slave morality thrives on a massive and institutional concern for the weak, the mediocre, and the mean.

But perhaps Nietzsche makes a mistake in his reckoning with Christianity. Slave morality was a reaction to a lapsed, late antique form of master morality. But should we not understand Christian morality as quite different from antique morality? To the extent that ancient morality deploys a system of norms, Christianity emphatically does not. When the so-called rich young man asks Christ what good he should do, the latter gruffly replies that there is no such thing as the good. Only God, only divine love is good (Mt 19:16–17; Mk 10:17–18; Lk 18:18–19—see also chapter 3, note 3). Now, this love is not simply the decayed form of the master's values, or even of any form of any morality. Love cannot be understood in terms of the ancient noble, of gentlemen's morality. So Christian love cannot be identified with slave morality either. There is no continuity between ancient master morality and Christian *caritas*.

Of course, this does not mean that they cannot be understood together. Only, *amor fati* must then be understood to the letter, stripped of any antique connotations. In that case, it is about lovingly embracing what life has to offer. I can see Christian morality as a form of this, in which I have to bear and endure not only my own fate, but also that of another. Fate is then no longer exclusively a matter for the individual.

Suppose we contrast the ancient fate (what is due to me) with the modern plan (how I design the future). The Samaritan (Lk 10:29–37) had other plans when he saw a heap of bloody flesh lying by the road, was "overwhelmed" by mercy, and became his neighbor. The heap of bloody flesh by the road may have had other plans himself when he encountered his robbers. Does this scene from that parable, then, not also somehow belong to the register of *fatum*? Is the Christian *fatum*, understood in this sense, so fundamentally different from the ancient, tragic *fatum*?[14]

The Pharisees asked Christ whom they should care for—the question that motivated the aforementioned parable. Nietzsche seems to reduce Christianity to the question of who is to take care of him. This is, after all, that slave instinct, namely, organizing a morality that ensures that the weak masses, according to a well-defined dynamic, overrule the strong minority. Christ, however, declared both questions invalid. Again, love cannot be derived from a moral system, be it that of masters or that of slaves. There are not even categories of love.

Surely, then, the great difference between Nietzsche and Christianity lies in that "enduring fate together," which is literally compassion, not in saying "yes" or "no" to fate. This "together," however, is not a simple addition of individuals. Christ says that where people are together in the name of God, well, there is God (Mt 18:20). The divinity of being together does not lie in the addition, but in the love that permeates such a gathering. This, then, is not an extra, but a foundation. Love changes the togetherness so profoundly that it makes a difference, literally, as between heaven and earth. In fact, the difference cuts so deep that love makes any morality superfluous—which is what Christ means in his gruff reply to the young man. In this way, from this perspective, love appears not as a derived form of morality, but vice versa. Morality then becomes what man needs to live together in harmony when love is experienced as being too challenging.

Now, I can mitigate this by referring to Paul, who smooths out this difference between love and morality in a very astute way. He starts not with master morality, because that would be impossible in view of the lack of a common moral basis, but with the already decayed antique slave morality of the philosophical dynasty that begins with Socrates, Plato, and Aristotle. They came up with a system of four "cardinal" virtues: prudence, justice, courage, and moderation. On the basis of these four virtues it appears possible to organize a well-functioning society, even if it consists of fully selfish individuals. But to turn it into heaven, something of a different order is needed. Actually, Paul states that those who actually practice *caritas* no longer need cardinal virtues, ethics, or even laws or politics in order to live together "heavenly."

In anticipation of the imminent return of Christ, Paul considers the ancient virtues to be superfluous. These virtues suffice to make a world run smoothly, but they do not turn it into heaven. For this to happen, faith, hope, and above all love are needed. But humanity cannot produce these virtues on its own; "divine invasion" is required.[15] Therefore, for a long time, these virtues remained the private domain of moral theology.

Now Nietzsche, of all people, translates those theological virtues into philosophy. In a later preface to *The Gay Science*, Nietzsche cites all three of them. He links them to the cure of a disease, namely the disease of traditional thought. Hope instead of planning and controlling, belief instead of calculation and proof, and love as in an outburst, as in a resounding "yes!" to life. He places hope, faith, and love—*amor fati*—over against Christian metaphysics. Thinking itself now becomes hoping, trusting, and loving.

In Nietzsche, then, thinking has become aware of a chance for salvation from an extinguished thought, from a dead God. But is not salvation an eminently Christian concept? According to Nietzsche himself, it is emphatically only the moral God who has died. Is there another God who is not dead, who could be the Name of a salvation?

5

Neurosis

Freud

Freud belongs to the exquisite club of "masters of suspicion." Like Marx and Nietzsche, he inflicted an irreparable injury on the autonomy of reason. In the nineteenth century, so gloriously launched by the great modern philosopher Hegel, three thinkers from outside philosophy—economics, cultural criticism, and psychology[1]—came to undermine the rational complacency of modern reason. This happens, nota bene, with the help of that same reason—which is something many scholars choose to neglect. Marx reacted to the "utopian socialists" with scientific analysis and, on the basis of this, formulated at least a decisive determination of reason from the socioeconomic sphere. Nietzsche diagnosed the Western cultural disease as the unfounded priority of the truth drive, which revealed the truth about that drive, namely the unfoundedness of that priority. Freud, in what he considered a purely empirical and strictly scientific way, "discovered" the unconscious as the individual's truth that remains inaccessible to consciousness.

Freud also counted himself among another club of revolutionaries such as Copernicus and Darwin. What these scientists have in common is not only that they deployed a new paradigm, a whole new view of the world, but also that they dethroned the human being—rather than reason. Copernicus's heliocentrism pushed humanity away from the center of the universe; Darwin took the crown of creation away from it and redefined human beings as a failed species of ape. Freud, in turn, made human beings the plaything of odious sexual urges. At least, that was the Christian perception.

Freud came up with the iceberg metaphor—a fine *trouvaille*, by the way. We admire a beautiful transparent cone of crystal floating the sea and fail to see how beneath the surface of the water a huge opaque clump of muddy ice is sailing along. A philosopher of consciousness is a psychologist who suffers from fear of water. For this philosopher, only the cone exists. If anything hides under water, perhaps, it has at best "residual value" as degenerated or immature consciousness. Reason, logic, and consciousness remain normative. For psychoanalysis the whole iceberg exists and the cone is rather the derivative of what goes on under the surface of the water. Different logic applies there—if one can still call it logic. Freud speaks of a process, specifically a primary and a secondary one. Crucial here is that the logic of consciousness, reason, is called secondary and finds itself instituted from the start as a derivative, as an effect of the primary process: the working of the unconscious, which does not care about the rules of that logic because they only come "afterwards."

This can be illustrated by the phenomenon of the dream. When we wake up, that is, when we regain consciousness, the secondary process sets in. We try to draft the dream contents together into a "plot," according to the rules of metaphor and "dramatic coherence." This is hardly successful and, curiously enough, after a few minutes we have completely lost the dream altogether. After all, the super-ego (consciousness, you might say) was deployed by the awakened self against all that primary stuff. The primary process is where the unconscious system tries to outsmart the slumbering self and force turbid but masked desires upon consciousness.

It is in this atmosphere that Freud attempts to answer the question that has arisen since modernity. If the notion of divine revelation has been discarded, what can still count as a true source of religiosity? Reason, with arguments like "intelligent design"? The romantic feeling, as with Friedrich Schleiermacher at the beginning of the nineteenth century, of being included in the Greater Whole, as a passive resistance to the very dominance of passionless reason? Or do the sources lie deeper, earlier, darker? At least Freud claims the latter. Both reason and feeling are firmly rooted in those layers of man and culture to which only psychoanalytic hermeneutics has access. A philosophical problem forms when Freud, somewhat like Marx, presents his insights as hardcore science. More specifically, he follows a typically modern strategy in which an existing scientific field is explained as derived from a stronger, more comprehensive, deeper field. The existing field then becomes a "special case" of the broader explanatory scope. That new field not only covers the entire previous field, but also taps into a previously unexplained field. Freud implicitly promises to explain all that psychology could explain until then and, on top of this, that which it could not satisfactorily explain.[2]

Desire

Desire is a psychological fact, a complex version of life's necessities. It is quite clear that an animal that is not equipped with the necessary tools to satisfy its needs faces a certain death. With Kierkegaard, I mentioned the impossibility of putting a lion on a vegetarian diet. This is less funny than it seems. If a lion, due to circumstances, had no teeth to eat meat, it would not switch to leaves, it would die. The furnishings available to an animal to meet life's necessities are its instincts. This survival kit is not flexible or negotiable. The object of need is fixed. In the case of a hungry lion: meat. The need, the instinct and the body of the lion are, as one system, exclusively focused on the object "meat." An animal that is hungry hunts and eats until it has eaten enough and then stops, right at the point of satisfaction. This cybernetic system works flawlessly, like a thermostat. Within that system, total satisfaction is guaranteed.

With humans, the situation is somewhat different. Our hormonal system works as with animals, but we are not entirely determined by it. We can delay gratification (*différer* in French, linking it to differentiation). We can postpone a meal until mother calls us. We finish our plate, even though we are no longer hungry, because waste is out of the question. We also declare ourselves emphatically dissatisfied with thrice-each-day kibble and a bowl of water, which is what we feed our dogs and cats for life.[3] In the morning we go for energy-rich, in the afternoon for light, and in the evening for tasty. The next day the same, but also different. Not savory again. Friday is leftovers day. On Sundays we expect something more fancy and chic, possibly with a glass of wine. And there's going out together for a romantic candlelight dinner. It's always about food, and then again it's not really. There are quite a few conventions involved that are not hormonally motivated. Hormones other than for hunger are also involved. This variation is not random, it responds to desire which works differently from need and cannot be reduced to it. Desire is need that has detached itself from "literality," from "one-to-one" meaning, from the total satisfaction. From instinct to convention, from need to desire, from literal to metaphorical.

A lion wants meat everywhere in the world; that is not culturally determined.[4] He is not going to pass up a tender leg of lamb because it tastes different than a giraffe's leg. But in England everyone gets port after dinner, as dessert, while elsewhere it is usually drunk as an aperitif. In France, everyone eats raw vegetables, *les crudités*, before the main dish, not during. English people pour mint sauce over their meat; French people bruise garlic in everything. I will keep quiet about German meat—suffice it to say that Hitler was a vegetarian. Africans eat locusts, the French eat snails, and still others eat shrimps—it all looks equally gruesome and yet there is a specific, culturally determined appreciation. And when it comes to what belongs in the haggis, again I prefer to remain silent.

What, for that matter, to think of the love meal, *agapé*, the basic format of the eucharist, the sharing of bread and wine, what Christ proposed to his disciples? In terms of symbolism, it does not get any stronger. Christ asked us never to forget how "they" broke his body and shed his blood as he had done with that bread and wine. Here, bread and wine no longer serve to dispel physical hunger and thirst. They satisfy a rather "metaphorical" hunger, in the register of Christian imagery and symbols. If desire had not taken food away from the strictly rational, cybernetic mechanics of need satisfaction, such liturgical metaphoric would never have been born. This is true of all metaphor, by the way. Human thought and speech maintains a certain distance from literal signification, making religious (and poetic, philosophical . . .) registers possible.

The transition from animal to human seems to run along these same transitions, namely from need to desire, from literal to metaphorical. The latter transition may help to understand the former a little better. Animals have language, as do humans. But it is sometimes said that people do not have a language so much as they *are* language. Humans are linguistic beings in the sense that rather than using a language as a tool, as an instrument, they cannot take up position outside language. Even by remaining silent, people still tell something. This is why the classical model of communication does not allow us to really understand language and linguistics to its full. According to that model, a message passes frictionlessly from sender to receiver. This is true for animal language and for a manual for kitchen utensils, but that is where it ends. Even IKEA instructions reach beyond this model.

Animals use fixed vocabularies among themselves. Each consists of a very limited character set. Consequently, they have little to tell each other. "Food," "water," "danger," and "I am considering reproduction," that's about it. Signs and their meanings remain constant. There is not the slightest variation in them. There is therefore no chance of misunderstanding between animals. Just as well, because that could cost them their lives. When a deer squeaks "danger" because a tiger walks up and another deer interprets it as "here is clear water," then it is "game over"—pun unintended—for both deer. Animals also never lie to each other; there is too much at stake. No bee has ever had the idea of dancing "there is pollen" when that is not true at all. Animals telling each other a joke only happens in Gary Larson's cartoons. Each word has one fixed meaning; each meaning is communicated by one fixed word.

The mating call in animal species is the same everywhere and always, whereas humans have composed a huge variety of love poetry. Even the nightingale's most beautiful song, even the arbor bird's most colorful love passage, are all a matter of instinct and not of creativity. Leaving aside the readers of the fiancé's manual that Kierkegaard spoke of (chapter 3, note 7), people are capable of the most "original" declarations of love. Centuries of poetry testify to this. Desire relates to need as Shakespeare's sonnets relate to mating call. You see, there is indeed no simple continuity or simple discontinuity here.

Desire keeps a greater distance from its object than need does. It can even "shift" or displace the objects. Desire, according to Freud, allows three possible responses: satisfaction, repression, and sublimation—or: the physiological, the psychological, and the cultural (ethical?) response. Physiological gratification, the first response, is the basic mechanism with Freud. This, by the way, makes him a true modern scientist, a purebred rationalist. The alleviation or reduction of tension is a basic mechanism in nineteenth-century physics. Both other, derived forms of gratification are also understood according to the classical scheme of tension reduction.[5] If satisfaction is denied because the object of desire is forbidden, then repression will follow. To displace desire, to shift from the forbidden object to a socially acceptable one, is called sublimation. We then write poetry, or philosophize. We owe our culture to the sublimation of our desires that are forbidden by that same culture. Crudely put, that is.

Unconscious

It is sometimes too easily assumed that consciousness is a "thing," an object about which we can say something, plain and simple. "Consciousness resides in the brain," for example. With consciousness, psychologists can perform the most amusing experiments in the laboratory, experiments that meet all the required scientific validity criteria—and these can be very strict. This neurophysiological reduction is subject of discussion elsewhere; here, we only deal with the possibility of the discussion. The question still remains whether consciousness is a thing or not.

This possibility disappears where the unconscious is concerned. "It" cannot be located anywhere, not in the brain, not elsewhere. It is not a thing; we can say little about it. It is certainly not a container full of unconscious contents, which we know to be there but we have lost its key. It never shows itself directly, as in experiments; only in traces, symptoms. And those symptoms are not even unambiguous. Freud wrote brilliant things about this. A book like *The Psychopathology of Everyday Life* makes pleasant and surprising, but firmly founded coffee-table reading. The dream, the joke, the slip of the tongue, not finding your car keys—Freud analyzes and interprets it all from the notion of the unconscious. Nothing provable, nothing repeatable, nothing measurable. Understandable, at most.[6]

The unconscious is not accessible through experiment or introspection. It can be accessed, for example, via the dream, to Freud even the *via regia* through which something can appear from the dark abyss of the unconscious. This can only be understood from the intriguing notion of repression. One can hardly say that the unconscious is "opened" by repression. The unconscious is marked by the denial of access to self-consciousness. In this sense, the unconscious (and the conscious) is a state rather than a thing or place. Certain desires present themselves and are promptly censored by a strict moral authority (the famous *Über-Ich*) for being culturally unacceptable. Every boy wants to marry his mother and is prepared to kill his father to do so—or vice versa in the case of girls. At the same time, everyone needs to understand that none of this is feasible in "real life." Fortunately, no one actually recognizes oneself in this scheme. Your conscience has done its work; you can carry on with your chin up. And yet, and yet . . .

This ambivalence is in fact, for those who wish to understand it, an appropriate qualification for a symptom. It is produced within oneself and enters consciousness as something from outside. The super-ego closes the front door at the behest of the occupant—the self—and the unconscious rings at the back door, disguised. In both these ways, what was repressed seems strange, different. Take an innocent example: fear of heights. There is absolutely no point in explaining to someone who is shivering on the third rung of a ladder that this position is completely risk-free—after all, that person knows this too. Yet time and again, cold sweat breaks out. The person in question cannot explain, let alone control, that fear and experiences it as something that attacks from without, like a virus, and makes one sick or crazy. In this sense, no one can do anything about it. According to Freud, however, this fear of heights comes from within and is a (primary) translation of a natural, albeit unacceptable and thus repressed desire.

This marrying and killing—by the way, do you remember Jim Morrison's famous exclamation in "The End"?—belongs to what Freud calls the Oedipus complex, the primal repression, the mother of all repressions and the repression of the mother. Oedipus killed his father and married his mother, not knowing that they were his biological parents. Teiresias, the old blind man, understood because he saw what does not belong to the register of the empirical, what constitutes the mystery of human existence. In comparison, the riddle of the sphinx was child's play.[7]

The complex sets the repression in motion. All those who have worked through this complex—in the case of girls, it would be the Electra complex[8]—can move on and should only hope that the symptoms they develop afterwards are socially acceptable. After all, the inaccessibility of the unconscious to rational-scientific analysis implies that we cannot possibly predict which symptom corresponds to which repression.[9]

In addition to the preservation of the individual, there is also the preservation of the species (linked to sexuality—anyone remembers Melanie Safka's *Psychotherapy*?). These two drive systems can come into conflict with each other. These conflicts cannot be resolved by (self-)consciousness. In order to prevent a paralyzing impasse, the "I" engages the super-ego, to which the "I" has outsourced the control over the drives, with the license to repress the sexual imperatives that are produced by but at the same time directed against the "I."

This is a very different approach to "madness" than models that hinge on juice distribution—from those of Hippocrates to more recent neurotransmitters—or on the intrusion of demons. Madness occurs when repressed contents try to bypass the super-ego and impose themselves on consciousness in disguise, as a symptom—which strategy of course fails because the "I" cannot decipher the symptom. In this case, everyone is mad. We lose our minds because of these normal desires, since some of these "forbidden" desires happen to be socially unacceptable. When people act in a way they cannot themselves explain or control, there is a good chance that unconscious contents, i.e., forbidden desires, are at play.

So it is not as simple as some think, to divide humanity into those who do not develop a symptom and those who do, whereby the latter must then go through life as "crazy." Our whole personality, whatever that means, belongs to the register of the symptom—it *is* a symptom, indeed our very own. Our individuality is basically symptomatic. Psychoanalysis completely overturns the distinction between "crazy" and "normal." It is normal to be crazy—and crazy to (want to) be normal—*Catch-22*, anyone? In its place psychoanalysis installs the distinction between (individually or socially) acceptable and unacceptable symptoms. A trait then becomes a symptom rather than innate nature. Thus psychoanalysis turns a modern prejudice completely upside down. Indeed, our culture has a biogenetic conception of personality, as if we are determined by some kind of psychological DNA that we are supposed to deploy, a pre-given core that we must live up to. Meaningless phrases like "be yourself" and "this is just the way I am" illustrate this.

Jacques Lacan, Freud's brilliant and provocative disciple, came up with a suitable metaphor to refute that biogenetic model. Personality, he said, is like an onion. Once all its peels are removed, nothing remains.[10] *Ecce homo*. Later in this book, we encounter a fairly frontal criticism of this, namely from Sartre, by no means a friend of the unconscious. But he also stated that the meaning of a human being, of their doings, their choices and convictions, of their identity and their existence, is not the deployment of a previously written definition or essence, but rather the opposite: that the determination of every single human being is the result of all those contingent—and therefore not necessarily derivable from something else—factors.

In other words, all that we do, think, feel . . . is in one way or another a symptom, a trace of something "other" that cannot present itself as such but only indirectly, namely as trace. This trace cannot be followed in "reverse direction," leading right back to a true origin. Behind the trace there is only more trace. There is no such thing as a "true" self that can be deciphered. The psychoanalytic talking cure can "unscramble" a complex but cannot bring back a pre-given and temporarily buried full truth about myself. The repression is not a logical process that can be reversed, as in a double negation. The repression is itself not conscious, is not the result of a reasonable decision. It belongs to the register of strategy, but that strategy is not an initiative of the conscious "I."

The fact that certain contents will never bypass this built-in moral censorship also means that there is what Freud calls "resistance" at work, and that prevents awareness. Whenever someone claims that I am exhibiting resistance to a particular thought or condition, I cannot refute that. Not only am I unable to reach this with my conscious reason, but I also cannot translate my thoughts, which I can consciously evoke, back into unconscious content, because the primary and secondary grammar are not commensurable. One is not translatable to the other. To connect a symptom directly and explicitly to a repressed content, consciousness would have to be completely eliminated, and this is impossible; it belongs intrinsically to the psychological system as Freud understood it. The bottom line is that the other person can never prove resistance and I can never disprove it. It resembles the existence of God in this. Some people apparently have a resistance to this and there exists no argument against it.

Psychoanalysis sometimes includes resistance in its apology. Psychoanalysts contend that those who criticize psychoanalysis suffer from resistance to the notion that there is a dark side to the human psyche that is not accessible to reflective or introspective reason. Of course, the idea of absolute and total accessibility to reason is an arrogant illusion. But to find in that resistance an argument against criticism of psychoanalysis is also an epistemological bridge too far. So we best turn to thinkers who operate in between these two kinds of foundationalism, beyond the rationalists-versus-irrationalists gap. While these try to convince each other of their respective point of view, we can quietly continue along our thinking path, about religion for example.

In *Totem and Taboo*, Freud wrote, "In one way the neuroses show a striking and far-reaching correspondence with the great social productions of art, religion, and philosophy, while again they seem like distortions of them. We may say that hysteria is a caricature of an artistic creation, a compulsion neurosis, a caricature of a religion, and a paranoic delusion, a caricature of a philosophic system."[11] To understand how religion works, then, we need to turn to compulsions, because there, according to Freud, we can look at religion as if it were under a magnifying glass. Freud is not saying that religion is a neurosis and philosophy is a delusion. Because of the structural analogy, compulsion can serve as an enlarged model for understanding religious dynamics. Freud does not reduce religion to mental illness, but rather to a phenomenon that can be understood from its analogy to a pathological dynamic.[12]

God the Father

Religion is certainly not the result of a rational, scientifically formulated plan that starts from a theoretical idea or shared empirical data. No, religiosity exhibits the structure of a compulsive neurosis. Behind neuroses, including compulsion, one concept looms in Freud's mind around which everything revolves: the infamous Oedipus complex. This is interesting for this research, because this complex is about the father and all that he represents. Like Marx, Freud offers a double explanation of religion, without ever really explaining that ambiguity. With Freud, too, there is an "opium" smell to it. Religion points to a real deficit, but also embodies its illusory fulfillment. Religion is in any case an illusion; sometimes it turns out well, sometimes not.

This deficiency can be understood quite easily. In childhood, we feel protected by the presence of a strong and reliable father figure, who can handle the whole world. When we become adults, that father figure loses his mythical power; he becomes human. The adult, however, finds this unbearable. Unconsciously we long for that father who told all those beautiful fairy tales where all ends well. The secret longing for that strong figure translates into belief in an omnipotent God. In religion a person retrieves that original security that has been lost during the coming of age (i.e., through the Oedipus complex). Freud finds it highly significant that in the Christian tradition God is addressed as "Father." Remember a similar reasoning by the later Feuerbach.

Those who read "Father" as a metaphor, and not literally, do not have to include the whole logical-scientific context. Then a Father can be non-human, non-man, non-person. Bio-logically, of course, it is difficult to imagine a father who is not a man; socio-logically or anthropo-logically it is difficult to attribute a father role to someone who is not a human being; psycho-logically it is equally difficult to imagine a father figure who is not represented by a person. Now, theo-logically this is perfectly possible.[13] God is experienced as Father because that word in the Jewish tradition stands for boundless, unconditional love. "Father" also has a second theo-logical meaning. Christ announces that he has come to cause discord between father and son and actually between almost everyone else (Mt 10:34–36; Lk 12:51–52). That sounds harsh. Actually, it means this: it is not the biological, psychological ties that are the most important. The most important bond is that with the Father, for only in that metaphor, in his Name, do all people become "sisters and brothers." I will come back to that soon.

The second explanation, specifically the illusory interpretation, is a bit more difficult, not only because there Freud wants to understand religion in a neurotic register, he also has to understand it as a collective fact, structurally analogous to neurosis. Actually, Freud is looking for a kind of cultural-historical Oedipus complex from which religiosity can be understood. If religion is an effect of cultural-historical factors, then a changed historical constellation can also make that effect disappear again, or render it superfluous and allow it to peter out. This recalls Marx's intent. In their case, in short, modernity made religion superfluous.

Like Russell (see chapter 6), Freud believed that we will get rid of this illusion that religion ultimately is, if in our culture, in our education, we replace religious contents with scientific facts. This is possible because

Freud does not consider religion a fixed anthropological phenomenon, as did Feuerbach, but rather a cultural-historical contingent phenomenon, as did Marx. For this, however, Freud bases himself on well-defined "scientific," especially mythological, archaeological, and anthropological, insights that were already outdated or at least doubted even in his time.[14] According to Freud, religion would, even had to, disappear. According to Lacan, however, it is an illusion to think that religion will ever disappear.

Does God Have a Psychokiller?

Still, it is undeniably true that for many, God is the comforting Father to whom they can always turn—which is not always possible with their worldly father. But that does not mean that this is the actual "function" of God. It certainly does not count as proof of his existence. Christian consolation is a grace, not something that can be enforced provided the right actions and words are used. The consolation obtained is not an effect, is not magic, but springs from faith and its sources themselves. In this sense, faith is a healer rather than a sickness. We already learned this, albeit in different terms, from Kierkegaard.

When a psychologist studies the phenomenon of "religion" he will naturally recognize only its psychological causes. Certainly he can help the person whose delusions are expressed in terms of faith to become healthy again. That still does not make faith a psychiatric syndrome. It is not because germophobes compulsively clean and wash that hygiene becomes a psychological disorder. So, pathologies with faith as their theme do not count as evidence for the nonexistence of God.

So what can or should we do with this Father metaphor? Does it also work outside faith? Recall how Žižek points out that Christianity succeeded in installing at the very core of the (now moribund) Roman Empire a viewpoint from which all people are equal. Where that Empire, i.e., the (socio-political, economic, legal, military) world, was marked by an inescapable social hierarchy, suddenly a vanishing point opens up in which the whole layered structure appears as if it did not exist (1 Cor 7:27–31). Those who stand there will see only brothers and sisters. That is precisely what the Father metaphor signifies. All will be (like) brothers and sisters . . . we also know this from Schiller, whose romantic-political "Ode to Joy" was monumentally exhibited by Ludwig van Beethoven in the fourth movement of his ninth symphony.

Freud must have sensed the greatness of Christian charity. At the very end of *Civilization and Its Discontents*, he expresses his concern about the possibility of total destruction of the human world, as it became manifest during the World War(s). He saw only one possible dam strong enough to hold back this terrible threat, namely Christian charity. Unfortunately, according to him, that does not exist. In fact, psychology considers universal love a perversion, everyone just loving everyone else. That recalls the hippie dream, with Stephen Stills singing "If you can't be with the one you love, love the one you're with." Freud could hardly reconcile such interchangeability with his views on love as a selective process. He never figured it out; Christian charity remained a mystery to him.

But God was never intended to meet man's desires, be it as reality, be it as illusion, be it at the intersection of the two. God is not a cultural-historical effect that would be too narrow and at the same time too conceptual. He is not meant to stop all violence in the world and in the meantime play father to everyone—here we get Bonhoeffer's "stop gap" God again, the one who serves to fill the holes, solve the problems, clean up the world, and make life bearable. Indeed, God is not obliged, aided by an army of saints and a few more auxiliary angels, to solve the tragedy of human existence. Perhaps, and at most then, God helps us to bear that tragedy, to endure it. We should not expect a leap from the world to bring the solution, so that we must organize our desire according to the form of a leap. The leap out of the world into faith, as Kierkegaard thematizes it, will not profit you in that world, for the world has in fact taken on a different meaning in that leap. That leap is not a trick. If the intention is to solve the existential tragedy of the lost father, then religion has chosen a wrong motive. Then you do not leap but fall.

6

Primitive

Russell

Russell was not short on wit and diligence. He was not only a great mathematician but also an esteemed philosopher. He was even awarded the Nobel Prize for Literature in 1950. For example, he wrote a socio-politically inspired *History of Western Philosophy*, which is still a bestseller. He wrote other bestsellers, in part to finance his self-founded school. These dealt with education, happiness, marriage, etc. He also wrote an essay *Why I Am Not a Christian*. This is a very interesting book, even for believers, because it lists just about all the wrong and invalid reasons to be Christian. Instead of arguing about whether or not to include the theory of evolution in the educational curriculum within the Bible Belt, it would serve everyone better to suggest this book as required reading there.[1] In fact, it is unquestionably required reading for anyone even remotely interested in theology. It is among the clearest critiques of almost all possible caricatures of Christianity, mainly because it springs from a caricatured reading of it. Most rationalists do not aspire to any other reading. They are hopeless, never getting away from their "reasonless passion for a passionless reason."

Together with another brilliant scholar, Alfred North Whitehead, he published a monumental work, *Principia Mathematica* (1910–1913), a voluminous standard in three volumes in which they would derive mathematics from logic. When you realize that in addition to being a mathematician and natural scientist, Whitehead also made a name for himself as a philosopher and process theologian, you can see that we find ourselves in the company of the very cream of the intellectual world at that time.

Russell was not lacking in social commitment either. He was an ardent pacifist and founded the Russell Tribunal against War Crimes—of which Sartre, among others, would later become president. For the sake of this morally laudable conviction, Russell was imprisoned. This is what governments do with people who have a conscience.

I think it is fitting here to insert a quote from *Why I Am Not a Christian*,[2] because due to its programmatic nature it can easily be intertwined into several thematic sections below.

> We want to stand upon our own feet and look fair and square at the world—its good facts, its bad facts, its beauties, and its ugliness; see the world as it is, and be not afraid of it. Conquer the world by intelligence, and not merely by being slavishly subdued by the terror that comes from it. The whole conception of God is a conception derived from the ancient Oriental despotisms. It is a conception quite unworthy of free men. When you hear people in church debasing themselves and saying that they are miserable sinners, and all the rest of it, it seems contemptible and not worthy of self-respecting human beings. We ought to stand up and look the world frankly in the face. We ought to make the best we can of the world, and if it is not so good as we wish, after all it will still be better than what these others have made of it in all these ages. A good world needs knowledge, kindliness, and courage; it does not need a regretful hankering after the past, or a fettering of the free intelligence by the words uttered long ago by ignorant men. It needs a fearless outlook and a free intelligence. It needs hope for the future, not looking back all the time towards a past that is dead, which we trust will be far surpassed by the future that our intelligence can create.

I am not concerned here with the "God or science" discussion. Before we can embark on this discussion, a great deal of preliminary philosophical spadework is required, to avoid any superficial meatball thinking.

Positivism

Russell wanted to eradicate religion root and branch. "Religion is something left over from the infancy of our intelligence. It will fade away as we adopt reason and science as our guidelines."[3] Harsh words . . . The tone became a little more moderate afterwards, but the program remains unchanged. Thomas Nagel notes, "It isn't just that I don't believe in God and, naturally, hope that I'm right in my belief. It's that I hope there is no God! I don't want there to be a God; I don't want the universe to be like that." Nowadays it is admitted that religion does have some beneficial effects, such as keeping people out of pubs and keeping lunatics in line. Yet even those people must eventually realize that religion is not true, because now we have evolution. Here, one may ask the pertinent question whether evolution has not gradually acquired the status of a religion. Science will reply "No, because the theory of evolution is *true*."

At the beginning of the last century, it was customary among scientists-philosophers (mainly from England, Germany, and also the US) to grant reason the status of absolute truth—and by this they meant logical-rational, more specifically (natural) scientific reason. Russell was convinced that knowledge—and by that he meant, again, scientific knowledge—is a structure that keeps on growing and will even be accomplished one day. Indeed, knowledge is considered cumulative, and not infinite. Reality is its exact reach—how modern, how Hegelian. The typical method of science guarantees its own rectilinear growth. More and more it conquers the massive domain of reality. More and more it overcomes ignorance. This ignorance also includes religion.[4] In a scientific perspective, religion can be little more than descriptions and explanations in rather imaginative terms.[5] The key question then becomes, again, whether the scientific view is the only one or, if not the only one, at least the best one.

Some time ago I read in an interview about "the resurrection of the flesh and other curious cosmological phenomena."[6] This misunderstanding is not only prevalent among so-called unbelievers. The generation that crossed '68 (spiritual delineation: the hippies) and '73 (material delineation: oil crisis) received catechesis until the age of twelve and then dropped out *en masse*. This means that their theological baggage is full of childish and outdated representations. And yes, those images of God can easily, even preferably, be refuted in adulthood.

We are no longer familiar with the "strategy" of catechesis. Baby Jesus in a trough, with an ox and a donkey who had to keep out the freezing cold, really serves as a very strong image . . . for children. They are not concerned with critical historical study—Jesus was not born in the year 0, nor on December 25; it was not freezing in that stable; there were no ox and donkey standing brotherly side by side blowing on the baby; etc. But to use this children's catechesis as an argument against theology is just intellectually dishonest and poor. Ricoeur argues here for what he called a "second naivety." In this context, this amounts to ensuring that our "imaginative reason" is not definitively stifled by scientific reason and kept alive even during adulthood. An eye for the miracle—the miracle of science included.[7]

But along with the first misunderstanding appears a second one. Not only is the cosmological God the adult version of the childhood God and of the so-called primitive nature gods, but this God is rejected on the grounds of cosmological and other scientific arguments, whereas it should actually be theologically and philosophically upgraded—and then accepted or rejected. If many have skipped half a century of theological reflection here, their argumentation suddenly skips a whole century of philosophical reflection. Scientific findings do not show the world-as-it-is, which is a Cartesian prejudice, but each theory or paradigm provides a lens through which we see and discuss aspects of the world. Therefore, the natural or human sciences can hardly be invoked to refute truths of faith. Wittgenstein reproached both Russell and most theologians for causing a great deal of confusion in that very area. Those who think that religion must disappear because it bears no explanation, as well as those others who still try to find such an explanation, have all fallen into the trap of the alleged monopoly of scientific thought.[8] The scientific proof of the existence of God is just as ridiculous as the scientific refutation of the existence of God. Sciences argue in terms of cause and chance, or as Kant said, in terms of determination rather than freedom. Consequently, a theology that conforms to the scientific register has a hard time trying to articulate Christian freedom in a meaningful way.

To claim that God has no (longer any) place within scientific reach also means that we should renounce any form of "proof" of his existence or non-existence. The validity of the evidence, in the strict and scientific sense of the term, does not reach further than (explanatory) scientific reason itself. In some sciences it is already very presumptuous to deal with evidence at all. Most of the evidential value belongs to elementary mathematics and logic. These are formal enough to be able to design for themselves the premises and definitions and algorithms that allow them to construct a conclusive proof by excluding any ingredient that does not possess the purity of mathematics or logic.

The resurrection *is* cosmological nonsense, of course. But remember Žižek, who was not too shy or shallow to acknowledge the culture-bearing significance of this event (see under Nietzsche). And that is exactly what it is all about. Those biblical texts need to be read in their own "sense." Reading these stories through a scientific, for example cosmological, lens is just as foolish as reading the Little Red Riding Hood fairy tale as a journalist's report. Creationists and other literal readers may indulge in this, but we all know by now how dangerous literal readings are. Take another classic: Jesus walking on water (Mt 14:25ff). The physical impossibility of a human body moving upright across a body of water does not detract from the exegetical truth that Christ's determination prevented him from sinking into the mythical representation of existential doubt.[9] The water here signifies the desperate, the absurd—in almost the same way as the forest in "Little Red Riding Hood" or, for that matter, *The Jungle Book*. This is the only way to explain why Christ, shaking his head in compassion, addresses Peter, who is sinking, and says, "You have so little faith, why did you doubt?"

The cosmological gods had a real, direct, physical impact on the world. At best, they could be appeased with sacrifices. In any case, the death of their god on the cross would never have occurred to any of them. This god would have driven nails through the foreheads of all the Romans and Jews standing around the cross. In the Synoptics, the first three evangelists, there was a thunderstorm at the very moment of Christ's death, but in John's case nature did not even sigh. In John's case we don't find any strange cosmological or biological phenomena either. He talks openly about love, without beating about the bush.

A scientific attitude is not suited for thinking about God. This is perhaps mainly due to the "instrumental" nature of that attitude. Scientific and technical calculation does not ask (any longer) for the meaning of everything (Why?), but rather for its usefulness (How?). It is very easy to profess a god who is useful—we already saw how Marx and Freud went that way. A functional god can serve to shield specific political systems from political criticism, moral rules from critical questioning, but also, using an army of saints, to solve everyday problems such as recovering lost objects (St. Anthony), protecting travelers (St. Christopher), and even curing toothaches (St. Apollonia). Those who merely ask about the usefulness of God, however, immediately lose him. Neither science nor technology finds a place for God. Social improvers who reduce the meaning of existence to a utility question, who thus seek a scientific and technical—in this case political, legal, economic, etc.—answer to the search for meaning, usually get stuck in a totalitarian model, by the way. This is not surprising. The utility question never leads to God; utility must be sought in the world itself. Whoever looks for God within culture "kills" him and closes off the world in a totalitarian system. This search is doomed—and moreover contradicts monotheism. Monotheism actually has nothing to do with the amount of gods; it mainly states that only God is God. There only being one (supreme) god is called "henotheism." I will come back to this important issue.

Some reservations here about the judgment "primitive" in its broader sense—that is, not only with regard to the phenomenon of religion. This presupposes a criterion, often historically formulated, that declares everything that is not modern or technoscientific to be "primitive." There is also a political version of this, namely, "How is it possible that, in 2023, they still [feel free to fill in, according to your ideological obedience]." In this way, politics wants to appear hip, with its scientific finger on the pulse of actuality.

From a scientific point of view, a "primitive" explanation is a clumsy one. This has to do with the idea that "God" is a kind of container term for causes that we have not yet understood scientifically. Thunderstorms used to be Zeus punishing the Greek or marital strife at the house of Donar; now they are electrostatic discharges. As science progresses, the explanatory impact of the gods diminishes, until it will have disappeared altogether—see Russell's quote above. As long as we had no concept of epidemiology, a plague was a punishment from God. The Bible Belt has tried to read AIDS into the same register. This is as nonsensical as a scientific or creationist reading of the creation story.

First error: God only serves to explain the unknown. Now, should that be the case, I gladly will join all those who hope that God may soon blow over. Spinoza also said that a miracle is a misunderstood reality. In mythical cultures, this has certainly been true. The earliest stories in the Old Testament, for example the expulsion from Paradise, are full of mythical explanations. But monotheism has another "function," which is to refuse the absolutization, the deification of any explanation. Strictly speaking, no explanation of the world can be found in monotheistic doctrine. Only God is God, and he is not available, even to offer explanations. God does not dwell in another world, because there simply is no such thing, philosophically speaking; Nietzsche took care of that. God keeps a critical distance from the world, from any world. God is indeed a name of this distance, of the refusal of a scientific or indeed any total explanation. This refusal can never be a human initiative. I will come back to this later.

Second error: history constitutes an "epistemological demarcation criterion" for truth. This assumes that what comes later can only be better and more true. Here the word "primitive" appears as a judgment. It is a typically modern judgment, since neither antiquity nor the Middle Ages were explicitly concerned with history as a defining source of meaning, of truth. Modernity is "original" in the sense that it wants to legitimize itself through the notion of progress and all the connotations that emerge in its wake: emancipation, evolution, growth, efficiency, innovation, etc. These are now considered as natural law, as a source of truth. These are now considered as self-evident absolute imperatives, whereas they really are historical constructs. Science fits into this modern scheme, but that is still no reason for unreasonable rationalist hubris.[10]

It is, by the way, very curious how science legitimizes itself by means of a teleology, as if the whole of history had worked its way up to this ultimate access to truth, while it denies any teleology in the world itself.[11] Science thus legitimizes itself on the basis of what it rejects. This paradox, of course, remains invisible to science, as well as to that philosophy that swears by the absolute truth claim of that science. I take this up further with Lyotard.

Heidegger has unraveled the aforementioned paradox. Briefly, he contends that categories and statements that are valid within the world cannot be transferred or applied to the world itself. Modern science is indeed very modern here by denying this subtle nuance, this difference in scope. The basic principles of reality are then presented as self-evident and as belonging to that reality itself, in the sense that they require no external legitimation. This, however, testifies to "totalitarian" thought, a way of thinking that claims to speak on behalf of the totality; it pretends to know, to explain, to describe, and to own reality in its totality—at least in principle. This self-evidence is essentially not evidence, but bears the structure of a preference, of a decision—these terms are from Derrida, who will be discussed later in this book—and therefore of an act of faith or conviction.[12]

So this modern self-evidence also has something of a *petitio principii*, the logical term for "putting the cart before the horse." Such evidence pretends to explain something, but secretly already presupposes that which it sets out to explain. Because progress, growth, evolution, etc. simply belong to the basic vocabulary of modernity, it cannot understand itself in any other way than in these terms. Indeed, what is "new" can only be better.[13]

The third error is an extension of this: scientific explanations are the best, because they are true—perhaps you should reread the reasoning about the theory of evolution above. This is called in philosophy "tautology," and elsewhere "foundationalism." What remains unseen here is that the criteria by which thought is judged happen to be those criteria that were installed and at work at the birth of scientific thinking itself: certainty through measurability. Indeed, that is the criterion for scientific thinking. But is it the best, or even the only valid one? Rather, it shows that when philosophy prescribes that thinking should become knowing-for-certain, then indeed scientific reason turns out to be the most suitable candidate. This has little to do with teleology and progress; rather, this looks like a "personalized vacancy."[14]

Here we stumble upon the philosophical knot in the discussion between faith and knowing, between religion and science. That battle is not yet settled because we have not yet moved beyond the discussion between Kant and Hegel: is there only one reason, one spirit—viz. the scientific one—or do several reasons co-exist, not reducible to each other or referrable to one overarching super-reason, each with its own register and truth claim?

Faith versus Knowledge?

The history of Western theology yielded two important formulas concerning the relationship between theology and philosophy. The first is *Credo quia absurdum*. I believe because it is incomprehensible. We also came upon this with Kierkegaard. This does not mean that we should believe anything that cannot be scientifically proven. It certainly does not mean that we should believe all nonsense—then Monty Python's Flying Circus would be a world religion. It does mean that when something meaningful emerges that is beyond the reach of science, something else is needed to receive and capture its meaning, viz. a sort of belief, or at least a religious way of thinking. The latter opens up an interesting philosophical perspective that I will develop later.

The first formula can be read together with a second one, namely *Credo ut intelligam*. I believe in order to understand. When I step outside the scientific range, I find another reason, another understanding with its own validity. In order to understand the world, I first have to accept some things about the world that I cannot understand—at least not in the same, for instance scientific, way. To claim that this "acceptance" is so absolutely legitimate that it borders on certainty, this transition from belief to certainty, this paradoxical ground of the bizarre system of objectivity, I will call "hyperreligious theism."[15]

Philosophy of science opened a very important debate that is relevant here, concerning the truth claims of human sciences. During what has since more than a century ago come to be known as *Methodenstreit* or "method dispute," human sciences (history, economics, introspective psychology, etc.) defended their own specific truth claims against the monopoly of natural sciences. The "understanding" of something in its singularity was recognized as equally valid as the "explanation" of something in its repeatability. Curiously, at that time James and Wundt had just opened their respective laboratories for experimental psychology and a few years later the fuses in physics would blow.

At the very moment when verdict was being passed on the value of scientific knowledge, Newtonian physics and its Euclidian geometry entered into crisis. Suddenly, at the very core of natural science, the prototype of certainty and unambiguity, two new theories emerge, each carrying their own paradigm, their own world view: aside from the old, tried and proven Newtonian world, a relativistic and a quantum mechanical world appear—perhaps thermodynamics should also be given a special place here. While the mathematical models that go with each world turned out to be derivable from each other, the same is by no means true of their images or metaphors. And it does not stop here. Within quantum mechanics itself, wave mechanics and particle mechanics were rolled out. Again, those theories are mathematically translatable into each other (along Werner Heisenberg's matrix mechanics), but their "worlds" are not. The metaphors "wave" and "particle" are mutually exclusive. And again it does not stop there: "strings" have surfaced in the search for a relativistic quantum field theory, bringing more promise but also more perplexity into science.

This fascinating scientific transition has entailed some weird marginal phenomena that turned out to be quite profitable in New Age circles. In the 1980s Fritjof Capra (*The Tao of Physics*) and Gary Zukav (*The Dancing Wu Li Masters*) became reasonably popular with their *macédoine* of quantum physics and traditional Eastern wisdom. Suddenly the scientific scope was stretched to include religion, which is quite a surprise. In the wake of Feuerbach's anthropological desire, Dinah Zohar recently "discovered" a neurophysiological constant, namely 40 Hz, as the frequency at which God invades our brain. After all, our brains have a lobe where all neural activity plays at that frequency, which is also the frequency of the background radiation, the electromagnetic echo of the Big Bang. Via socioeconomic and psychological and other functional pathways, God has finally settled down in a remote corner of our brain. The science of God has revealed to us the neurotheological truth. You may laugh, but preferably not too loud and certainly not for too long.

In any case, since the end of the nineteenth century, many philosophers have pointed out that scientific thinking has its validity, but only within its own territory. Therefore, the theory of evolution is only "true" within the scope of scientific reason and during modernity—which is already quite a lot, of course. Rationalists, however, wrongly equate the range of scientific reason with "total reality."

Morality

As a consistent secular thinker, Russell is faced with the problem of where to find a valid alternative basis for morality outside of religion. Just being nice to someone else does not make substantial moral headway, he thinks. Morality must be firmly founded. He finds a rather ambiguous, yet typically modern solution by retaining the religious goal of religion but renouncing every traditional religious ground—especially the metaphysical foundation and its institutional embodiment, in a word: the church and its magisterium. He christens this the "free man's worship." This refers to the feeling that causes individuals to merge into a larger moral whole that transcends their selfishness.[16]

In several of his texts, Russell denounces the concept of sin, the fact of original sin. He finds it demeaning and just plain wrong. We do not all commit bad things at all; we are mostly people of good will, some a little more than others. But that is not the point here. I am formulating a possible theological response. Perhaps Christianity is not about sin *per se*, but all about salvation. Everyone will be saved, which is why everyone needs to live in a state of sin. "Sinful" then means "standing in the promise of salvation." This has nothing to do with "naughty" or "criminal."

The philosophical response is even simpler: original sin, the sinfulness that we inherit just by being born, is nothing but innate selfishness. So Russell and the (other) magisterium are actually pulling the same string. Where Russell elaborates on his "free man's worship" and argues that policy-makers should use the ever-increasing technical potential purely for good rather than to increase personal power, wealth, and prestige, he even explicitly refers to the model of Christian charity. This is all the more striking when one considers that a little earlier Freud had written something similar at the end of his study on *Civilization and Its Discontents* (see Freud). There he stated that only one power could possibly be deployed against the newly arising, real danger of the total destruction of the earth and the extermination of mankind. That power, you will remember, is Christian charity. Only this can curb such a threat with success. But Christian charity does not exist according to Russell and Freud, except perhaps as an "ideal" but then it loses the very character of guarantee. So the view they take remains rather dim . . .[17]

Hyperreligious Theism

If I may be naughty for a moment now, I would call Enlightened modernity "hyperreligious."[18] During a debate with an atheist (flat version), he stated "I am convinced, I am certain that God does not exist." I found that highly significant. The almost imperceptible transition from conviction (belief) to certainty (knowing) hidden in that comma is a sign of hyperreligious thought. This is the certainty not of mystical devotion but of the Cartesian, natural-scientific method. The aggression with which modernity sometimes "proves" the non-existence of God cannot be compared to the poetic devotion with which, for example, Anselm formulates his proof of God in the form of a prayer. The shortcut that runs from conviction or belief to knowing and certainty shows me how scientific rationalism is not so much an areligious atheism as rather a hyperreligious theism. By theism, I mean a system that installs an entity, such as God or Reason or Law or whatever, as Supreme Being. This involves something great that can be considered normative for all meaning. The way God functions in theism—with theology of creation, moral theology, dogmatics, etc.—and the way Reason functions in atheism are both very similar. The "a-" of "atheism" then simply means that God has been discarded and replaced with some other Supreme Being. This atheism, however, maintains the theist system and structure. I will elaborate further on that "a-" in the final chapter.

Instead of a faith that hinges on surrender and grace, with prayer and dance, here we have certainty and evidence, with inquiry and measurement. Therein lies the hyperreligious character of theism, not in a better or more powerful or higher God, but in an absolutely certain belief in their system and the enclosed guarantee to make absolutely certain statements about God—without even thinking about who or what or how God might also mean something. Most of the time, "flat" atheists remain satisfied with the most infantile images of God and then, rightly in fact, continue to criticize those. Many intellectuals even hang on to those images, refraining from upgrading their theological and philosophical baggage . . .

When someone asked Russell how he would account for his atheism before God, he replied, "Not enough evidence, God!" Richard Dawkins considered this a reasonable reply. Yet there is still a difference between these two. Russell was more modest in his atheism and would rather call himself agnostic. From that position he did not find good reasons to organize a religion based on God—or on any god, in fact. He actually thought that it was better to assume that there is no God, an idea that is agreed on by, among many others, Sartre. In this sense, he takes the "other" wager than Blaise Pascal, who claimed that in the case of agnosticism, one is better off opting for the existence of God anyway. After all, in that case the believers "win." And if it turns out that he does not exist after all, believers have enjoyed a better, in spiritual and moral sense, life than non-believers.[19] The word "wager" suddenly brings Kierkegaard's leap into view. There too, we have no guarantee, no proof. Neither wager nor leap can be called project.

I would like to clarify this by means of a well-known but often misunderstood ritual. At the sickbed, when the doctors leave the room, someone lights a candle. When science and technology fail, someone makes this gesture. That is not magic, that is not outsourcing health problems to the man with the magic wand, to that "one ruler" whom Nagel complains about. That gesture should not be read in the register of technical mastery; quite the contrary. That candle expresses hope and trust, not necessarily in Something or Someone—in a theistic entity—but in a "good outcome," without knowing what that should consist of, because then one falls back into technical mentality. The candle is not a device to fulfill my wishes, but a sign that says that, however things may come out, we trust that it is for the best, according to whatever categories that lie outside our existential range.

The question then becomes: does that candle have any valid meaning at all? Is this superstition, primitive, cowardly, or anything like that? Or is lighting a candle also a form of thankful thinking, of thought other than technical-scientific?[20]

7

Silence

Wittgenstein

Like Kierkegaard, Wittgenstein grew up in opulence. While the former's home was very Lutheran and dutiful, the latter's—thanks to his Catholic and culturally active mother—played host to the entire Viennese *beau monde*. Both initially indulged in the luxury of a fortune made available to them, but then both soon chose a sober way of life that seemed to suit a philosopher better. Wittgenstein even passed on his share of the inheritance to his sister, justifying this decision with the excuse that she already had pots of money.

Like Marx's Jewish father—and many others, including the "father of phenomenology" Edmund Husserl—Wittgenstein's Jewish grandfather had converted to Protestantism to secure his social position. Whereas Marx asked few questions about religion except as an element of his social criticism, Wittgenstein was genuinely concerned about the question of religion; it affected him not only logically but also personally. Here Marx is more like Freud, who also comes from a secular Jewish context, and Wittgenstein is more like Kierkegaard—whom he admired, by the way. Like Nietzsche, the young Wittgenstein read Schopenhauer, but it was ultimately Russell who led him toward philosophy. It was the latter who confided to Wittgenstein's sister that her brother was expected to be the next great step in the history of philosophy. He was not that far wrong . . .

As a great thinker, he has often been, of course, misunderstood. Most people still think that Wittgenstein considered religion, ethics, and art to be pointless items, about which it is better to remain silent. He would then belong to the positivist schools. But on the contrary, he found these things more important than logic. Logic was merely a tool to clean up philosophy so that we could fill our lives with the true, the beautiful, and the good that can only be cultivated and lived out outside of theory.

Wittgenstein soon convinced the greatest minds of the British academy of his analytical talent, but the reverse left much to be desired. Either because he thought he had solved all problems in philosophy or because he felt misunderstood, he took up teaching after the publication of his *Tractatus Logico-Philosophicus*. When that did not really work out he even took up gardening with the nuns. But as with Heidegger, his thoughts took a rather drastic turn and he went back to university to continue thinking, debating, teaching, and writing. Having just read Freud, we could ask the question whether his philosophy is sublimated homosexuality, but who cares. And yes, maybe he sat next to Hitler on a school bench.

Thought and Silence

There is, of course, much disagreement on that well-known statement "About which one cannot speak, one must remain silent."[1] It may sound a peculiar thing to hear this from someone who thought he had solved all the fundamental problems of philosophy by describing and prescribing very precisely how to speak clearly. Surely the latter is the trademark of so-called analytic philosophy? But as I said, Wittgenstein cannot be fit into any particular tradition or school, like the logical positivist school known as the *Vienna Circle*.

Rudolf Carnap, a German philosopher, was a famous representative of this school. He bluntly declared every "metaphysical" statement meaningless. This included all statements about God, the Truth, the Good, the Beautiful—in a word, the basic concepts of metaphysics. After all, such statements could not be "decomposed" (the literal translation of the Greek "analysis") into the kind of elementary statements that would produce purely sensory knowledge. That is why this school is called: logical empiricism (or also positivism).

Carnap also had the strongest reservations about the typical Heideggerian use of language, which still irritates philosophers who like to make things easy for themselves. For example, he mocked phrases such as "The thing things." Before one can extract any meaning from this, one must indeed abandon the whole analytical set-up. All demands for transparent conceptuality, sensory foundation, and grammatical purity (the "well-formed formula" or "wff," pronounced "whoof") then disappear, and the possibility of a meaning other than scientific (or "equivalent") then appears. But positivism does not recognize any other than scientific meaning. Heidegger's "thinging of the thing" opens an essential dimension of the world around us that cannot be disclosed by scientific analysis. The "essencing"—the essence of something is not itself a thing but an event, see Heidegger—that a thing gathers into itself, and through which it can appear to us as a thing, belongs to a caring proximity to things rather than to sterile, analytical detachment. It leaves the initiative of meaning to the world itself, not to (Cartesian) consciousness.

The strict analytic tradition employs a rather radical and brutal critique of metaphysics by rejecting as meaningless all that lies beyond an empirical approach. What one cannot speak logically-empirically about can only be nonsense, so about this everyone must remain silent. Categorical imperative of Anglo-Saxon philosophy.

This positivist version, however, is only one of the possible interpretations of Wittgenstein's famous statement. But as I said, he could not be captured by one camp. I will offer another, more recent approach or interpretation. There has to be one, since Wittgenstein himself calls his first main work nonsense instead of gospel, no more than a ladder that should be thrown away once one has climbed beyond philosophy. In its seemingly endless—after all, it has been continuously trying to explain the world for some 2,500 years now—attempt to explain the world, philosophy has created more problems than it has solved, Wittgenstein observed. Time for some major cleaning up. As a volunteer during World War I, he decided to do some serious work between heroic adventures, so he started jotting down notes, which he later collected and composed as the *Tractatus Logico-Philosophicus*. He claimed that this work had solved all philosophical problems. He found he had to save philosophy by lifting thought beyond it. Since its problems could not be solved anyway—after all, their solutions have eluded generations of brilliant minds—they could better be avoided. Logic cannot be used to solve problems but it can show how hygienic thought is not affected by them. Problems are not solvable but either dismantlable, thus reducible to fake problems, or just plain unsolvable. And in the latter case it is indeed better to remain silent. Wittgenstein himself considered this insight the most important achievement of his research. Not an imperative, rather a philosophical observation.

But What Exactly Should We Keep Silent about Anyway?

Actually, Wittgenstein's basic philosophical question, like Heidegger's, is still the same as Plato's. By the way, did Whitehead not preach that all Western philosophy could best be qualified as a set of footnotes to Plato's work? The latter was perplexed by the fact that reality as such was comprehensible—but not on human initiative (as the sophists held). Most people spontaneously assume this intelligibility and chatter about this and that and about so-and-so—what Heidegger calls "idle talk." But the fact that this is actually happening, people understanding each other and communicating about a more or less "same world," whether it is a barroom brawl or an insight that could lead to a Nobel Prize, that is precisely what a philosopher wants to think through—so Wittgenstein too. Surely, when Wittgenstein has dissolved the whole of philosophy and, literally, has urged it to evaporate, we find ourselves back at the source, at the wonder and the gratitude that constitutes the basic motivation of Plato's thinking?

In any case, Wittgenstein did not want to draw this perplexity into philosophy, as a theme, because it resists logical analysis. Amazement does not allow itself to be "abstracted" into a philosophical system. The same Wittgenstein who only published on hygienic thought also noted that his really fundamental thoughts are not to be found in his publications—exactly as Plato writes in his seventh letter. So in his two major publications, which, again, he himself thought were nonsense—a kind of Swiffer cloth that one throws away after it has cleaned up the mess—and literally beside the point, he carefully examines the rules that govern hygienic thought looks like and then argues that the unsolvable philosophical problems are due to violations of those rules.

Alfred Tarski put it aptly afterwards, so aptly that we may wonder whether one needs to have studied philosophy for years to do so. "P" $\Leftrightarrow$ P. There you are. The statement "P," necessarily a "wff" of course, is true if-and-only-if P is the case. A sentence like "It is raining" is true only when it is indeed actually raining. Well, as simple and obvious as this sounds, there is a lot of discussion about this that I am happy to leave out here. What matters is that Wittgenstein did not stop there. He wanted to know whence this "if and only if" came. He questioned, as a right-minded philosopher, the obvious, the evidence, what is taken for granted, thoroughly and radically. If what is "true" is what is "grounded," then that ground itself is neither true nor false. True and false do not in the first place refer to agreement with the facts, but rather to what that agreement entails.

What makes our thoughts mean something when expressed? Apparently there is something at work that ensures that certain true statements—that is, only those and no other—correspond to facts and states of affairs, as Wittgenstein calls them. We could call this work "logic."[2] But this logic that makes the world intelligible can never and nowhere itself become part of the world. Nor is it a mere statement, like "It's raining." Nor is it an object, or a fact, or a situation about which something can be proposed. It is to be found outside or beyond the system of signification. This is why we should keep silent about it. That which provides meaning does not have itself any meaning—an insight that Derrida will take up.

Of course Wittgenstein did not mean by this that philosophy of life, ethics, art, and so on would be meaningless; quite on the contrary. If he already thought critically about this at all, then it was critical in a Kantian sense. His critique concerns the demarcation of the domain within which statements are valid. The correspondence with his pupil and friend Maurice Drury shows convincingly how crucial religion and art were to Wittgenstein. It is just that, according to him, one cannot theorize or philosophize about this because you end up with unsolvable absurdities—precisely those problems that have kept metaphysics going on for centuries without any real result. Wittgenstein wanted to put an end to this fruitless quest. Silence, then, not because life is meaningless but because its meaning falls outside the scope and operation of logic, of analytic language. It is not a question of saving thought from what is noble, but quite the reverse, of safeguarding what is noble from logical, scientific analysis. It is impossible to reflect upon what is important in a sterile, hygienic, and analytical way. Art, ethics, and religion have to be *lived*.

Two centuries earlier, Kant had shaken the foundations of the entire metaphysical edifice by daring to question the scope of theoretical or scientific reason. He called this study "critique of pure reason." The story goes that his servant Lampe lamented that God was apparently, at least according to his master, beyond the reach of reason. Kant would therefore devote a second study to the reach of yet another reason, not theoretical but practical, not scientific but moral—which, incidentally, turned out to be just as pure as the first one. God does fall within the scope of moral reason.[3]

The insight that thought is motivated or, to use a Kantian term, regulated from a "domain" that remains inaccessible to that thought itself, lives on in a tradition that hardly takes its inspiration from the analytical tradition. This just shows how Wittgenstein cannot simply be placed in this tradition. Derrida speaks of a "law" to which thinking submits without being able to thematize, analyze, or present that law as such. Elsewhere he calls that which from within directs the event of thought "theological" in nature, if only to distinguish that operation from the philosophical event and to close that domain off to philosophy. When Derrida speaks of theology in this way, he is not using it at all in any institutional or doctrinal sense.

Before moving on to Wittgenstein's next phase, we stay with Derrida for a moment. What is usually referred to as "postmodern" thought has been under suspicion of anarchy from the very outset. Those who look away from the crisis into which metaphysics has entered of its own accord—that is, not from the outside, through a cultural-critical or subversive-political putsch—fear that the critique that strikes traditional philosophy is destructive. They fail to recognize that this critique must, again, still be read in a Kantian sense, which is that metaphysics seeks to examine its own scope and validity and to reflect on itself, its pretensions, and its ambitions. Someone like Derrida then convincingly demonstrates how philosophy has always employed certain strategies to "anchor" its propositions and models. Derrida does take the death of God seriously and describes how the concept of God is used to exempt a particular system—what I call a "theistic" system, more or less following Nancy here—from critique, from "deconstruction." This turns out to be the only way to secure "certainty." This strategy has now been "unmasked" as such, as a strategy—or at least it seems that way because is not itself unmasking a strategy to "find" real truth behind every other strategy, as Nietzsche realized while unmasking the unmasking. In any case, we now know that these strategies were tacitly employed and we can therefore never again resort to those strategies. This crisis of thought is not one that can be reversed. Traditional metaphysics can no longer be restored. This is not about an error of thought that can be remedied, nor about a problem that can be solved within metaphysics. I take this up again when we read Derrida himself.

Those who do not understand the crisis go in fear that it leads to "anything goes." If God as Supreme Being is removed from the structure of knowledge then anything is possible, they cry out.[4] Fortunately, their fear is unfounded. It is true that, because of the aforementioned critique, the old mechanisms that declare one proposition true and all others false no longer work in a strict sense. Whereas previously "meaningful" and "true" coincided or at least the former constituted a condition of possibility for the latter (see "wff"), Derrida overturns this rigidity. He examines a meaningless sentence "Le vert est ou," something like "The green is or." In French, however, this possibly sounds like a question, namely "The green is where?" or even "The glass is where?" depending on whether "ou" is heard and contextually interpreted as "où" (by the gardener) and "vert" as "verre" (by the waiter). Derrida analyzes this sentence to the bone and comes to the most curious conclusions that I am not going to unfold here. What Derrida does argue, and rightly so, is that this famous sentence has in the meantime acquired a specific and explicit meaning, namely as a canonical example of a meaningless sentence.[5] This attitude toward what was previously excluded from meaning also occurs elsewhere in French thought. Gilles Deleuze, for example, was not at all concerned with God. Yet he did not state, as is all too often articulated in meatball thinking, that theology has no meaning. For him, theology only passes muster as conceptual container for all notions and models that have little or no (philosophical) relevance. Continental thinkers, at least, are honest enough to include everything in their thinking and refuse to exclude in advance that which threatens any pretended purity—even if, in Wittgenstein's days, there was not yet this outright chasm between continental and analytic philosophy.[6]

Basically, what it comes down to is that for Derrida, there is no such thing as absolute meaninglessness—nor absolute, total, eternal meaningfulness, of course.[7] This does not imply that everything is simply "true." However, we lack a nonnegotiable criterion that decides between what is definitely true and what is definitely false. There is therefore no such thing as absolute, eternal truth. Nevertheless, we cannot "move forward" without any experience of truth. This ambiguity is expressed by Derrida in his famous "Il nous faut la vérité." We need truth, even if we can never fully possess or access it.

Playing and Speaking

Wittgenstein's work is usually divided over two periods. Handbooks will introduce the reader to Wittgenstein I and II, or the first and the second, or whatever. In any case: two Wittgensteinisms. After all, when Wittgenstein in his *Tractatus* had cleaned up all problems in philosophy and started teaching and gardening, he never stopped thinking, of course. A philosopher does not possess an "off" button. And meanwhile, he had begun to doubt the existence of this "work" about which one cannot speak, namely that logic from his early work.

Wittgenstein did not suddenly discover a method by which he could break open this logic; no, he even gave up on that logic. Why would philosophy need this sort of "outside ensurance" of meaning? Why cannot thought itself regulate meaning? Perhaps every way of thinking (and communicating) has an "inner" logic. Perhaps there exist even more than one logic. And then perhaps the most important possibility: perhaps all those logics behave like games.

Wittgenstein is not the first and only one to employ the metaphor of the game to tackle serious and profound philosophical questions. Nothing is more serious than a game, philosophically speaking. After all, a game has its own rules that apply only within that game and without which a game would just not be that particular game. Those rules are not imposed from outside the game. There is no rule outside of chess that governs the behavior of a bishop or rook, no rule outside of a game of cards that governs the relationships between the cards. Nor is there any major rule that is necessarily transferable from one game to another. A rook can never become "trump" in ping-pong. But of course there is a greater similarity between chess and checkers than between chess and ping-pong. Family resemblances, so to speak.

That is all there is. This too makes "game" such a strong metaphor. There is no basic format of "the game," of which all possible games are applications or derivations. There is no metarule that governs all games. Even any winning strategy can only apply to games that are totally uninteresting. The game is a strong metaphor precisely because it rejects any reduction to a prior unity. The game can therefore never be "tested," as in verified or falsified, it can only be played as in won or lost—or even better: well played. Translated to thought and speech: they generate their own effects, but outside this game (e.g., science) there is no arbitration, no agency that assigns an "objective" truth value to the game of thought and speech.

Wittgenstein speaks of "language games" in his second *magnum opus*: his *Philosophical Investigations*. When speaking, depending on the theme and circumstances and other (imponderable) parameters, the language game is determined and the corresponding rules are obeyed. According to the German philosophers Jürgen Habermas and Karl-Otto Apel, this constitutes an ethical attitude, but I think Wittgenstein himself would not go that far. Lyotard also prefers to speak of an agreement that is not necessarily explicit, and Derrida in a similar context will recognize it as a promise. What the Germans consider a commitment, Lyotard a kind of contract, and Derrida a promise, Wittgenstein treats as just given: speech happens. People live together, communicate with each other, and this happens in language games. The intended ethical moment, if any, has already taken place—and it is rather a pragmatic moment. Ethics is a language game that has its own rules, but Wittgenstein no longer accepts an explicit set of "meta-rules" that directs all (other) language games.

Lyotard formulates three remarks about language games: 1. The rules of the language game are the object of an agreement between the players; 2. The rules determine the game—without rules, no (language) game; 3. Every statement counts as a "move" in the game. The game is not determined by either form or content. Such a decision would take on the form of a metarule. Contents (politics, science, art, church . . .) require forms (journalism or recitation, explanatory or understanding, painting or poem, sermon or confession . . .), which then overlap or remain far apart, etc.

Of course, this should not be caricatured as if one chooses a particular language game from the universal menu and then seeks like-minded people who want to play along. To begin with, a language game is not a theory, a description, or an explanation of things and states of affairs. Wittgenstein explains it this way: we do not know that there is a tree in the garden; we do not learn that there are books and hammers. We sit under a tree, read a book, and hammer a nail into the wall. In other words, meaning is not to be found in outerworldly ground but arises from our dealing with that world. We are now getting very close to Heidegger's analysis of how we relate to the things around us in the world.

What then remains of truth? After all, before, there used to be Logic—with capital letter because it now manifests itself as transcendent in outerworldly sense—that guaranteed the correspondence between statements and states of affairs, between speech and the world. But now Wittgenstein has become somewhat "milder." He asks himself the philosophically frugal question why a person would doubt the truth of a flower in the garden, or the truthfulness of a recipe for soup.

It is important to realize that no language play can be called "better" or "more true" than others. That would only be metaphysics again, the self-professed True Language Game. As long as the rules are respected, what is said within the language game remains valid. There is no (longer any) Logic outside the play of language games that directs all language games and evaluates their truthfulness. The production of meaning is purely a matter of each language game itself; it operates and applies only within the appropriate language game. This production is never either totally transferable or absolutely not, given these family resemblances. The religious language game will more easily "spill over" into the poetic than into the scientific. The analytic-religious language game will be very difficult to translate into the continental-religious language game.

Note that there is such a thing as a religious language game after all.[8] Within that game, religious statements do make sense, but this sense cannot be simply and totally transferred to other language games. So it is quite normal for a religion to be unable to formulate scientific arguments, let alone turn them into strong arguments or proofs. Meaning, then, is not universal—this is a first conclusion. Logic is not a universal substance that operates from outside between world and language; in each case it governs the workings of each language game from inside. So there is no single, eternal, universal, autonomous, "divine" Logic after all. That "God" is dead. Curiously, the death of that God called Logic allows for religious speech again. This is a second, in this context important, conclusion. If logic still exists—after all, philosophy has been cleaned up, logic has done its job—it is still purely as a name of the fact that language games exist and that they work according to some mysterious coherence—coherence that is not a human accomplishment, but is also no longer produced by Logic. Logic is no longer a philosophical detergent that dissolves fat philosophical problems, but each time simply yet another form of speaking (about speaking).

Some consider this a clean break with the first Wittgenstein, mainly those who want to categorize him into logical empiricism or ditto positivism. Others discern more continuity. After all, in the "first Wittgenstein" the validity of religious statements was not guaranteed by an external logic, nor was it in the "second Wittgenstein"—in the latter case because there is no "external logic" anymore. Actually, Wittgenstein's attitude toward religious language does not change all that much. It may not fit within a logic, but it does fit within its language game. At most, one might suspect that previously obedience to or distance from a universal logic could be a measure of truth, of validity, or of meaning. His attitude toward analytic philosophy does change, in as far as with its external referent (i.e., Logic) it suddenly loses its absolute truth claim as well. This referent is no longer that about which we must remain silent because we cannot speak of it, but that of which there is simply no more to be said. So, Logic is dead, long live all logics![9]

Are we running into some sort of relativism here? Not at all, because every relativism still presupposes an external absolute reference point, a position outside the field of language games from which all language games are seen to have the same truth value. That would again install something about which it is better to remain silent, and that does not help us any further here. For it is no longer about a truth claim with the simplicity of a "correspondence" between words and things. Just as there is no such thing as an absolute "winning strategy" in games, there is no such thing as an absolute truth guarantee in language games. As long as the rules are respected, the game plays itself out. Of course, there are difficult games, like chess, and easy games, like blackjack. One game already lends itself more easily to strategies with high chances of success than another. Compare it with a religious or philosophical language game on the one hand and the instructions for a shoehorn on the other. The latter language game allows for a quick decision whether the statements make sense or not. But in philosophy, in faith, or in art . . . we do not know at first sight whether we are dealing with meaningful, let alone "true"—whatever that may mean from now on—play of language games.

The end of all certainties . . . that is what Nietzsche prophesied, right? He led the way to thinking without any guarantee of certain truth. Well, we no longer enjoy the comfort of certainty, but we do have confidence in "the Law." What and how we think is not "wild" in the sense of "random." It only seems so because we do not know, and certainly do not control, the laws of thought itself. We have no access to what ultimately motivates thought. Hence the naivete out of desperation among the Last of the Rationalists, who apply scientific (in a broad sense) argument and proof not only within science, but also to thought and its laws themselves.

Perhaps this is what Wittgenstein means when he states that although he is not religious, he still views every problem from a religious position. As awkward as that may seem to some, we just have to accept the fact that what drives our thinking is of a "theological" nature. We can only thematize it as inaccessible; we cannot analyze it as an object of thought. More specifically, we can never completely "clean up" the way toward that Law by means of logical or scientific operations. In this sense, Wittgenstein considers the ambition to find a definitive answer to any question of the form "What is X?" too lofty. All that is acquires meaning within language games and no further; there is no world outside the play of language games where a prior, original truth about X rules in eternity.

The religious language game is legitimate because it is "played," period. God exists because he is spoken of, not because an establishable substance has installed itself outside that game. As I will point out in the last chapter, God is a name that walks in and out of all language games uninvited. That name disturbs every language game, even the theological and the religious.

Believing and Acting

I already mentioned that Wittgenstein admired Kierkegaard. To a faithful friend he explained that two persons who each stood in their own faith should not so much argue with each other as that their lives should be significantly different from each other. So again, faith is a matter not of theory, but of praxis. Therein lies the distinction. I am now rereading Wittgenstein along with Kierkegaard in order to move on to "life."

Wittgenstein called Kierkegaard the most profound thinker of the nineteenth century. This invariably surprises many who think that the former was concerned only with logic and the latter only with faith. The mistake they make is still tangled up with that "silence." Indeed, that we should remain silent about something does not mean that it would not be interesting; quite the contrary. It is precisely here that Wittgenstein agrees with Kierkegaard, namely where he is convinced that what matters in life is not accessible to theoretical explanation or logical description.

The analytic schools, to which Wittgenstein never belonged, tended to consider what could not be said within the logically consistent use of language as nonsense. Wittgenstein considered logic to be a tool for purifying philosophical speech, not for invalidating any other than philosophically purified speech. In this sense, then, Wittgenstein corresponds very well to Kierkegaard, because the latter too wanted to "purify" life, faith, and thought, especially in his "pseudonymous" works. Kierkegaard unrelentingly exposed the inner inconsistencies of any aesthetic and ethical justification of existence; Wittgenstein unrelentingly exposed the inner inconsistencies of speculative philosophy. He thought he had solved the philosophical problems by reducing them to fallacies, so actually he abolished philosophy *de facto*. The old philosophical problems are fake problems, and their old solutions can therefore be little more than beside the point.

The issue at stake is religion, ethics, and the "good life" in all its senses. That is manifestly not a philosophical problem, nor does it bear theoretical treatment. Faith or religious existence does not depend or hinge on metaphysical propositions. The good life cannot be derived from a set of faith contents or doctrinal propositions. Rattling off the creed simply because you believe you have to, but without living by it, would have irritated Wittgenstein just as much as Kierkegaard.

Wittgenstein compared his *Tractatus* to a ladder that is no longer needed after having reached the highest step. At the end of that book he says unequivocally: whoever follows my reasoning beyond the propositions in the book, that is, beyond philosophy, suddenly recognizes all those statements in it as nonsense. Wittgenstein's whole philosophical enterprise, imagined as a ladder, consists in getting beyond philosophy, not so much to arrive at another, better philosophy, but to arrive at a morally and religiously fulfilling life, unhindered by so-called philosophical problems. Logical analysis should only make itself superfluous, once thinking has been cleaned up.

Not that this is a goal in itself. Wittgenstein is not a nihilist. It is not his intention to abolish thinking. Rather, he seems to be trying to "liberate" faith, morality, and art from the straitjacket of metaphysics. For Wittgenstein, ethics is the investigation of what is valuable, not of what is true. To him, a value is not a fact. This distinction is much older—already David Hume warned about the confusion between value and fact—but it is sometimes forgotten that Wittgenstein considered ethics and religion more important than logic, usually because there is nothing about them in his *Tractatus*. According to Wittgenstein, there is no explanation for religion. "Any such explanation I would reject," he says, "not because the explanation is wrong, but because it is an explanation." In a letter to his friend Drury, he writes, "The symbolism of Christianity is beautiful beyond words, but when anyone tries to turn it into a philosophical system, I find that disgusting."

In his diary, Wittgenstein noted that belief in God comes down to the recognition that there is more than just facts. His last words are "Tell them I have had a wonderful life." In the gratitude of one who leaves such a tormented life, should we not recognize a certain spirituality beyond all logic? If so, it is now time to turn to Heidegger.

8

Nothing

Heidegger

Heidegger was not a great fan of biographies. When a student asked him for some background on Aristotle during a class, he gruffly replied, "He was born, worked, and died. Now back to the lesson." Perhaps Heidegger, one of the pioneers of what is called existential philosophy, was not convinced of a meaningful connection between a person's concrete existence or life on the one hand and his thinking or philosophy on the other. For him, the act of thinking cannot be reduced to an initiative of the subject. Just as well, perhaps, since he has made at least one serious misstep in his life. In 1933 he was elected Rector of the University of Freiburg and a week later he joined the NSDAP (commonly known as the Nazi Party), which may indicate at least a certain opportunism.

We are not going to talk about "that" here. When my students, who usually only know that Heidegger was "a Nazi," get restless when his name is mentioned, I justify myself with the words of Levinas. This Jewish philosopher lost almost his entire family in the extermination camps and nevertheless said of Heidegger that he was the "Himalaya of twentieth-century thought."[1] Furthermore, I would like to refer here to the pile of apologetics that have appeared since the work of Victor Farias until the aftermath of the publication of the so-called "black notebooks." Here I will make do with the remark that in philosophical circles it has by no means been decided whether his leaning toward NSDAP has a significant, even relevant influence on (the reception of) his thinking. As a matter of fact, one finds in his work a great deal of criticism of regimes such as Nazism (and communism, capitalism, Americanism, etc.).

Heidegger, like Nietzsche the son of a sexton, studied at the expense of the Catholic Church, which at the time almost automatically meant a seminary education. After an unsuccessful attempt to enter the Jesuits, he took up the study of theology, only to turn to philosophy two years later. It was not until he was thirty years old that he publicly distanced himself from what he called "the system of Catholicism." He had just then become Husserl's assistant, after the Jewish Edith Stein—who had become Husserl's assistant on completing her dissertation on empathy—converted to Catholicism and entered a convent of the Discalced Carmelites. She turned to the God of the *New* Testament.

Heidegger had it noted that the God in philosophy is another than the God to whom we dance and sing and kneel and pray. In an extremely subtle and original way, he explores how the latter was able to transform into the former. How did God get into philosophy to become a Supreme Being in a rational structure? That is the question Heidegger explicitly asks himself in a key text, *The Ontotheological Structure of Metaphysics*. It sounds complicated, but once we become familiar with how Heidegger thinks and writes, things will clear up.

Although Heidegger probably knew very well how he made many people dizzy with his writings, he himself claimed that his thinking was closer to the essence of man than technoscientific thinking. Despite the fact that this latter (un)thinking determines our world, it actually alienates us from our true humanity. That is not so much because of what he called "calculating thinking" in itself, but because of the inflated status that we are used to giving it in our thoughtlessness.

Heidegger has been accused of being an incorrigible nostalgic who wrote reactionary pamphlets against science and technology in his mountain cabin in the Black Forest. Not so. For one thing, Heidegger was wise enough to realize that science and technology cannot be reversed. Abolishing technology, for that matter, would become a highly technical matter and thus self-defeating at the root. Second, technology can and will abolish itself, as a historical phenomenon. This is destined. That is precisely the revolutionary insight that Heidegger advances. Reality, or the world, is not an unchanging structure "over there, before us" (*ob-iectum*) that we unravel bit by bit, with science serving as our ultimate tool. We must take an appropriate attitude toward this phenomenon, toward that way in which we think and in which things appear to us—a way Heidegger calls "resignation," with reference to Meister Eckhart's *Gelassenheit*. Third, many ignore a curious fact. Generally speaking and certainly in phenomenology, the living world (*Lebenswelt*) is opposed to the scientific world. I went into this when presenting Russell, but here I need to nuance that alleged opposition.² For in both worlds, technology plays a crucial role. Hence Heidegger sees in technology an umbrella term, a way of being and thinking that fundamentally marks our world, in which we live and do science. It is not an arsenal of tools, but a "techno-logic."

Technology, according to Heidegger, is the motif or baseline of Western metaphysics. Asking about being became ordering being. Dealing with reality, i.e., the event of world, has become dominated by exploitation, calculation, planning, control, extrapolation, and so on. Modernity has reached its completion in marketing and management. In this completion it has also suddenly exhausted all the possibilities of modern metaphysics.

Surely we are inclined to think ourselves, moderns, very successful. After all, we have completely mastered technoscientific control after centuries of plodding away in the dark. According to many—that is, Russell and his heirs—this finally leaves all "inferior, primitive" ways of thinking behind. Now Heidegger finds this a most questionable thesis, in the sense of ill-considered and thus still to be thought through. He rejects the superficial "yes" or "no" to technology in favor of a "yes" *and* "no": resignation.

Being

It typifies Heidegger's path of thought that he does not directly ask the question about being, as traditional metaphysics does. For whoever asks "What is being?" is actually already asking about a thing, a well-defined "that." So this question is not really open, because the answer is already largely contained in it. No, he asks why and how metaphysics has forgotten about being, precisely by asking about it directly, with the wrong question. After all, being is not a thing of which philosophy can request a determination. This, according to Heidegger, is the tragedy of metaphysics which asked the question about being in the way you would ask about beings. The answer to this question automatically arrives at a Supreme Being. This step betrays what he calls the "onto-theo-logical" structure of thought. According to this structure, any rational system (-logy) will always refer being as a whole (onto-) back to a Supreme Being (-theo-). Heidegger wants to push thinking through this structure and set it free again. Being is not a thing but an event, namely the event of meaning, of world, of truth.

Now why is this so important, turning being from noun into verb? Well, Heidegger does take the death of God—Nietzsche, remember—seriously and recognizes the nihilistic, auto-destructive tendency in Western thought.

Fitting thought into a fixed structure time and again leads to nothing less than suffocation. The Supreme Being becomes exhausted and loses its power. The structure collapses. The system implodes.

Those who prefer to look away from this cling to the modern idea that thinking is "moving forward"—remember evolution, progress, etc.—toward (the scientific representation of) the true world. The history of philosophy then consists in a steady process of purification. Systematically all irrational and illusory elements are eliminated. Religion belongs to these elements. So does poetry. The world, in turn, is nothing but the object, that mute and inert thing. Mute because it is completely detached from thought. It lies completely sunk in indifferent complacency, ready to be unraveled by whoever knows the right code. The right code must be science, because that is simply the culmination of the process of purification. That is a typical element of the modern self-image—which has no legitimation outside itself.[3]

Modernity installed a historical dynamic that understands everything in terms of progress, emancipation, evolution, rationalization, etc. Romanticism has never been able to deflate this notion. Modernity employs this specific dynamic in response to the question concerning its own status. However, the dynamic reveals an ambiguity that Heidegger was able to unmask. On the one hand, it seems that the history of thought is a noble, speculative affair. Man seeks knowledge for the sake of knowledge—what Nietzsche called the truth drive. By systematic elimination of primitive impurities he arrives at science. Coincidentally, in the wake of this disinterested search, a technology also develops that profits immensely, without any ethical reservation, from the results of science, in order to promote the prosperity of nations. On the other hand, this history can also be read "backwards." In the work of Aristotle, the seeds of a tendency are already appearing whereby humanity wants to explain the world in order to control it. Control then becomes the criterion of progress. Thus, science becomes the effect of technology, not the other way around. At the moment when algebra and experiment were presented to reason, they proved most suitable for meeting the requirement of control that has motivated thought since Aristotle.[4] Technology, in this view, becomes a hermeneutic ontology instead of the sum total of all tools on earth. It is the way in which we think about the world and in which the world appears to us, as two sides of the same coin. As I said, because of this destiny or historical tendency, we no longer receive being, we have come to order it.

This way of thinking eventually produced the system of objectivity in which, on the one hand, the world exists independently of thought and, on the other hand, thought is granted direct and complete access to that world, at least as long as the correct—i.e., scientific—method is used. Who or what guards this access, no one knows or even wants to know. The system of objectivity translates the question of legitimacy into evidence and thereby renders the question superfluous. The question of objectivity is not heard in metaphysics, even considered unheard(-of). Heidegger, therefore, calls objectivity "unthought of" and, precisely for that very reason, worthy of our closest attention.

All through metaphysics, that is, since Aristotle, philosophy has thought of being in the way of a being. How is that? Being was understood as "being-caused." Being existed only because it was caused by another being. According to Aristotle, each being has four causes, each in their turn a being. He gives the example of a statue. Its causes are the substance (e.g., a lump of marble), the maker (e.g., a sculptor), the idea or representation (e.g., a man with a beard), and the purpose (e.g., worship in a temple). For everyday life, this model amply suffices, but philosophy soon finds this model too superficial. After all, if we try to imagine a "causal chain" along which we arrange all causes, realizing that each cause has four causes, we get an exponentially expanding and unsurveyable stream of being. This would make any standard metaphysician dizzy—and nauseated. Hence Aristotle allowed himself a trick that, in many guises, has lasted for more than two millennia. For Aristotle claimed that everything exists for the sake of one Unmoved Mover, a perfection in and on and for and by itself, which is itself not caused but which can count as the final cause, as the "because of which" of everything. No wonder that when Aristotle's work made its way into the West via an Arab and a Latin translation, theologians of that time—Thomas Aquinas being the most famous—immediately identified this Supreme Being with God. Still much later, Spinoza continued to call God *Causa Sui*, his own cause. Christian metaphysics, that is: Western philosophy and theology held on to this system for centuries. The order of being and the order of knowing shared a parallel structure with God at the top and all the rest underneath. God provided the basis of being and the explanation for all being in the form of a plan of salvation including a natural law—thus also a moral, political, and aesthetic . . . order.

This structure was assumed to be the perfect representation of reality. In other words, reality was supposed to behave according to this structure. Much depended on this, especially the intended grasp and control of that reality. Remember Hegel, who claimed to have mapped out all of reality and its history and was sometimes reproached that reality did not always behave according to his system, to which he then laconically replied, "Well, too bad for reality!" The system trumped reality. We have already seen how Kierkegaard tried to think beyond such constructions. Whereas Kierkegaard offers the leap as a way out, Heidegger proposes a "step back." This step back renounces total systematization, structuring, rationalization of the world.[5] Thinking stops before the enclosure of the world around a Supreme Being and thus avoids the ontotheological trap. This keeps Heidegger within thought, within metaphysics that is, rather than jumping out of it into a sort of faith.[6]

If being can no longer be made present, but only retrieved as decay, as exhausted, as dismantled, then of course it makes no sense to keep on frenetically deploying one system after another. Then we must help thought to break free from that system, from logic, and from objectivity. The "dismantling" and the "abyss" show an opportunity, a liberation.

Truth

Heidegger began where Wittgenstein stopped, with man finding meaning in his dealings with things.[7] We can only understand something, only think something, in our capacity of being-in-the-world. Truth does not come from another, higher world. Both Heidegger and Wittgenstein realize that we receive the meaning of a hammer by hitting a nail with it. Heidegger starts from the world, here and now.[8] He calls this "facticity," which has nothing to do with facts or *data*.

This still does not contradict Heidegger's reticence about the connection between biography and philosophy above. "Facticity" is not yet what Sartre made of it afterwards, the sum of all my actions and thoughts, i.e., my strictly individual autobiography. By facticity Heidegger means that thinking does not fall from heaven; it is always already happening around us.[9] Indeed, the world is the whole web of meaning that is going on. There is no thought outside the world, also no world outside thought. What remained "unthought" is *unheimlich*, does not belong to the world. This has become a basic thesis of so-called hermeneutics.[10] This is where the Cartesian model of the world on the one hand and thought on the other implodes. Heidegger's hermeneutics do not reduce the world to things that obey laws laid down by physics (materialism) or ideas that follow mental laws (idealism). World and thought are "reunited."[11]

According to Heidegger, technoscience has occupied thought to such an extent that the essence of actuality remains out of sight. For if we think that science and technology are simply available to us, we are gravely mistaken. We ourselves are completely determined by what Heidegger calls technology. We are available to technology. Technology is not an arsenal of scientific models and technical instruments, but a way of being and thinking, of existing. Technology is a name for our world. Our world comes about thanks to an indexing of things; our world has the form of a file. The world consists of things that we can retrieve as from a menu. It is not that our world is digitized, but the other way around: the computer has become the metaphor of our thinking because it best represents what the world has become, how being is delivered to us.

None of this means that science is the ultimate and total explanation of the world. Science has, at least so we suspect since Kant, a well-defined range that it cannot calculate itself. After all, outside that range nothing exists, nothing persists, and what means nothing to science prevails there. This is, however, precisely why Heidegger considers this nothing of essential importance, because where nothing prevails, being is to be found.[12] This is where Carnap and other analytic philosophers began to feel very uncomfortable . . .

Being is not a thing and cannot be thought of in the way we think of beings, for example scientifically. Heidegger called this insight "ontological difference." So being cannot be thought of as a cause, a condition of possibility, or a total, etc. of all beings because then it would still be thought of as a being—a Supreme Being indeed, but still a being. Actually, we cannot formulate an epistemological relation between being and beings and vice versa without falling into the trap of the traditional metaphysical approach. Heidegger tries very hard to avoid that trap, even though he realizes that the entire grammar of Western language seems to be tangled up in that metaphysics. Nietzsche had also noted that as long as our language hangs on to the word "is," we remain tied to metaphysics and theology. By this he meant that whenever we utter a sentence or proposition like "X is A," its truth should always be guaranteed by an otherworldly authority, a divine arbiter. This is less true of statements within our daily world like "John is sick" or "This pancake is tasty" but becomes relevant when we deal with statements about the world like "Being is becoming" or "Everything is relative" or "History is awareness" or "Truth is agreement between thing and idea."

Truth for Heidegger is not "propositional," not primarily a property of statements. It is not a question of parallelism between reality on the one hand and a theory or model or proposition on the other. The latter can at most be "correct," but never fully true. Full truth is reserved for a more "essential" (*wesentlich*) thinking. Ontological difference shows that being is not a being, but essentially no-thing, a not-something. It communicates itself to beings. Being can be seen as meaningfully presenting beings to thought. Being is then the unthought in Cartesian dualism. Heidegger also likes to draw on a poetic version of phenomenological jargon. Being then becomes lighting up beings. This means that beings arrive in thought as meaningful without any well-defined intention on the side of being or any identifiable mechanics of being behind it. Things just appear in a meaningful context called "world." World is the event of meaning—better: of sense, of a sensible coherence of meaning. When and where world happens, "it makes sense." Whether that is scientific or something else, there is nothing to be done about that. World is destined.

Aristotle was not too stupid to shoot rockets at the moon. The way being was understood then, the way being presented beings to thought—in short, the world of antiquity—did not allow for this approach at the time. In the ancient world, the earth was not an exploitable lump. To Aristotle, the "supernatural" was the sphere of the perfect, of the divine. Stars were eternal because they moved in perfect circles that have neither beginning nor end. No mortal shoots sublunary things up there. Step by step, the partitions between the supernatural and the natural were broken down. Petrarch went up Mont Ventoux in April 1336 and found the landscape there as alluring as it was below. Nothing special, nothing divine. Just the same nature but slightly different. In April 1961, 625 years later, Yuri Gagarin left the earth's atmosphere. He testified that he did not find God out there.[13] Stars and planets lose their sacred significance. They become mere lumps. No objection to shooting things at them; after all, that has become purely a matter of calculation and exploitation.

The "huge" event is the arrival and reception of modernity, of modern thought, of the "other," modern world; to shoot missiles at lumps is at most spectacular. The first event concerns the event of world, the *truth* of being, the world *as* event; the second is merely a matter of calculation, of being *correct*. Technology, *the* motif and motive of metaphysics, has turned the earth and all celestial bodies into lumps. Space travel was never organized for the sake of cosmic poetry or knowledge-for-knowledge, but had a very explicit agenda: exploiting space. As Carl Sagan proclaimed on television in the 1970s, to tremendous applause: when we have made the earth uninhabitable once and for all, no problem, we will all go to Mars and start all over again.

Being becomes, with Heidegger, an event to which calculation has no access. It cannot be understood through causes, because being has none.

The grand principle of Leibniz applies to technology: *Nihil est sine ratione*: nothing is without reason, ground, or cause. In other words, everything has a reason, ground, and cause and is as such justified not only in existence but also in intelligibility. All that is, therefore, necessarily has a ground, is grounded, and can therefore rationally be accounted for. Even God, the ground itself, is grounded in the understanding that there must be one principle from which all the rest can be derived.

Heidegger, however, turns this grand principle inside out. He rephrases: nothingness is without reason, *ex nihilo*. Recall that this nothingness does not refer to a denial or absence of being, but to the element where being dwells and science has no access. Finding ourselves in a technoscientific world, we cannot propose otherworldly reasons for this. Then no suprahistorical evaluation of modernity applies. There *is* technology, it makes up our world, period. When Heidegger was asked what is the most important word in his famous title *Being and Time*, he answered (of course): "and." Behind the event of being, that is, behind the reception of the world, no agency or mechanics manages this event. There were ancient Greeks, there were Middle Ages, etc. Those are different worlds. Behind those worlds resides no "true" world of which all worlds are merely historical-geographical or cultural reflections or instances. Worlds come and go.[14] There is no reason to assume that "our" world is the last and best. But then we must think being not in the way of a thing, but as event.

Freedom

Just as Heidegger sets truth apart from epistemology, he takes freedom out of psychology and ethics. He is not concerned with freedom of choice, not with the choice between coffee and tea, or even between good and evil. Like truth, true freedom belongs to ontological difference; that is, to being as event rather than as a fixed structure that determines freedom—insofar as that is not a contradiction. In this sense, then, Heidegger fully stands in the modern tradition where freedom and emancipation are key concepts.

Freedom could be opposed to alienation. If freedom belongs to the essence of man and thus to thinking, then taking away that essence constitutes an attack on freedom. For Heidegger, alienation is due to the forgetting of being. Metaphysics is the history of alienation in that it denies man his own destiny. To even see that, we need to think beyond metaphysics. But there is no thought beyond metaphysics. That is why Heidegger, as mentioned above, goes in search of the unthought *within* metaphysics. So, how can we think the unthought? How can we liberate thought?

Heidegger himself, who liked to retreat to his cabin on Todtnauberg in the Black Forest, uses the image of a *Holzweg* as a metaphor for thought. This almost untranslatable word refers to overgrown paths in the forest along which wood is dragged out of the forest. They are the effect of that dragging; they do not lead from A to B, according to a plan. They suddenly stop in the middle of the forest. There are many of these, winding through every forest. They are often deceptively similar and cannot serve as specific landmarks. In German, *auf dem Holzweg* means "lost track." In any case, it refers to the opposite of a well-trodden path, the beaten track, the "road most traveled."

Holzweg refers to what Heidegger means by the unthought. This is not some well-defined content that lies waiting somewhere to be divulged but has not yet become articulated in the prevailing philosophical systems. The unthought is not, as with Hegel, something that still has to be appropriated in order to obtain a fuller picture, a more complete explanation. The unthought is what thinking has forgotten, albeit not in a psychological sense. It is not about trying to remember a shopping list and then forgetting the milk. It is about a complex of not wanting to think, not being able to think, and not being allowed to think. Derrida called it the "unheard-of." This has a double connotation—and Derrida always liked that. It means that which is not heard, but also that which is deemed inappropriate. It is about what "cannot be" in an epistemological as well as in an ethical sense. But again, more on this when we come to Derrida himself.

Even if science shows us a sterile, mechanical, senseless world, everyone still accepts that this is the "true" world. It is simply thought of this way, period; it constitutes a rationalist evidence, an article of faith, *the* scientistic creed. This thought results from a long history of research, a process of systematic purification and elimination of so-called primitive elements. The possibility that science is only one discourse—or language game—among others, that it is simply the way in which things in a certain consistency—which I called "world"—appear to us, remains unthought. Technoscience is then no longer objective reality but the way in which being and thinking belong to each other in time. Not only does this remain unthought within science, it is also considered unheard-of to dare suggest this. After all, it makes no sense, since it is about nothing—that is, about being. Current thought then behaves exactly like a "fashion," a temporal validity that rejects what does not "fit."[15]

Only from the unthought can another thought sprout. More precisely, the contemplation of the unthought makes it possible for another way of thinking to come into view. Since Heidegger believes that metaphysics has exhausted its possibilities, another way of thinking must present itself. This becomes exciting since it follows from the inherent nature of any really other way of thinking that it cannot be included within or derived from current thought. Metaphysics cannot think beyond itself without going "under deconstruction." Levinas and Derrida will teach us more about this "other" as the place where metaphysics wants to break free from itself. This detachment is supposed to facilitate the appearance of that other way of thinking.

The question remains, of course, how then we are to receive a thought that does not (yet) belong to our thinking. If another way of thinking comes into view, as I phrased it, it cannot be a "full view." Here Heidegger uses the word "wink." This "other" thinking, not translatable into ours, will arrive in a form analogous to a wink. What does "wink" mean? It has no content; it only "points." It points to something that is about to happen, an opportunity, an opening, a promise. What event awaits us? Well, here Heidegger indulges once again in a clever wordplay. "Event" in German is called *Ereignis*. But Heidegger reads a second meaning into it: the mutual appropriation, namely of being and thinking: *Er-eignis*. Thinking and being were separated from each other. When thinking leaves behind all rigidity of the metaphysical system and starts contemplating the event, this counts as essential liberation, as liberation from metaphysics' determination of mankind, alienated and amputated from being.

Being lasts; world does not last, not even God. Did not Nietzsche teach us that gods also decompose? Dead gods decay, just like everything else in this world. But being is also always arriving and a new world announces itself. In *Ereignis*, a wink will become visible. Therefore we, as thinking beings, must be vigilant, for the event approaches like a thief in the night.[16]

God, and Also: the Last

Heidegger himself shows a certain "modernization" along his thinking path. First, philosophy used to underpin theology—perhaps because the church then "underpinned" his studies financially. But then suddenly philosophy becomes the only ontological reading of the world, whereas theology, along with all other sciences, is put down as an ontic approach.[17] After all, theology is concerned with a being, albeit the Supreme Being. At the end of his life,

Heidegger entered what could be called a third phase in which philosophy and theology were allowed to stand side by side. In a conversation with students in 1951, Heidegger once admitted that he would like to write a theology without the word "be"—that shortest word of which Nietzsche claimed that, as long as we continue to use it, thought will never escape the yoke of theology.[18] Here we have an interesting starting point.

God is not affected by being. The fact that, according to Heidegger, God only "happens" from within the essence of being does not mean that "being" is expected to become a predicate of God. For him, God is a matter of experience and being is a matter of thought. The identification of God with a being, even if that being is a Supreme Being, stands in the way of any true question concerning God. How did this identification come about? And if it disappears in the "end" of metaphysics, does this mean that the God of the Christians suffers the same fate as everything else in the world? Or does God transcend being after all?

Being, then, is not God, and vice versa. The God who was alive once, namely the Supreme Being from metaphysics, is dead. The question concerning the God of faith remains open, undecided. Heidegger shows himself to be as ambiguous as Nietzsche, as if God could be introduced in philosophy, but not as God of faith, although dependent on this God. It seems as if for Heidegger the God of the Christians will disappear along with the God of metaphysics. But does God immerse in theology? If not, philosophy can never decide whether the final god, the liberation from metaphysics and Christianity, is also the God of the Cross.

The dissolution of all metaphysics, God included, has long been underway. Heidegger speaks of de-godding as the historical framework of that dissolution. He describes this process as follows: on the one hand, during modernity, the worldview becomes Christian, by attaching it to a Supreme Being; on the other hand, Christianity becomes worldview by appropriating a metaphysical system. In this way, gods have fled. De-godding prepares modernity, not the other way around. Modernity is the world in which the concept of God itself is elaborated, and murdered. The whole world implodes and all systems and structures erode. Both the organization of a system around God and the denial of the existence of God are figures of de-godding.

De-godding is not a human activity; it cannot happen on our initiative. The gods leave, this just happens, their departure arrives. There is no god who at a certain point gathers his things and leaves. The last god is the event of the departure. From that moment onwards, believers only hang on to their God in a theoretical model, among others. This specific form of theism, namely the rational argument for faith, has then become an option. So has atheism in its superficial formulation. Between these two, there is no decision. Modernity is the undecidability concerning God. Moreover, says Heidegger, within the realm of thought we would be better off remaining silent about God, for what are we talking about when God has fled and is dead?

Heidegger considers theology and, in fact, metaphysics symptomatic of an inability to deal with finitude. For Heidegger, therefore, the step back also involves staying away from Christianity, remaining in the question (philosophy) and renouncing the hope of an illusory, otherworldly answer, which is precisely *the* theological premise. The step back must prepare for the coming of the last god.

That last god is our only salvation. In an interview with *Der Spiegel* that was not allowed to be published until after his death in 1976, the self-proclaimed atheist thinker Heidegger spoke the famous words, "Only a god can save us."[19] What would or could a last god do in a world abandoned by or of God, from which God disappeared, in which God was murdered? God indeed had to disappear from the metaphysical register of presence, had to let go of being. But Heidegger's God is no longer defined by being—remember his statement about a theology without "being." God need not be a being, which is perfectly consistent with monotheism, which says that God is not to be sought among beings because only God is God. It simply means that God can return, but in an other-than-metaphysical register. If God returns, it is not as the same divine substance that had become momentarily forgotten. Just as de-godding makes up the meaning of God, now the last god is fully understood under the sign of arrival, without being. Philosophically speaking, the last god is completely determined by his advent, in the event of his arrival, in the announcement of the event—without this determination implying any statement about the event, about its content and nature. The last god arrives winking; that is all he "does." To discern this, thought must let go of metaphysics, must take the "step back." Only then does the space open up in which alert thought can catch the wink and the divine can arrive. The last god can only return or arrive as departed. The arrival is the departure.

That space is the realm of the sacred. Philosophy can open that space, but it is up to the poet to name the sacred, to invoke it. Cannot poetic thought and speech then also be the place where philosophy reconnects with theology, even though Heidegger calls them opposites? Does not something like "theopoetics" appear in theology today? Indeed, this involves a renunciation of overly rigid rational categories in our thinking about God and an acceptance of the rich metaphors that the treasure of faith harbors.

Heidegger suggests in *Identity and Difference* that this god-less thinking that abandons the God of metaphysics is perhaps closest to the divine God. That divine God is the God to whom we pray, sacrifice, kneel, dance, and sing.[20] It is therefore advised to read Heidegger, at least those who seriously want to get to know him, in a religious register. We surely would do better to follow the religious rather than the logical path of his discourses. Those who follow the religious path enter a future that is not one of calculation but one of reception. Those who follow the logical path merely get a headache.

All of Heidegger's basic terms and fundamental insights breathe Christianity. It begins with the chosen status of man, the thinker. Does not "belonging to being" resemble the image of God that we find in theology of creation? And what about decay as a natural state of man, which he can authentically transcend in contemplation? In contemplation, then, the world appears as the being-given of things, which should make us grateful. Living among things, being in-the-world as marked by care, seems to be inspired by the idea of finitude as it is elaborated in Protestant theology.[21] Resignation, this strange word of Eckhart, is considered the only true late-modern attitude toward technology. The idea of salvation as the last god in *Ereignis*, which happens as advent, gratefully received in the basic confidence that we will never be left behind in utter absurdity, in total forgottenness of being, in meaninglessness, in hell. And how this trustful confidence urges us to look forward expectantly to the arrival of a new being, which announces itself in a wink, in something that does not say anything, like a baby in a manger. By thinking of being as forgotten, as a "Deus absconditus," we withdraw it from total forgottenness without restoring it to its full presence as a being.

Let us consider the special position of the human being that is chosen as the unique location of being that gives itself to thought. A human being is, of course, a being but is not completely absorbed in or determined by that being-ness. A human being is in, but not of the world, to put it biblically. That is why a human can never become a complete object of scientific inquiry. With Heidegger, humans reach beyond beings through their belonging to being. The religious register resonates clearly here. At least, it complies with the first two chapters of the book of Genesis. In the first creation story, only man is created in the image of God. All the rest was already there, unformed, and was simply divided, separated, opened, and produced. Life was created, but not in the image of God. Creation refers to an organization of world, as it were, within which things can acquire meaning. This, by the way, is the philosophical meaning of the Flood: when man forgets God, the waters above and those below unite again. Creation is undone; there is no more world and no more meaning. Also in the second creation story, much older and much more mythical, all nature is already there but only man receives divine breath, spirit. Transformation, separation, and so on, can be read as analogous to Heidegger's givenness of world, where man finds the names for things, their meanings. Unlike the Bible, however, Heidegger does not stage a giver or creator.

Thinking is considered the path of redemption from the fallenness of banal existence, from what Heidegger calls forgottenness of being, from what seems to be a philosophical fall from grace that constitutes the "original" belonging together of thinking—*Dasein*, human being—and being. His thoughts on guilt within the framework of care also refer strongly to the theology of sin. The initiative for this redemption does not befit man, however; rather, it befits being itself that nevertheless remains nothing without thinking. In thinking, being appears as the nothingness of the world, as what means nothing to the world. One can easily compare this with the first chapter of the Gospel of John.

Later, Heidegger recognizes this fallenness no longer in existence but in metaphysics itself, no longer in the attuned (*gestimmt*) life from where thinking sprouts but in all that is (to be) thought. This thought has not yet heard the good message, namely, that true thinking, marked in the first place by hope, trust, and receptivity,[22] prepares the advent of the new understanding of being. That thinking should take on resignation à la Eckhart and vigilance à la Paul.

Of all the philosophers in this book, Heidegger is the most religious. It is mainly from him that I learned to think further about a philosophical vs. "flat" atheism.

9

Unfree

Sartre

It was considered *bon ton* in postwar Paris to roll out life without reference to God. Nevertheless, it is said that Sartre, at the end of his earthly existence, opened the door a little to a certain transcendence on the ground of moral considerations—rather Kantian, in fact. It is also rumored that Simone de Beauvoir, with whom he was known to have had a literary-philosophical relationship—and more—tried to "suppress" his notes on the subject, dating from as early as 1947 onward. Sartre's notes were published posthumously in 1983 as *Cahiers pour une morale* or *Notebooks for an Ethics*.

It may be typical of Sartre that, as an original thinker, he did not leave behind a fully accomplished system. Indeed, at the end of *Being and Nothingness*, he indicated that he wanted to work out an ethics on the basis of that book. It was never published. In *Critique of Dialectical Reason*, Sartre tried to reconcile his individualistic existentialism with a rather collectivistic Marxism—courageous, complex, and sometimes quite abstract. However interesting, the intended reconciliation was never achieved. It should come as no surprise that some people started to fill in the blanks in Sartre's work themselves.

Sartre's star, rightly or wrongly, has since waned considerably. His alliance with communism, like Heidegger's flirtation with Nazism, has infected his credibility. Communism was then the trend among Parisian intellectuals. When Albert Camus, in *The Rebel*, rejected communism along with all other totalitarian regimes, it led to a split with Sartre. Relations with Raymond Aron, a fellow student of Sartre's and his co-founder of the journal *Les Temps modernes*, also deteriorated because of Aron's leanings toward center right-wing liberalism. Another co-publisher, Maurice Merleau-Ponty, later described Sartre as an ultra-Bolshevik. But then again, Louis Althusser, for example, was a prominent member of the Communist Party. Derrida recalls that the latter denied the brutal suppression of the Hungarian uprising (1956) by Warsaw troops—left-wing negationism—because that would have implied that the party had made a mistake, and this was inconceivable. It is a pity that a philosopher of that stature could be tempted to such dogmatism. Sartre may not have gone that far, but his political myopia regarding the communist regimes still remains unworthy of an intellectual of such stature, however culturally "excusable."

Sartre was vehemently opposed to the French colonial regime in Algeria—where, by the way, Camus and Althusser, but also Derrida, were born. He even condoned anti-colonial violence. "Shooting a white man wins twice. It destroys an oppressor and an oppressed. What remains are a dead man and a free man." He was arrested during a demonstration, but President de Gaulle let him out, explaining that "One does not imprison Voltaire." Perhaps the general was considering the quote from Voltaire where the latter said of someone whose opinion he did not share, "I despise what you say, but I would give my life for your right to say it." Or was he rather thinking of Herbert Marcuse's repressive tolerance where the powers that be pamper critics with praise and prizes to take the sting out of them.

Heidegger, after an initial enthusiastic response to *Being and Nothingness*, is said to have characterized Sartre afterwards as a "rather talented journalist." Is this a sneer at a philosopher's political commitment? Or did the great master of the Black Forest denounce the little writer from the Parisian café? Did Heidegger think that Sartre exaggerated factuality by picking his philosophical examples off the counter? Or did the Nazi thinker recognize a younger colleague also going down the wrong path?

Sartre never made the mistake of boldly stating that God does not exist. He does say that if God exists, I cannot be free. He also says that a human being is "condemned" to absolute and radical freedom—and the crushing responsibility that goes with it. Finally, he warns us that submission to God counts as bad faith, what he calls "mauvaise foi." We must therefore live "as if God does not exist." This, then, is the "other" wager than Pascal's—but not "other" in the same way as Russell. Pascal claims that those who do not know whether God exists are better off pretending that he does. Sartre regards the non-existence of God not as an "ontological" but as an existential proposition.

Existence, Essence

Two world wars gave pause for thought. In less than forty years, all of Europe was shattered. Suddenly, great ideals, structures, and systems appeared dangerous rather than worth striving for. *Dulce et decorum pro patria mori?* Not any longer, no. After all, was it not in the name of those great systems, referred to in Horace's quote as "fatherland," that both world wars broke out? Apparently, as Nietzsche foresaw and Heidegger thought through, those systems have lost their credibility, their potency. Consequently, humans can no longer turn to those great systems—or narratives, see Lyotard—to disclose the meaning of existence and society.

Then the question rises whether our life has or receives any meaning at all. This overarching being that produced religious, political, and moral structures and systems appears to have collapsed. God is dead, so we are told, but we shall see that Sartre does not quite include this insight in his philosophical project—he considered Nietzsche a mad poet rather than a philosopher. The consecrated and worldly representations of Christ on earth, together with natural law, turned out to be exhausted essences. Previously, these were the most essential signifiers that organized the scholastic and feudal world. Modern rationality threw them out and took over the organization of the world itself. The cultural-historical motif was now translated into terms like social engineering, progress, secularization, etc. No matter how Sartre tried, and apparently that was his ambition, he could not lift his existentialism beyond this motif. Just as Marx turned Hegel "upside down," so Sartre turns the classical form around where the meaning of existence used to be derived from pre-given and original (read: decreed by creation) instances, truths, and norms: the essences. But he never really reached beyond metaphysics, even if he allowed existence to precede essence in the ontological order.[1]

Sartre's contemporary Levinas also plays with the tension between these two. They both borrowed this tension from Heidegger. But where for Heidegger the vocation of the thinking human being comes from being, for Sartre and Levinas being rather represents the inhuman, the non-thinking, the enclosed, the mute. Pre-modern essence—which Heidegger rephrased as a verb: "being"—has simply been left empty for them. Whereas with Levinas being is an unthinkable thing, a bare and undifferentiated being, with Sartre being is attributed to things in opposition to consciousness, which withdraws from being. Not only can consciousness achieve this, it even has to because otherwise it too would be objectified as a thing, as just a being.

Heidegger, Sartre, and Levinas thus all agree that in the case of humans, being is not the last word. With Levinas, human is what emancipates from being with the promise of an ethics; with Sartre, human is consciousness that resists being; and finally, with Heidegger, human is a being that not only is but, as thinking being, also is a "to-be."

Things are just there. We set things up and in doing so, furnish a world. Whereas with Heidegger we receive meaning from a meaningful tissue of meaning in which we are included along with things, with Sartre we are supposed to hand out meaning to things ourselves. Hence Sartre, who had also studied Husserl's phenomenology, understands consciousness "intentionally," as the signifying relation to things.[2]

Consciousness as a relationship is ongoing; it is never "accomplished." Conscious existence precedes the existence of things, resists objectification. More specifically, consciousness refuses petrification into a being. It resists any "precipitation" in what traditional philosophy calls "essence." To Sartre, this precipitation would mean nothing less than death. Where death for Heidegger meant the possibility of impossibility, for Sartre it is the impossibility of possibility. Having died, we can no longer refuse the determinations by others. Sartre's philosophy proved "autoprophetic" after his own death, when the battle broke out between the "camp" of his secretary Benny Lévy on the one hand and that of Simone de Beauvoir on the other. At stake was his so-called intellectual testament, *L'espoir maintenant* (translated as *Today's Hope: Conversations with Sartre*). Here, the old and sick Sartre is said to have admitted that history needs a transcendental openness in order not to get stuck and that Jewish messianism can contribute to a philosophical understanding of this openness. De Beauvoir blew a fuse and sharpened her pen. Lévy, a Maoist converted to Judaism, was supposed to have put those words in the mouth of the blind and dazed Sartre and forced him to have them published. *Enfin*, the matter was obviously never cleared up, and Sartre was right in suggesting that consciousness after death is at the mercy of uncontrolled determinations.

Essence, the ultimate determination of a being, belongs to things. A stone is just a stone and if no one does anything with or to it, it will still be the same stone tomorrow. A thing does not of itself seek another thing, lending it meaning. Only consciousness finds the things and the others and gives meaning to them. Those things have no say in this. They cannot refuse or resist the meaning given to them by consciousness.

The option to exist therefore belongs solely to consciousness, in that it continuously crystallizes its essence into an "I." The fact that consciousness realizes that it exists creates a distance between this consciousness and existence—as a thing, that is. That distance is the project, life, freedom and responsibility, *act*. Again, the notion of existence as project stems from Heidegger. By not just existing as a thing, consciousness can "think ahead" rather than remaining inert and restlessly coinciding with what it "is." Consciousness always leaves behind an "I."

Consciousness can exist in a proper or in an improper way—a popular distinction in philosophy that was questioned by Derrida. Proper consciousness always defers its determination, whereas the improper consciousness betrays itself by yielding to its determination as a thing. This forms a betrayal because consciousness consists precisely in not being, in its "notting," in its withdrawal from any kind of final determination by itself or by others. "That's me!" can, or rather should, never be thought by a consciousness. Such statements are denounced as illusions.

Consciousness also looks for the other consciousness, but treats them as things: conscious things. So it is alright for consciousness to declare of another consciousness, "That's you!" or even "You're that!"—"that" being any predicate. Our coexistence is inevitably a categorizing, a predicating, an evaluating, etc. In the encounter with the other, the question automatically arises: "What can this other signify to me?" Even with Levinas, this question indeed rises automatically, immediately, but it is never final. Levinas's ethical encounter has a different finality; it has the other and not the "I" as its end. It is true that with Sartre consciousness cannot take the place of another consciousness. The relation between consciousness and a conscious thing is by necessity dialectical: the former wants to objectify the latter. But consciousness cannot be determined as a thing and must therefore resist this objectification. There is, according to Sartre, no determination that consciousness cannot refuse—which may be a bit optimistic, as the example below should demonstrate. But that also means that I cannot count on the other, precisely because his consciousness eludes my determination. Statements like "I can trust him because he is also a communist" do not work in Sartre's model.

Consciousness is not a thing. The "I," on the other hand, is. It is, in fact, the "ontic" side of consciousness. Consciousness cannot say "That's me," but it can truly claim "That is (my) 'I.'" As with Levinas, that "I" carries a certain ambivalence with it. It is the necessary precipitation of the consciousness that precedes it. The "I" does not *have* consciousness; it is its effect. Without an "I," consciousness would remain an abstract or spiritual thing or fact. This does not imply that the "I" therefore belongs to consciousness—or vice versa. I am the ever-changing, ever-deepening determination of "my" consciousness—"my" in the sense that it precedes only me and not another "I." Hence the title of Sartre's 1936 book, *La Transcendance de l'ego* (*The Transcendence of the Ego*). By this he does not mean that the "I" belongs to another world, but rather that it lies beyond consciousness, namely among things. Thanks to consciousness, however, the "I" is never definitively determined—except by "mauvaise foi." Only, the "I" cannot determine itself on or off its own. The "I" is an always momentary crystallization, the sum of all my decisions, thoughts, and actions up to that point. Every time consciousness acts, the "I" changes. Whenever "my" consciousness acts, I change. And by the way, the whole world changes with me. That is for later.

According to Sartre, we should not rely too much on his own autobiography. After all, its subject is not Sartre's consciousness, but his "I." We must not integrate this *ex post* into his philosophy. It is true that in *The Words* (*Les Mots*) we make acquaintance with a fantastic "I," such a fabulous "I" that "its" consciousness has refused a Nobel Prize for its sake.

The individual here is marked by an ambiguity, by being and at the same time not-being—it will never sound more Heideggerian than this.[3] Early on, in *Being and Time*, Heidegger had already explained that a human is of course, by nature, a being, but that any human being, by thinking properly (*eigentliche* or *denkende Denken*), also transcends this being-a-being and stands out toward being: *Dasein* ek-sists. With Heidegger thinking reaches out toward being that dwells in nothing; with Sartre thinking forms a not-being that precipitates into being-a-thing. This "I," however, is so ephemeral that it cannot be said to exist at all. In Sartre's own words from *Being and Nothingness*: "I am the one who I will be in the mode of not being he."[4] In this way, consciousness "undoes" the "I" into what it is not (yet/anymore). In the same way, memory and expectation undo beings, consciousnesses, and things that are not present (yet/anymore).

With Sartre, nothingness takes the form of a relation to being; with Levinas being is also a kind of nothing in the sense of an undifferentiated ontological layer; with Heidegger nothingness belongs to being in a liberating way—amazing how Christian a supposedly atheistic philosopher can sound. The "notting" of being keeps Heidegger's beings away from science's total explanation—which we also found in Russell's thoughts as an implication of monotheism. Recall how nothingness, as distance from being, reveals freedom in the essencing of truth.

Existence precedes essence, says Sartre: "L'existence précède l'essence."[5] Actual concrete, conscious existence precedes being and the determination thereof. Existentialism elevates concrete existence to a principle, to an autonomous source of meaning. The meaning of existence is never given *a priori*; it always arises from existence itself—not the other way around, as in traditional philosophy where the concrete and individual was always derived from the abstract and universal. Everything and everyone was supposed to become what was "written down" in some form of blueprint. This refers to, among other things, so-called natural law. This states that our existence is intended—specifically by God—and that we must try to decode this intention and arrange our existence accordingly. Such existential design is rejected by Sartre.

In *Existentialism Is a Humanism* (*L'existentialisme est un humanisme*), he notes that there can be no such thing as a universal, eternally pre-given human nature because there is no God who can conceive that nature. That still does not mean that humans without nature cannot be thought together with a God without essence, without blueprints of people or even of anything. It comes down to thinking of humans not as created in any image, but rather as a never completed self-design. An admittedly spectacular reversal. In order to pitch it strong, however, Sartre did feel obliged to deploy metaphysics. The individual, which Sartre declares to be absolute, is unwittingly inscribed in a theistic register. Humans acquire a divine status; they each become their own *causa sui*. Apart from consciousness, one needs nothing to design an "I." To Sartre this is not simply a neutral observation but also a moral imperative. As happened so often in the twentieth century, whenever metaphysics was waved off at the front door, it simply came back in through the back door.

As I said, another consciousness can also reduce me to a thing. A form of objectivation that everyone has had to deal with sometimes is diagnosis. Let me take the example of alcohol addiction. Primo, someone is always more than the diagnosis; he may also be a philosopher, or an artist—I do not want to suggest that all philosophers and artists are heavy drinkers . . . Secundo, no one is ever completely determined by that label, in the sense that there are endless varieties of addiction. Tertio, an addict can always step "on the wagon" and become an abstainer. But what if that diagnosis survives your efforts, haunts you, and the people around you continue to regard you as a drunk and thus "by definition" treat you as unreliable as well? If you are not of unusually strong fiber, you may eventually or even probably relapse. Consciousness then renounces the "notting" of determination and succumbs; it determines itself as always-already and forever a drunk, which no one ever is until consciousness fails. In the case of an addiction, the "I" starts to determine and deploy consciousness in function of the search for alcohol. We can then no longer speak of an "authentic" or proper consciousness. When consciousness gives up its "notting," this becomes a case of self-betrayal, a betrayal of the moral imperative of the perpetual design of self.

Sartre calls this improper mechanism of betrayal bad faith, "mauvaise foi." It is the surrendering of oneself to objectification. It consists in outsourcing one's consciousness to the world. Consciousness suspends its "notting" and hooks the "I" onto something it is not. In bad faith the relationship between consciousness and "I" perverts. Consciousness imposes on the "I" a determination that it cannot reverse. Consciousness then renounces the existentially imposed distance between thinking and being. It merges with its "I" in that determination and becomes a thing, irrevocably. Consciousness stops there, because it is no longer a no-thing, it has become a "that" from then on. Consciousness paradoxically (ab)uses its freedom here to outsource that freedom and proportional responsibility.

This outsourcing can happen to anything, to an addiction, but also to a religion. Someone who calls himself a Roman Catholic and obeys the relevant magisterium in a well-defined way, that is to say without the slightest doubt, no longer counts in this philosophy as a properly conscious person.

But the reverse is equally true. Is there no such thing as "bonne foi," good faith? Yes, but that does not solve the problem because even in all sincerity it is still essentially about outsourcing. It remains a reliance on something outside consciousness, in this case the own "I," which is no longer an effect of consciousness but its determination. What I want to be coincides with what I already am—and to the extent that my desire belongs to my being, here we are again with a paradox that marks improper existence. It is a relapse into the old "from essence to existence" scheme. The "I" then acquires a prescriptive function from which consciousness cannot escape.

Good faith, therefore, also belongs to improper existence, along with bad faith. The opposite of (bad or good) faithfulness is properly existing in full freedom and responsibility. So it does not help here to consider Sartre as an atheist "in good faith," for he continued to permanently question his atheism.

Like many atheist thinkers, Sartre wrote more about God than most theologians. Sartre kept looking for the legitimation of his atheism—without ever finding it, of course. Did this stem from insight? From the study of authors who carried the seventeenth-century French controversy over true lived spirituality into the twentieth century? Or rather from indifference? Or from a persistent adolescent aversion to religiosity as he saw it lived by parents and grandparents? So he certainly cannot be put in the same atheist camp as Russell, who was rather an agnostic because he defended his atheism on epistemological grounds—remember: "Not enough evidence, God!" He certainly cannot be added to the list of those who mysteriously know for sure that God does not exist. I suggest that Sartre urges us to pretend that God does not exist because that decision takes option for freedom and responsibility. It is an emancipative decision. But then, when we take all this into account, we see three transcendences from consciousness: things, the "I," and God. A slice of Kant, anyone?[6]

Freedom and Responsibility

Unlike the equally crushing but at the same time liberating responsibility with Levinas, the responsibility with Sartre concerns the whole world and all of humanity. This is what I meant above when I wrote "Whenever 'my' consciousness acts, I change. And by the way, the whole world changes with me." Everything that a person does or fails to do changes the face of the world. Despite this crushing responsibility, no one can legitimize actions by a reference outside consciousness. Such legitimation would subject the person as a "thing" to a system that would then bear full responsibility for my thoughts and actions. This happens when people exclaim "Befehl ist Befehl!" or "Wir haben es nicht gewusst." They mean that their consciousness was turned off.

This, of course, fits well into the modern ideology of autonomy. Sartre took this notion very far. If my act changes the whole world, that is indeed a heavy burden. If we consider the world as the instantaneous result of the actions of each individual, this questions just about all philosophies of history, idealistic as well as materialistic. For then there are no longer any historical factors outside the individual sphere, the whole never being anything more than the sum of its parts. In fact, history can then no longer be studied as a science but sinks into a sea of unsurveyable big data. But then there is also no point in reacting to, for instance, a colonial regime; we can only counteract enslavement around us. That is why Sartre first introduced a transcendent moment in history. The person becomes the result of a tradition and experiences itself as a project submitted to a vague teleology that pulls at its consciousness. However, Sartre never published this idea during his lifetime. His next historical study, the *Critique of Dialectical Reason* (*Critique de la raison dialectique*), was supposed to be an existentialist correction to Marxism. In it, briefly, individual consciousnesses are upgraded along the lines of a violent restriction of freedom into a community that then becomes the subject of a self-designed future.

Dostoevsky contends that if God does not exist, everything is possible. There is no longer any authority that restricts human nature. There is no longer a generally accepted, overarching moral authority within a community. Sentences like "This is absolutely not done!" remain devoid of any meaning. After all, whether or not something is "done" depends entirely on one's own moral sense. Thus, according to Dostoevsky, without God every moral sense fails; there is no longer a morally privileged line of conduct. For the Russian writer this meant hell: in the absence of God, one can expect anything. The most hideous then becomes just as normal as the most beautiful. Sartre took another view: if man is free, then God cannot exist. If God exists, man is eternally objectified in a creation plan, and can therefore never be free. Absolute human freedom demands that there be no pre-given set of standards of any kind. So even if God did exist, in some mode of being, we must live our lives *as if* he did not exist. Only the non-existence of God guarantees that for each consciousness everything is possible; hell is everything that stands in the way of these possibilities. Each "other" is part of that hell. Hell actually is those others—"L'enfer, c'est les autres."[7] Postwar Paris, turned cynical by the second bankruptcy of Western civilization so soon after the first, could appreciate this message.

Sartre himself went beyond that cynicism, for consciousness always has the freedom to refuse any determination. It even has the duty to do so. In his political phase, Sartre drew the conclusion from this that anyone who experiences oppression is allowed to revert to terror. It becomes difficult here to still morally justify such an interpretation of freedom. But first I try to articulate the underlying mechanics without reference to violence as it appears with Sartre. When we see an African, we cannot *not* see him as an African. That would be one form of racism: to deny the "difference"— the other form of racism consists in stretching this difference in terms of subordination. But when I meet an African at a bar having a beer, or at a demonstration against racism, I have two situations where the relevance of an "African identity" is not the same in each case. In that difference lies the freedom to consciously relate to objectification. When I meet a concrete, singular African, I am not at all obliged to fix both my "I" and the other in a racist schema. What racism does is to lock up *each* African in a schema of inferiority, usefulness, caricature, etc.

Sartre defended a strong connection between freedom and responsibility. His idea of freedom is therefore a purely moral freedom. It can only grow when no agency subjugates a person and takes over responsibility. Sartre, when in German war captivity, noted that he enjoyed more freedom than his guards. He meant, among other things, that within the camp he could still bear more responsibility for his thoughts and actions than those soldiers, who could only obey orders.

It seems as if Sartre's existentialism put forward, primo, a moral imperative: to continue to fight for individual freedom; and, secundo, a political imperative: whenever a system seeks to objectify consciousness, to safeguard the first imperative. However, when Camus pointed out to him that communism did not obey the second imperative, but rather had become the object of it, it led to a rift between both intellectuals.

And What about Love?

Freedom with Sartre is so absolute that it even overrules love. Love in all its shades seems to Sartre to be found in the religious, so illusory, element. The one who loves, says Sartre, actually wants to be God, and wants to be absolutely everything to the other person and thereby objectifies, becomes the object of the other person's total and unconditional love. To love, says the dialectician Sartre, is to want to be loved.[8] I want the other to regard me as the necessary ground of this other's existence. This means that the other too must give up freedom and dissolve all distance between us. This entails that the other also delegates all freedom and hands it to me "second-hand," as if to repay my objectification with mock currency. The sting lies in the mutual suspension of freedom, which is according to Sartre a false sacrifice to love—a sacrifice he consistently refused to make, apparently to the delight of Simone de Beauvoir, the Castor of his Pollux.

Even in love, in coexistence, and in intimacy, the other still remains my hell. In this case, it is a distanceless non-relationship between two things that chose to hang on to a shared dream. The love relationship is not a relationship because there is no freedom and no distance that allows for free self-determination. The asymmetrical relation, which makes mutuality an illusion, is different from that of Levinas, who recognizes the divine trace precisely in the other, and not in the self.

It seems as if Sartre's existentialism is marked by a "certain undecidability," and is fueled by a terminological ambiguity. On the one hand, freedom is the absolute source of existence that keeps consciousness alive and saves it from the threat of being; on the other hand, we are condemned to a freedom that entails a responsibility we cannot possibly bear. Given this ambivalence, some call Sartre an optimist of total emancipation; others consider him a pessimist of moral suffocation. Somewhat along the lines of Sartre's fellow existentialist, the Catholic philosopher Gabriel Marcel, we might suggest that this ambivalence is ultimately due to the inability to transform the asymmetry between my consciousness and all the rest of reality, other consciousnesses included, into a rather Levinasian asymmetry.

What Sartre does, in Levinas's jargon, is to extend egology to its extreme consequences and make egology itself the absolute moral imperative. In Marcel's terms, then, Sartre has totally reduced love, coexistence, and the recognition of the other to the sphere of eros.[9] Eros, absolutized and stripped of the other dimensions that essentially belong to "full" love, boils down to, again, the objectification of the other—and therefore of the self. Could it be that Sartre was deprived of the grammar of full love, that his first childhood years—this is provocative, bringing in Freud now—were so devoid of "nest warmth" that he experienced love within the family only as turning each other into a project? Some passages in the autobiographical *The Words* do not really contradict this possibility . . .

God remains with Sartre, in analogy to the model of human love, the Supreme Being to which we delegate our freedom and which demands from me absolute recognition as the ground of my existence. And since God is, put philosophically but bluntly, a being to which we attribute consciousness and therefore (or: because of that) also freedom and responsibility, it remains an illusion, possibly one of which we will never know if it cannot, in some register, acquire some sort of reality after all. In that case, Sartre would have to acknowledge that there are discourses that remain closed off to philosophy but disclose, beyond or even within the dichotomy consciousness–thing, a reality that endures the name "God."

Whether God exists or not does not really matter, according to Sartre. The point is to reclaim the individual human being from the stranglehold of religion. Just as we cannot stand in the place of another consciousness and therefore can only objectify every other consciousness, we do the same with God. Even if we were to love God so fiercely, we do not escape love's dialectic as analyzed above. Sartre's existentialism had already passed judgment on this dialectic in its own moral imperative—albeit that in the implications of that imperative the Supreme Being returns altogether. God is then the only consciousness that demands of all other consciousnesses that they acknowledge God. Thereby this Supreme Being objectifies all humans as creatures, subjected to his natural law. In this way, then, God is the only freedom in the whole world, giving up his freedom in the requirement of love and thus contradicting the freedom of every human being. He even claims it as compensation for his own lost freedom, which is only reaffirmed (as lost) as long as each man indeed definitively gives up his freedom in faith.

In *Existentialism Is a Humanism*, Sartre writes that during the seventeenth century God still captured all meanings in "essences." During the eighteenth century, God disappeared but philosophy held on to the essences. Even though Sartre set his philosophical research on the tracks of a critique of metaphysics, he ended up with a firm traditional metaphysics of consciousness. Perhaps this is so because, like so many, he did not include the death of God in his reflection. After all, Sartre still believes that the death of God only allows a person to live fully. Nietzsche states at the end of the first song of *Thus Spoke Zarathustra*, "Dead are all gods, now we want that overman shall live!"[10] Not humans, but overman can exist without gods. Because the gods are dead, overman cannot become Supreme Being either.

In the end, the dichotomy between thing and consciousness burdens Sartre with a dualism that continues to work at the foundation of his moral and political considerations. It even leads him to reject psychoanalysis because he recognizes in the opacity of the unconscious the dumbness of the thing. But it also raises serious issues that Sartre cannot evade. His idea of a political community, for example, that he wanted to work out through a combination of existentialism and Marxism, cannot really be called successful. The morality that he wanted to work out as a follow-up to and elaboration of *Being and Nothingness* has never been published. Whoever asks for a universal, eternal moral norm finds nothing, no trace, and no sign. Furthermore, says Sartre, even if believers reply that there *are* signs, it is still my consciousness that gives meaning to those signs. Now, if all others are hell and it already takes a lot of philosophical acrobatics to keep oneself out of that hell, then it indeed becomes extra difficult to formulate a moral or political model from there. Again, personalism comes to the fore here. After all, the person is a "broader" and "deeper" concept than the individual. It could be a remedy against the crudest consequences to which Sartre's existentialist position leads. It starts from a commonality that is not a collective and not from a conflict between mutually objectifying consciousnesses.

Some fifty thousand consciousnesses—although, *en masse* . . . ?—formed his ultimate procession of objectification. But then suddenly numerous followers turned against him. They took his own philosophy out on him . . .

10

Face

Levinas

Levinas did not really connect with Kierkegaard. Nor did he have any philosophical use for mysticism, Jewish kabbalah included. He distrusted the irrational and pietism. Although his thinking was obviously impregnated by Jewish religion, he insisted that his philosophy was basically Greek. He therefore explicitly inscribed himself in the tradition of Western metaphysics,[1] but just like Heidegger or Derrida, it was impossible for him to repress (his) religious roots, even though he tried so hard, again just like Heidegger or Derrida.

As a child Levinas had known the pogroms in his native Lithuania; in France he experienced the underground rumblings of anti-Semitism.[2] He noted how many Jews in the French and German academic and cultural milieu converted rather eagerly to a Christian denomination in order to secure their social status—like his philosophical teacher Husserl, the "father of phenomenology," did.[3] When Levinas was deported to Germany in 1940 as a prisoner of war, he experienced anti-Semitism in its rawest form. Although the regime in the camp could still be called relatively humane, the Jews were treated as inferior beings. When Levinas saw the camp dog cheerfully welcoming them into the barracks each evening after the labor-that-sets-free, realizing how only that dog could still recognize universal human dignity in the Jews, he remarked ironically about the faithful quadruped: "The last Kantian in Nazi Germany . . ."

As much as Levinas did not connect with Kierkegaard, all the more he did with Heidegger, albeit as his stern critic. He introduced the then politically still uncontaminated German master in France in 1932. Little did he know that barely a year later Heidegger would join the NSDAP. Despite the fact that Levinas lost almost his entire family in the Nazi gas chambers, he regarded Heidegger as the "Himalaya" of twentieth-century thought. He never set foot on German soil again, though.

Perhaps we can say that Levinas operated according to Greek philosophy; that Jewish wisdom inspired him; and that outrage at Nazi horror motivated him. He employs the Greek conceptual apparatus and accompanying philosophical grammar to articulate his Jewish indignation at the dehumanization under a totalitarian political regime. Levinas has always continued to emphasize that any thought or belief that is not concerned with concrete responsibility for the other generates a dubious philosophy or theology—among which, despite mutual sympathy, he counts Christian faith.

In 1974, performance artist Marina Abramović explored the limits of Cartesian dualism as well as the limits of a public's appropriation of the artist. This performance was called *Rhythm 0*. She stood in a room with an audience and declared herself to be an object amid other objects that she had placed on a table, including a pair of scissors, a scalpel, nails, a metal bar, and a gun loaded with one bullet. During this six-hour session, she was treated inappropriately, to say the least. She was cut so that someone could drink her blood; another pointed the gun to her head and plied her finger around the trigger. She remained totally passive throughout. When the performance ended and she started to move on her own again, the audience shied away and fled the room, unable to bear the confrontation with a person that they had treated (and who willingly behaved) as an object.

This experience is confirmed by some significant anecdotes. A Tutsi testified after the 1994 Rwandan genocide how he hacked at one Hutu after another with his machete, until suddenly one of them looked him straight in the eye. The weapon stopped; the man could kill no more. In 2002, a student walked through a school in Erfurt, Thuringia, shooting at anything that moved. When he pointed the weapon at a teacher, the teacher shouted "Look at me! Look me in the eyes!" The student looked at him, lowered his weapon, and walked on.

These episodes illustrate what Levinas wants to show us. Suddenly a Face appears, an "other" who does not simply fit into my plan, a person who cannot simply be inserted into my project. That is precisely why he is "different." Now, "other" has gradually become a keyword of French philosophy over the last century. Until then, "other" in traditional metaphysics always meant other-than, with a "self" as norm. Different was always different from a self, from the subject, from the norm. Surely the relation between "same" and "other" always consisted in the reduction of that other to the self—whether that relation was called "knowing," or "using," or "having," or anything else in that register. The other was never understood in, on, and by itself—insofar as this is at all possible—but merely from the position of the same.

Western philosophy has forgotten about the other and continued to engage too much with being, Levinas argues. That was partly a sneer at Heidegger, who wanted to "transcend" modern philosophy with its instrumental rationality but still remained stuck in being. For Levinas, the ethical moment overrules ontology. Whereas Sartre said that existence precedes essence, Levinas asserts that ethics precedes ontology.

From "I" to "Me"

Levinas and his French colleagues no longer think of this "other" as a function of a self. The other resists total incorporation. There is a rest that resists.[4] The other is never totally recoverable or completely reducible. Levinas goes on to work this out in a very particular, ethical way.

But as I said, he does place himself in the Greek tradition and thus starts from the self, from "I." This "I" inhabits the world in a rather centripetal, appropriating way. The world revolves around that self. Levinas calls this an egological relation. The "I" presents itself as the knowing and possessing center of the world. Around that center the world is organized as a totality, in which there is no place for the other as such. But this self is not "original," although it usually feels that way. Whereas Heidegger considers the experience of anxiety as the *via regia* toward an experience of being, Levinas refers to insomnia. When unable to sleep, we sink into the *il y a*, which is the Heideggerian being à la Levinas. We have seen that with Heidegger, being has a very positive, liberating, appealing, event-urous or even advent-urous meaning. Not so with Levinas; here it is a cold, anonymous, almost threatening sediment, marked by indifference and absurdity.

Of course, we should not take this insomnia too literally. It is not as if between the moment of getting into bed and dozing off, I can be reached in the *il y a*. Levinas uses this image because, of all experiences, it most resembles the confrontation with meaninglessness. After all, in the dark I can see no things; there is no world in which I find myself among things. Nothing separates me from anything else or distinguishes one thing from another. A great sense of senselessness overwhelms me, for I cannot initiate sleep on my own or from my own self. Sleep eludes me, as some sort of denied grace. The world does not appear to me as a space in which I can build up my existence in a meaningful and relational way. There is not even an "I." As Kierkegaard says of the aesthetic stadium, there simply is no relation here, not with a self, not with another. Sleep is just that of which I cannot make a project. I can only lie in wait for it and undertake nothing. Space and time lose all meaning in this bare and barren being. Levinas does not consider being in terms of "es gibt zu denken,"[5] contrary to what Heidegger suggests. There can only be thought once the human being is awake. Only an "I" can catch sleep and wake up on the other side of that sleep.

If Heidegger says that the thinker and being belong to each other, that this is the ultimate human vocation, then Levinas says something completely different here. Being is in the latter case where human and world, thought and meaning are absent. Whereas Heidegger sees being as the essencing of *Dasein*, Levinas claims almost the opposite. For him, being is meaningless. The essence of a human being, the vocation, speech, does not come from being but from the "other" side of being, from beyond being. A person must first pass through the phase of "I," away from being, in order to hear this calling.

In this sense the "I" is not absolutely and per se evil, because it means at least an emancipation from absurdity, from the meaninglessness of being. Whereas superficial readers of Heidegger still thought they were allowed to identify being with God, with Levinas this is not possible at all. If God is to be found somewhere, it is beyond being, where human vocation also resounds. The transformation takes place in the encounter with the other. This is characteristic of Levinas's position. After all, finding God in *il y a* almost smells of mysticism, of a direct access to an otherworldly entity, and Levinas distrusts all this deeply. God can only be a trace. We can only trace God when he leaves a trace in the world. We find that trace in the Face—with capital letter to underline its metaphysical status.

A certain dominant tendency within Christian metaphysics, a tendency that Wilhelm Dilthey once expressed literally in this way, runs from the (antique) exteriority to the (Christian, increasingly modern) interiority. Augustine's "intimior intimo meo" demonstrates this sharply. There is a deeper-than-deepest point within me, beneath the bottom of my soul. Returning to earth, Yuri Gagarin declared that he had not seen God out there. Of course not. God is not to be found out there in the cosmos. God lies beneath my soul, even deeper, in a deepest depth that I myself cannot even reach. This is, paradoxically, the de-centered center of my existence. God lives in me, where my center is no longer mine and I no longer occupy the center. Anselm also put it this way, opening the way to mysticism: if you want to meet God, throw out everything you find inside yourself. The inside of our interior appears to us as a strange "outside" that calls on us. Compare it to the symptom in psychoanalysis. This hides so deep that we no longer consciously recognize it as "ours." Yet it moves, literally: motivates us profoundly.

Levinas adds his own twist to this. Finding God indeed remains a matter of decentering, but this does not take place within the interior but outside, in exteriority (from the subtitle of his first main work, *Totality and Infinity*), where the other appears as what cannot be appropriated. That is the meaning of exteriority here: not "outward appearance" or "objective givenness" but "outside my( )self." God is to be sought not in a spiritualized interiority but in a phenomenological exteriority. He reveals himself in the Face that testifies to a need and also asks me to do something about it—without therefore articulating exactly what to do, so in the first instance to just "be there for the other."[6] I can only meet the other, the track of/ to God, in-the-world.

The Face is not just a face, a "mug." The exteriority of the Face must not be understood as a "facade." The Face has nothing to do with attractiveness, with mimicry, with skin color, with any of all that. Let us remember that eyes are traditionally depicted in poetry as gates to or mirrors of the soul. It is a question not of reintroducing that notion "soul" back into philosophy or psychology, but of the experience that those eyes reveal something, that through those eyes we can see/hear something that calls from beyond any empirical order.[7]

In the encounter with the other, the "I" can either maintain itself, because it concerns an obligation without coercion, or transform into a "me"; in other words, the other takes over and puts me in the "accusative": I am guilty without fault. I can only blame myself, I cannot transfer this guilt to others, accuse others, for then I would relapse into egology.[8] After all, the other is in distress, but I did not (entirely, exclusively, intentionally, etc.) organize this distress myself. I exist and the other is in need. This makes me irrevocably guilty and that realization calls me to account: what am I going to do about it? I am expected—to put it mildly—to respond to that call, to take up my responsibility for the other person. I owe that to the other person.

Ethics cannot be derived from ontology; it fulfills it, or even more so, justifies it. The fact that the Face cannot be constructed from an egology entails that the imperative, the call, cannot come from myself—on the contrary.[9] In this ethical relation I do not have the (first or last) word. I must not go and "ex-culpa-te" or start preaching; I must act. Levinas's ethics is not a theory, but about the transformation of word into deed. I must not sit at home pondering the suffering in the world; that is just too shallow.

We saw with Sartre how for him the encounter always involves an assessment. We ask ourselves immediately what the other can mean to me. We look and weigh. The cruelest thing we do to each other is to "classify" each other, to push each other into boxes, to stick a label on the other. After all, these classes and boxes and labels do not even belong to the other, they belong to myself. I hand them out. Of course, no one can argue that labels are not done. It is just as well that at the sickbed of someone with a kidney stone there is a sign that says "kidney stone" and not "possibly a certain medical condition." But when two nurses invade the room of that "kidney stone" and unfold their love life to each other while rolling that "kidney stone" in a clean sheet without even looking at the person and asking "And how are we today?" then something is clearly wrong. That is not "caritas." If all we want to know about the other person is that he suffers from a kidney stone—or is a drunk, an immigrant, an unemployed person, a psychiatric patient, etc.—then we are missing a very important dimension: the dignity, what makes someone a person and not a thing. This dignity is obscured by the labels. In fact, classifying a person deprives him of his dignity, of his being-other. This "otherness" has little—always something, but never everything—to do with another language or skin color or gender and so on. After all, these are again classes and categories in which otherness belongs to and is determined by a system set up by a self. Otherness does not need, does not even tolerate, any determination because every determination is inevitably always again an appropriation. It is about irreducibility that is never literally, physically visible. The dignity-as-other, the alterity as irreducibility, hides and shines in the Face of the other.

The other puts an end to egocentric violence. Measuring up others and fitting them into my project in order to make the world a Sartrian hell of mutual oppression is a much too pessimistic model. Ethics suspends this violence. The roles are not reversed, but given up. The other stands there simply *as other*, without a message.

This dignity shows itself as fragile or vulnerable, but a fragility and vulnerability that are capable of holding us hostage. These are terms that

Levinas himself uses. The other appears to us as other, as a not-I. The other is not another I, because then he would relate to me within the same logic as I relate myself to him. Then there would be two selves fully engaged in the egologica. It is precisely this logic that is broken down in the ethical relationship.

The other suspends my egological position; he does not belong to the world that I want to know and that I can control. The ethical relationship starts at the moment at which I refrain from taking advantage of the other (financially, socially, sexually, etc.). And this "refraining" should not even be understood as too active. It is hardly more than just opening myself up to being overwhelmed by the other. The weakness of the other is so strong that it takes me completely "off the hook." The world no longer hinges, as a project, around me.

In Latin, a hinge is called "cardo." As long as the world "hinges" around me, the "cardinal" virtues suffice to live well and virtuously with others within an egologic world frame. These virtues were reduced by ancient philosophy to a basic set of four: moderation, justice, courage, and prudence. Christianity, in the figure of the great theologian Paul, added three theological virtues: faith, hope, and love, of which love is the most decisive (1 Cor 13:13). Levinas did not go that far. He was far from hostile toward Christianity, but considered incarnation a bridge too far. That is for later.

In the parable of the Good Samaritan (Lk 10:25–37), Levinas recognized his own ethical position. In Jesus's days, the Jews looked down on the Samaritans—today there are less than 1,000 of them. The Samaritans took a dim view of all the rules that the high priests cited from the Torah and imposed on the chosen people. By making a Samaritan the protagonist of this lesson to the Pharisees, Christ is sneering at the Pharisees' complacent moral superiority. While the representatives of the Temple walk around the scene of the crime for what they consider to be valid, because religious, reasons, the Samaritan stops near that pile of misery that he finds along the road. He is no outcast, by the way, since he travels by horse.

What matters here is that the Samaritan suspends his project (recreation? business? visitation?) for this almost-nothing.[10] No idea who that is . . . male or female? rich or poor? solidly Jewish or merely Samaritan? powerful or at the bottom of the social ladder? circumcised or with foreskin intact? There is nothing to see, to understand, to deliberate, to decide. There's only one thing to do: act. In any case, there is no guarantee of any reciprocity, of any form of service returned, of compensation or reward. Nor could the Samaritan rest assured that his concern was religiously correct.

After all, suppose that bleeding sucker were a gentile, an uncircumcised and thus unclean human being, imagination boggles when considering the consequences . . . And yet.

Let us now look at the framework of the parable. The Pharisee asks Christ who "his neighbor" is. He wanted to hear Christ answer "Everyone, gentile included." Then they could accuse him of blasphemy without further ado. After all, touching goy was just as taboo as touching Torah—which raises a very interesting problem, unfortunately beyond the scope of this book. To "delimit" the denotation of "neighbor" is a very egological strategy. It allows me to care only for those who can benefit me—my family, my friends, my superiors on the social ladder . . . But Christ brilliantly replies by turning the whole question around. At the end of this short parable, which must have made the Jews around him turn purple, he does not list the categories that determine "neighbor" but answers with a counter-question: "Who was the neighbor of this pile of misery?" And the Pharisee can only admit: "The Samaritan . . ."

This is what Levinas means by the call or appeal. From the other, once stripped of his political, economic, social, etc. categories, comes an appeal that compels despite the fragility and vulnerability of someone who can no longer hide behind labels. This is what Levinas means by "hostage": the other will not let you go. Optics opens an acoustic, one sees someone who says something that I cannot see, only hear. And this "hearing," says Levinas, that is what Western philosophy has forgotten.[11]

Divine Majesty

God, with Levinas, is wholly Other, "Tout Autre." This has far-reaching implications. First, that God can never, ever, in any way, even partially, be present in the world as such, as the object of our looking or thinking. This is implied by the term "monotheism." We cannot possibly make an adequate image or idea of God. Secondly, it is as if God ensures that the other can never again be completely integrated in or reduced to our plan, project, image, or idea; as if behind every Face there is a force that resists my tendency to reduce that other person to what I control, understand, desire, etc. And that force is absolute, in the sense that although we can refuse the Face, we can never surpass or nullify the force. We can appropriate the other in the unethical, egological relationship but we can never capture God.

God is not a noncommittal option, according to Levinas. Once the Face is "opened," God's voice cannot be muted or erased. This is because in the Face "my" initiative is taken over. Not that I transfer or outsource my management to another; the whole system of management is suspended. Management becomes hostage.

God does not coincide with this or that other; he remains other than all possible others. Perhaps that is one meaning of infinity as "different" from totality: we may, so to speak, go down the whole row of others, but we will not encounter God who infinitely eludes us. God is not different from the others; then he would just be at the back of the line. God is not so much other *than* the others as the irreducibly otherness or alterity *of* the others. God is the refusal to reduce others to egology; God is resistance to totalization, the total reduction to the "same."

God resists understanding and he resists being. Just as well, because the God that belongs to epistemological and ontological systems is dead. This is why Levinas does not like theology that engages in concepts and proofs of God. For him, as for Heidegger, the God that is revealed there is a being, a scientific object—theology then being a science. Whereas Heidegger initially rejected God in order to spare theology, Levinas rejects theology in order to preserve God. Whereas Heidegger thinks he can expect the divine to arrive in the new thinking of being, Levinas always seeks God beyond being.

Now there is a problem with a "wholly other" precisely inasmuch as I take that alterity seriously. First of all, something that is "completely different" would automatically be completely unreachable, even to thought. Surely there must be at least a sort of "line" or "trace" along which I can recognize that otherness and along which that otherness can reach me. Of course this does not necessarily presuppose the modern position of "subject," since that is what Levinas criticizes. The other is different precisely in the sense that "it" cannot be integrated into my determinations and definitions as an object. So the other does differ from what I expect, desire, or need. The other "decenters" me and "dispossesses" me in the sense that I am no longer the master of myself and my relationship to the other, and that my existence no longer coincides with my project. This is where God happens.

God never becomes simply the theme of my speaking or thinking. This does not mean that we cannot speak or think about him, but rather that the actual meaning, the sense of that other, is not constructed by speaking or thinking in itself but is offered from behind that thinking and speaking. We cannot lock up God in a set of propositions. The other is understood not by saying but by listening. Levinas's ethics is not about stopping thought. He does reveal a vanishing point in thought, an openness through which thinking cannot penetrate, where meaning can only arrive in the form of the demand for a (non-theoretical) answer.

The originality of Levinas lies in the attempt to thematize God in philosophy without "understanding" him. God *is* not, he works. God never presents himself directly to our thought or our perception. God leaves a trace, but not a trace that ever arrives at the "thing itself," at God. The trace always remains trace. Derrida loves this idea: if a trace indeed refers, then always only to other traces. Every time a trace "ends up" somewhere, it never turns out to be an end point but always an "otherness," thereby unavoidably becoming a trace again and again. Derrida turns the trace into a linguistic phenomenon, but for Levinas it is all about flesh and blood. God is not so much a trace that refers but a trace that points or redirects, namely to the concrete other before me. God is that pointing, that calling. God is not a thing that can be approached propositionally, even in a sentence like "I believe in God." We cannot even enter into a relationship with God apart from the concrete other. Therefore, because God is a trace that never comes into full presence, we cannot erase the name God. Even when we ignore the call, even when we kill the other, we cannot reduce the name to the same, not encapsulate it in our egology. We cannot kill God because he is nothing but a barely and preferably unpronounceable name of a trace that does not even "is." As Other-than-being—the title of a book by Levinas: *Autrement qu'être*—God remains unapproachable.

"God" is a name for the call to give up the self for the benefit of the other, any other. It is not up to me to categorize that other according to a system of criteria that determine the extent to which the other deserves my care. That would be, after all, egology again. God saves care from merit. Responsible care, that responds to the call, is not the conclusion of a syllogistic argument in which every human being is qualified as a sufferer who has a right to receive care, as a universal anthropological category. This is an egocentric design of care that is soon bogged down in a mere technique of care. Then heteronomy is in danger of being lost altogether. In the tradition of Plato and Kant, heteronomy finds the source of the good in the sacred.

Levinas, by the way, sees an interesting distinction between sacred and holy. Anthropology does not make that distinction. There, the sacred stands together with the holy against the worldly, the profane. The torn veil (Mt 27:51; Mk 15:38; Lk 23:45) removed the distinction between sacred and profane but did not throw holiness out of the world. For Levinas, desacralization means that the world casts off its irrationality, its magic, its moral distortion, and its arbitrariness. Holy is the pure ethical relation, the divine claim, without fuss. Holy anger is not sacred anger, holy violence is not sacred violence, responsible indignation is not irresponsible arbitrariness. Holiness sprouts from the desire for God insofar as I allow myself to be redirected from the desired toward the not-desired, toward the other who invades my existence.

It is worthwhile to involve René Girard in this distinction. He works on the notion of desacralization, retaining what Levinas roughly means by holiness, as follows. For Girard, the Bible brings us, apart from a spiritual message, the following anthropological message: violence belongs to humanity and the world; true love has a divine, holy source. His first thesis, that at the basis of every culture lies a mechanics of religious violence, became immediately very popular in intellectual circles. His second thesis, that Christianity was an exception, met with silent disapproval. And when he "outed" himself as a Catholic, intellectual France turned its back on him. But he bravely persisted in his "anti-religious" argument.[12] According to him, in the passion, peace and violence each play their own role. In kenosis God renounces sacred violence.[13] In the whole process, from the entry into Jerusalem to the preface at Pilate, Christ shows man how the worldly spiral of violence works. When Christ announces from the cross that "it" is accomplished, the old religions could not follow this at all. Their God would have poured out thunder and lightning over the Jews and the Romans, would have organized a flood or at least would have scorched the city with napalm in a sea of fire. But this God does not even lift a finger, does not even speak a word—if only because that is again precisely what we would expect of him.

Levinas and Girard unmask sacred explanations for both natural and human violence, where strangers bring storms and plagues and war is good. In the same world, the gods must be placated with sacrifices. It is against such religious bribery that Christianity protests. As already mentioned (see under Nietzsche), Christ loses his temper only once, in a passage called "temple cleansing." The sacrifice is for Christ the greatest shame, the crudest form of blasphemy. A God who is all about love cannot be appeased with a dead bird. In a desacralized world those practices do not "work," those strategies do not exist. The transcendent is free from violence.[14] The sacred or divine with Levinas and Girard is free from any form of violence—insofar as such pure peacefulness can be articulated philosophically. This is not to say, however, that they are theologically identical. The Torah is not Christ.

Levinas has both sympathy for Christianity and a fundamental criticism of it. He rejects every theology that does not take my responsibility for the other as its foundation—all the more when it takes personal salvation as its foundation instead. Also, the idea of incarnation bothered him. God does not become flesh but remains in the Word and thus becomes Law. In the Law God reveals himself to reason. God does not incarnate in the other human being; rather, there is "discarnation." God tears off the flesh to open the track of the Face. God disappears in the call. The Face lies "behind" the flesh; the flesh itself is never an ethical motive. It only becomes an ethical motive through the divine majesty—later Levinas speaks of the glory—of the withdrawing and referring or redirecting trace.

11

Metanarratives

Lyotard

Jean-François Lyotard has been called the "pope of postmodern thought," actually mostly by himself. He was a philosopher who liked and used the word "postmodern" a lot. Other great thinkers shuddered at the word, but Lyotard wallowed in it. For him, the postmodern feeling for life was so self-evident that he titled one of his books *The Postmodern Explained* (*Le Postmoderne expliqué aux enfants* or ". . . explained to our children").[1] Actually, that was a sneer at all philosophers—more specifically the German Jürgen Habermas and the American Richard Rorty—who had difficulty leaving behind the original Enlightened and Enlightening ambitions of modernity.

Lyotard first summarized what he means by postmodern in the word "pagan." By the way, the term "postmodern" comes from architecture, not from philosophy—Lyotard was also and perhaps primarily a philosopher of art. The word has a philosophical birth year, namely 1979, when *The Postmodern Condition: A Report on Knowledge* appeared. Soon, however, the term became a philosophical meme. It also perverted into postmodern*ism*, a pseudo-philosophical cultural hype. *Pomo* became *arty-farty*. Lyotard suddenly preferred to speak of "rewriting modernity,"[2] and with this he came much nearer to what that prefix "post-" is supposed to mean.

Late modernity, our actuality,[3] is marked by the realization that the basic ambitions of modernity will never be realized in their entirety, as a package deal. This is indicated by the prefix "post-" in its many compositions: post-modern, post-metaphysical, post-Christian, post-secular, etc. It cannot simply mean "after" because we are still in modernity; we are indeed not beyond it yet. It does mean that something is happening to "the modern."

One of his "definitions" of the postmodern has earned a place among the one-liners of philosophy: the "end of the metanarratives." Metanarratives, for Lyotard, are stories that pour the course and purpose of history into one Idea. However, these metanarratives, created 200 years ago as "ideologies," no longer work. Not that they were abolished—the demolition or abolition of those great stories would probably have to be a metanarrative itself. These stories are still being passed on, they still circulate, but now we know that these giant projects will never be fully realized. Socialism, nationalism, capitalism, liberalism, and so on, are still ideas that motivate politics and social criticism, but their fundamentalists have become romantic curiosities. It is no longer a matter of "dulce et decorum pro patria mori." Nazism and communism, for that matter, can also pass for metanarratives.[4] And postmodernism actually threatened to become one too, however internally unstable that term would be. After all, Lyotard's postmodernity leaves behind every -ism, its pretension and ambition included.

Even Christianity is sometimes considered a metanarrative. But is this justified? A very important difference lies in what theologians call eschatology, the final and ultimate victory of good over evil. This completion of the world does not itself fall within history, within the modern world. The triumph of good requires, on the one hand, "just going around, doing good" but also, on the other hand, a radical enduring of evil in the world, in attendance of the Final Judgment. This was just totally foreign to those great narratives, since they demanded immediate installation of the One Good (all modern revolutions, from the French Revolution with the terror of Robespierre, via the thousand-year Reich of the Nazis, the five-year plans of Stalin, and the cultural revolution of Mao, to the "Power to imagination" in May '68) and the elimination of evil (e.g., feudality, racial impurities, capital, authority . . .).

Knowing

Modernity is where and when knowledge becomes science, an institution that sustains itself thanks to a system of legitimation. The latter is outsourced to modern philosophy, to Descartes's model of certainty and the critical discussion between Kant and Hegel about the status of reason that should provide and even guarantee certainty. This ambition generated some "utopian" models, which Lyotard calls "metanarratives." This notion remains close to ideology, but the meaning of this latter term has, especially since Marx, collapsed under its own inflation. Then again, the meaning of the word "narrative" spreads out so far that Lyotard can easily deploy it in his own philosophy.

Those metanarratives are, for example, the Enlightenment as a philosophy of history in terms of progress and emancipation, of idealism and materialism, of socialism and liberalism, of capitalism and . . . perhaps of Christianity, though I seriously doubt this. These stories still circulate, but they have lost their legitimizing and recruiting power. So it is certainly not the case, as many people think, that those great stories have disappeared, or have made way for a scientific objectivity that sticks to facts instead of singing out ideals. It is precisely science, Lyotard claims, that has eagerly but paradoxically availed itself of these metanarratives.

And what might that be, a metanarrative? Which demands does it have to meet? To begin with, Lyotard considers the metanarrative typical of modernity—which makes it all the more curious that he includes Christianity in this, but more about that later. Each time it concerns stories with a universal pretension, the subject of which is nothing less than the whole of humanity. The story is always emancipatory, which means that it holds out the prospect of an improvement for humanity. Humanity takes up its own history as a strategy of self-elevation. Finally, the great story also shows strong logical coherence and conceptual transparency. It contains a solid analysis of the initial situation and a sharp image of the final situation, of the goal to be realized. In all these features, the metanarrative differs from mythical narratives, for example. These consist of different story cycles that stem from oral tradition and are not concerned with logic; at most they have a local explanatory and prescriptive value. Such stories that originate from an indefinable past, sing of the capriciousness of gods, and maintain the inescapable circularity of time find no grace in the modern mind.

To the extent that these metanarratives belong to the modern mindset, Karl Löwith may help to understand them. He argued that they are all secular versions of the Christian doctrine of salvation. In that case, all those "-isms" would literally be innerworldly, historical versions of the Christian scheme of salvation. History as the vector of liberation is then a Christian idea that has detached itself from its transcendental reference.[5] It is no longer God, but mankind itself that, within a predetermined lapse of time and according to a scientific-technical recipe, will install heaven on earth—remember Feuerbach.

It is interesting to see how Lyotard connects science to these legitimacy narratives. There might be some confusion here since some hermeneuticians consider science itself a story among stories. If there exists such a thing as a story about science—which is not the same as science-as-a-story—it would be the philosophy of science. This branch of philosophy does not yet legitimize scientific knowledge, but considers its rules of play. Lyotard means that science does not get its legitimacy, its truth claims, its epistemological status from itself. Science cannot justify itself, but needs grand narratives to do so, stories about truth, about power, about money . . . Nor is it science itself, as a practice, a profession, that claims to be able to explain all of reality—that contention would indeed be a philosophical instead of a scientific one. Scientists put on a white coat at 9 o'clock in the morning, switch on the equipment in the laboratory, and go to work until 5 o'clock in the evening. It makes little difference to them whether their daily tasks brings science closer to a truth or total explanation. They get paid; their project is subsidized; the industrial spin off is assured; everyone is happy. The truth claim is barely an extra feature. Truth? What is truth?

It is not science that presents itself as the normative form of thinking. We have already learned from Heidegger that the scientific world happens to us and cannot be considered the result of the actions and publications of a few geniuses.[6] But it is undeniably true that the only form of thinking that does not have to legitimize itself on the public forum today is scientific reason. In this sense, a philosophical or theopoetical "argument" will never be compelling, whereas a scientific argument will. Even if there is no "objective" reason for this.

In modernity, thought has become knowledge. This depends on measurement and proof, on method. Its rules do not apply outside the scientific game itself. To demonstrate its relevance, science must appeal to something stronger than itself. As a result, it must, paradoxically, relinquish what it pretends to do: knowledge for the sake of knowledge. Science is a matter of power and money, not truth. No truth without money. Laboratories cost money; firms pay for research; publishers of scientific journals are sponsored by industry. Appointment of academic staff is made not always according to scientific merit, but rather on the basis of the likelihood of securing funds and grants. Lyotard points out that these are not marginal phenomena but are an essential part of the scientific dynamic, of science as business.[7]

Science thus seeks its legitimacy where, according to its own philosophy, no valid knowledge exists, namely in stories. Narratives do not provide knowledge because they themselves do not obtain legitimacy anywhere on that level; they do not even consider it necessary or desirable. Science works differently, of course, at least according to the philosophy of science.

But science solicits its legitimacy, its arguments for why it is "more" (more reasonable, more true, more relevant, etc.) than all (other) narratives, from what it considers "less" than itself. That is science's blind spot, but in its hubris it completely ignores this.

Perhaps, on the other hand, that spot is not so blind after all, since science does "know" that stories offer less truth, at least according to modern criteria that are all about science; but it also knows that that is an effect of what makes stories interesting for science, precisely that they are immune to logical-rational operations and evaluations.

Science, so modern philosophy teaches us, shows us the world as it is, not as it should be. Yet that is not quite right. Science shows us a world as it fits into the scientific frame. Science could only arrive, only happen in a world that was pre-arranged as measurable. Science carries a moral imperative within it. Thinking must conform to the determination of the world as scientific. This scientific framing resembles a "false application" that was drawn up so that the headhunters are sure that their candidate will appear as the only suitable one. Modernity only means progress according to its own criteria, such as technical control, makeability, predictability, prolongation of life, increased mobility in every field and on any level, telecommunication, big data, expansion, and so on. To the modern mind, these goals are all obvious and self-evident.

Other modern effects such as loneliness, anonymity, pollution, depression, inequality, and climate change should then remain solvable side effects. About truth and knowledge and reality, narratives were written out in which only science fits. A slogan like "Knowledge is power," attributed to Francis Bacon in 1597, can hardly be considered neutral. Newton's main work, *Philosophiae naturalis principia mathematica*, did not come out until ninety years later. The title is a metanarrative in its own right. The contention that science is actually natural philosophy, hinging on mathematical principles, distinguishes it from earlier scientific formats now considered primitive. Remember the progress narrative. But again, the legitimating power of that narrative has been totally used up.

We learned this from what happened to anthropology, for example. This modern human science was originally intended to investigate "primitive" peoples—and thus accentuate their difference from modern culture. At least, that was the "metanarrative" of anthropology. Until Claude Lévi-Strauss discovered that there is no structural difference between a supposedly primitive and the modern-scientific culture. Modernity, the modern story, undermines itself here.

The legitimacy of science these days lies entirely with the system of objectivity, namely with the belief that there is a real-world reality independent of thought, in itself. This is not a grand narrative but a Cartesian model of reality. Science then has the liturgical mandate, as the only sacred knowledge, to roll out the full truth about this reality, to reveal its true explanation. This objectivity is just about the toughest nut to crack in metaphysics, because it has the aura of self-evidence. "It is so because it is so." It is the most unnegotiable and inaccessible system that metaphysics has designed, the most evident, the evidence of evidence itself. The ultimate dream of reason. If things are as they are—first dogma of modern rationalism—and there is a "winning strategy" to unlock things as they are—second dogma—and not as they are presented in erroneous, unhygienic discourse (narratives, that is), then—third dogma—a total explanation must be possible.

This raises the question of the guarantee that science does indeed describe that objective reality and not a psychotic variant of it. The answer is of a very different character than the ideological gravity of objectivity, namely the lightness of "Well, it works!" This is the criterion of legitimation by performativity, as Lyotard calls it. Karl Popper argues that falsifiability must be the basic trait of scientific thought. A statement can only be recognized as scientific if it can be refuted, at least in principle. Non-rebuttable statements can never be scientific. "God exists" or "God does not exist" are not scientific statements. While the scientific praxis presents itself outwardly as vulnerable, falsifiable, it draws its legitimacy from stories that are not falsifiable to secure its truth claim, as we understood. Now that those stories still have the power of an echo, only the pragmatic cynicism of instrumentality remains. "It works." But the meaning of life does not "work."

Not Knowing

According to Lyotard, modern metaphysics or the legitimate operation of science depends on the design of a system. Only the reduction of reality to system provides the necessary stability to make control, proof, extrapolation, measurement, experimental repeatability, the lab, etc. possible. The system of objectivation then proves to be the most successful. It provides the basic format of a system that holds the promise, or rather the guarantee, of a total explanation. After all, as mentioned, "It is what it is . . ." resonates perfectly with ". . . and it works."

Of course, the reduction of reality to system, of thinking to planning, leaves out something important, namely the unpredictable event. More specifically, this is about what happens but cannot be inferred from the system, something that happens *in spite of* the system. Lyotard's type example is Auschwitz. It happened, despite all negationism.[8] But it cannot be integrated into the modern narrative of progress and the liberation of all humanity.[9] When the story goes around that all of humanity benefits from the extermination of a part of it, something is clearly wrong.[10] Lyotard points this out. The grand narratives have cracks in them; their systems can no longer contain full reality. For Lyotard, Auschwitz constitutes no exception, it is only the most lurid blow-up of an event that does not allow itself to be inserted into the system.

There is another facet to Auschwitz that Lyotard does not deal with, but that is indicative of the event and its relationship to history. This name, "Auschwitz," stands for three meanings or perspectives that are absolutely irreconcilable: Final Solution, Shoah, and Holocaust. The first is the political decision to solve and definitively eliminate a well-defined problem, literally. It is not (officially) about hatred, but articulates a rational decision. It is carried out in an exemplary efficient manner. This instrumental mentality meets all the demands of modernity; it only forfeits human dignity. But modernity *is* in a way the problem concerning human dignity, and how to understand this without any external reference such as the experience of us being created in the image of God—remember how fraternity, one of the pillars of modern political thought, has fallen completely under the radar of that same thought. Remember also how Freud suspected that only this fraternity could form a dam against the threat of mass destruction. That is why it is a great pity, perhaps even dangerous, that fraternity does not seem to be accounted for in political decision making.

The second, Shoah, is a people's experience of its total destruction as a verdict. This experience is related to the experience of God's abandonment, of God unilaterally breaking his covenant with the Jewish people. The film *God on Trial*, based on an idea from a book by Elie Wiesel, portrays this brilliantly.[11] This experience is not "translatable" outside Judaism. It is an internal experience, an authentic religious resistance.

The third, Holocaust, is the allied experience of a cinematic spectacle that first meets with disbelief and then is put beyond moral evaluation. It is the ultimate barbarity, something that does not belong to the European spirit. Yet it concerns a "full-fledged" modern recipe, a clever example of cold, calculated instrumentality that reduced human beings to their usefulness. The allied position suffers from ambivalence precisely because of the confusing and overwhelming nature of the argument. When dead Jews are efficiently "upgraded" to mattress padding, soap, and gelatin, and all their goods are recycled and redistributed to the greater honor and good of the German people, a heartfelt "But that's not possible!" can only sound pitiful, at least according to the hard line of rationality. Human dignity has no ground outside philosophical and religious discourses—just try to find a trace of this in any human science, you will not find it. Perhaps because it is impossible to reason against such lucrative recycling machine in terms of human dignity, the church chose to help as many people as possible in silence. It remains striking that modern politics, however it might have wished, could not formulate an adequate response against this. Indeed, traces of Nazism still pervade modern political practice.[12]

There is no universal, unambiguous meaning of this event. Today, we would probably choose 9/11 as a suitable name for the inability to insert extremist terror into history and to understand it from our human-scientific models. With each analysis of yet another act of terror, we notice the same inability. We do see certain patterns, such as indoctrination, provocation, and the use of social media. But it is impossible to draw a useful profile of "the terrorist." It is of course still very short-sighted to identify religion with violence. That is a typical case of ideological myopia.[13]

After Knowing, Thinking?

That "post-" is a vicious prefix. Literally it means "after," but that does not really work. Primo, postmodernity is still modernity, only with a prefix that indicates that something is happening with—not "to"—that modernity. This "post-" signifies at most a modification—Lyotard himself uses the term "rewriting," as does, curiously enough, Rorty—of modernity. Secundo, modernity is indeed not over. To the extent that science and technology are still normative, we still fully belong to modernity. To the extent that the status of science and technology is under discussion, modernity is in crisis. Tertio, since History, a definitive and total indexation according to a well-defined chronology and therefore with capital letter, can be called typical of modernity, any historical classification outside modernity is probably nonsense. Indeed, postmodernity emerges when that History is no longer an evident fact but has become a question. Postmodernity marks the disintegration of history into small narratives, without central coordination, without excessive pretension, and without absolute extrapolation.

"Post-" therefore refers rather to the self-questioning of modernity than to a chronology according to which modernity should transform into its historical successor.[14] This scheme is already fairly absurd, since chronology and succession are typical figures of modernity itself. The search for an inner-world system that gathers the events of reality into a single History exclusively befits nineteenth-century thought. Words like progress, (r)evolution, growth, emancipation, *Bildung*, etc. belong entirely to modern self-understanding.

The "post-" marks the "end" of modernity, with late modernity as its last phase. Again, unlike an ordinary end, this "end" does not belong to a history, because then we would find ourselves caught up again in the paradox of the "after." The "end" is precisely the "end" of history and of all establishable ends. We must not fall into the trap of postmodernism, as if it were the accomplishment of a strategic dismantling of original modern ambitions, the liberation of its programmatic origins in a utopia of relativism. Postmodernism is the caricature of postmodernity. The "end" of modernity or indeed of the whole metaphysics, with modernity as its culmination and turning point, could well become an "endless ending"—I will take up this idea explicitly with Derrida. Perhaps it is a transition, a mutation. In any case, we do not know any better now, if only because that "end" cannot be overtaken by a modern "knowing," by scientific reason. We cannot "know" if and when modernity will end.

We then have two options. We can, beyond rigorously systematic thought, relate to what happens in spite of the system—Lyotard refers to Heidegger's "ereignet." Or we can nostalgically throw ourselves back into a restorative system, which unfortunately can only be a derivative of grand narratives. Which -isms are still at play today? Nationalism is doing well, so is populism;[15] another fine example is "marketism," which in its turn refers to globalism. And are not fundamentalism and extremism also excesses that point to an overcompensation for capitalism?

I maintain that these latter excesses have very little to do with religion, with a god, but all the more with politics and industry under a sociopathic sauce of which we just cannot figure out the recipe. Served on a bed of Koran, admittedly, but that should not be exaggerated. The religious indoctrination on this side offers little theological nourishment, and once in the Islamic State, every missionary gets only military training. Now, this is not about Islamism, a grand narrative that seeks to legitimize terror beyond the validity of modern legitimacy. This is about the erosion of legitimacy. And this can be done in religious terms, such as paganism and polytheism. As I will argue, it is not by mere coincidence that the critique of the grand narratives and of modernity, that is, the critique of metaphysics, is cast in religious terms.

Before Lyotard successfully coined the term "postmodern," he briefly used another term, namely "paganism," as related to "polytheism"—both religious terms, but in each case in their philosophical, politically relevant sense. He contrasts this paganism with the philosophical, even political, belief in an overarching outerworldly principle that can be invoked to legitimize well-defined practices (religious, political, scientific, etc.). There is no such one overarching theoretical scheme that allows every (political) event to be explained and given a logical place within the political field that does not lose its coherence because of any event. In other words, Lyotard's paganism involves a critique or even the dismantling of philosophical theism. In still other words, Lyotard is defending a philosophical atheism—what has been announced as the actual theme of this book. This is an atheism that has heard and thought through the death of God.

Lyotard is not necessarily talking about worshippers of the sun or animals or trees. His paganism is no more about Wicca than Nietzsche's autopsy is about the biblical God. Not quite, but then again not quite not. What is typical of paganism, in philosophical terms? It is free of the obsession with unity, rationality, transparent concepts, logical stringency—in short, of theistic metaphysics. Paganism thus points to a culture which was not (yet) infected by (mono)theism, by the notion of a Supreme Being that directs the world from above and from outside (see Anselm in the chapter on Derrida). This then refers, though not necessarily, to polytheism.[16] I can, however, safely state that this polytheism is not a theology but a religious ontology, albeit permeated with postmodern hermeneutics. What elements come together here? There is no identifiable otherworldly and therefore inaccessible origin from which the world can derive its meaning and which continually brings the world back to its own God-intended unity. Rather, there are countless stories going around that are not mutually translatable into each other, that do not relate to each other within a logic, that are called divine and have an elevating effect—not in a moral sense but as existentially constitutive. It is about our way of being, as evoked in stories, in narratives. Diversity is also irreducible there. A polytheistic hermeneutic ontology is in and by itself differential.[17]

However, differentiation is often misunderstood, as a negation, an imperfection, a lack of unity yet to be remedied. It should therefore cause no surprise that traditional metaphysics takes a very dim view of differential thought.

And Thinking God

Lyotard is not a religious thinker. He is too much of a human-scientist. It is therefore not so much his philosophy as such but his idea that Christianity could be a metanarrative that interests me here.

It seems to me that Christianity is still rather a fundamental critique of the metanarratives than a metanarrative itself. Of course, this does not mean that there exists no "modern version" of it. The "moral" reduction of Christianity, against which Nietzsche famously fulminated, could be that modern version and as such qualify as a metanarrative. Deism, the doctrine of a God who, as a watchmaker or an architect, puts the cosmos into motion and barely interferes with it in any other way, is also a modern version. Both these versions are joined together on Kant's tombstone, "The starry sky above me; the moral law within me," the domain of theoretical and that of practical reason. Lyotard is primarily concerned with Kant's third reason, judgmental reason. His question becomes, therefore, how can we pass judgment when we no longer have universal criteria at our disposal, in any field? When is something good, or beautiful, or true? After all, the metanarratives that used to inform us about this no longer work.

Is Christianity then a metanarrative? For Lyotard, the story about redemption of original sin through love may count as such. Before questioning this interpretation, it should be pointed out that redemption did indeed begin to show signs of strategy or even economy at a certain point. Perhaps this is why it is not so much Luther's protest against the sale in indulgences that started off modernity but rather the trade itself. In their most caricatured form, indulgences are about a calculable cost-benefit analysis of that salvation, about the possibility of a balanced worldly investment in eternal salvation. But it is precisely this economy of salvation against which Christ fulminated.[18]

In order to become a metanarrative, Christianity had to throw out its tradition, its *depositum fidei*, and install a rational origin. After all, tradition was a bag of prejudices and, as Gadamer once said, modernity suffers from only one prejudice, namely that against prejudices. Now, if anything is all but modern, it is the uncritical acceptance of religious truths. These rational origins became the cosmic and the moral order. These two systems, the external and the internal, nature and culture, necessity and freedom, the starry sky and the moral law . . . became the baselines of modern religion.

Such origins, averse to tradition and otherworldly revelation, fit the metanarrative. The title of an important book by Kant, *Religion within the Bounds of Bare Reason*, says it all. When religion wants to present itself in the public sphere, it first passes the tribunal of reason. There it cannot legitimize itself by invoking tradition or Magisterium. Enlightened reason does not care about these things. What Kant and what Enlightenment ask of Christianity is precisely that it transform itself into a metanarrative, that it become modern. Religion is tolerated only if it becomes hyperreligious, a rationally founded religion—see Russell.

The Bible itself is another stumbling block—the meaning of the Greek *skandalon*—to modern culture. Enlightenment wanted to reduce it to a moral prescription. Beside this moral reduction, there are other forms: the socioeconomic and the political reduction that want to turn the Bible into a revolutionary pamphlet; the cultural-historical one that wants to check the stories for "authenticity" in the sense of "actually happened" historically; and even a psychoanalytic one (as with Eugen Drewermann). The actual contribution of each these perspectives is rather marginal. My concern in the present context is with the status of events in the gospels. Many events in the gospels are not "integrable." From a rational viewpoint, they even sound absurd. The star of Bethlehem is cosmological nonsense; the virgin birth of Jesus is biological gibberish; Christ riding into Jerusalem as a king on a donkey is political nonsense; the meek inheriting the earth is military subversion; the poor widow's mite is economic nonsense; walking on water is physically absurd; and so on. To speak in modern terms, those pictorial events disrupt any rational discourse. The gospels tell not a metanarrative but an anti-metanarrative. How would Lyotard react to this? By taking events as its basic theme, Christianity actually strips events of their eventual character. It then belongs, as it were, to a *plan* of salvation. He considers the Jewish narrative more open because there the Messiah is still expected whereas Christ, the last word of God, has already come. But one could also state that the Jewish narrative is closed around the absoluteness of the Law, whereas the Christian narrative of love is open because neighborly love ultimately also implies receptivity, hospitality, openness and thus a focus on the other. To close a narrative around love should belong not to the order of grace but to that of the human sciences. It could deal with psychological love, sociological altruism, economic solidarity, or political fraternity.

But then Lyotard also seems to include grace within this enclosure because it is promised and thus guaranteed by God himself. Grace, in the modern version of the Christian narrative, is no longer an event, an "advent," a divine gift, but an economy. It guarantees, for example, eternal salvation as the reward after a dutiful and morally high life—or for the purchase of an indulgence.

Be that as it may, as a metanarrative, Christianity has exhausted its potential along with all the others. The modern version of Christianity has had its time—its time being modernity. Does this mean that Christianity *as such* has had its time? No. Could there be a postmodern version that is not a mere copy of the pre-modern one?[19] Yes. And that version is in line with contemporary French philosophy.

Attention to the event—does this not require a "religious" attitude of thought? Not ignoring what does not fit the system, does this not sound Christian? "Meontology," the study of being(s) that engages with the "infinitesimal" that is to be found at the limits of every (mathematical) model and under every (human scientific) radar, is that not what we find in the Bible?[20] The "option for the poorest," is that not what following Christ is all about? It should be noted here that this option is different from Levinas's Jewish spirituality, which tends to see every human being in its vulnerability, so that the latter is more of an anthropological category than a theological one, as in Christianity.

It will come as no surprise that I am borrowing from Heidegger again. At the beginning of his academic career he taught about the perception and experience of time in the letters by Paul. The latter thematized the event as a thief in the night. The event, in this case the "parousia" or the second coming of Christ revealing the full truth about man and the world, cannot be calculated, predicted, scheduled, or put on the agenda. Thinking the event is something else than planning. What is required here is watchful, attentive thought. Heidegger translated that vigilance into his thoughtful openness to a new understanding of being that is about to happen and that announces itself as a wink (see Heidegger).

Christianity needs self-criticism to avoid its own modern reduction to metanarrative. Postmodern hermeneutics presents Christianity as the prototype of a story that cannot and will not be "grand."[21] The Christian story is not one and is also not a totality; it will never be finished or completed; it contains no rational and transparent roadmap; and it keeps its core away from the world without installing another, true world. After all, the latter is what modernity has left behind; and postmodernity, as Nietzsche taught us, has yet to abolish the notion of true world itself.

Now, at the end of the first chapter of his *The Postmodern Explained*, Lyotard says something that is not easy to understand. What, after all, is the postmodern about? About saving the honor of the name, says Lyotard. Not saving the name, but saving the honor of the name. How did the name become dishonored? By theistic metaphysics, I suppose. It prefers concepts, as general as possible. These concepts allow things and states to be indexed into a system, into a file. God is a name; *Causa Sui* is a concept. Christian metaphysics hardly distinguishes between those. An important postmodern insight now concerns the localization or incarnation of thinking (and speaking and writing and painting and dancing and singing . . .), that is, its particularity and materiality, as opposed to its universality and spirituality or ideality.

Could Lyotard be referring to kenosis here? We already encountered this notion with Levinas. A philosophical reading of Phil 2:5–11 could reveal the following. The Christ hymn that Paul quotes there relates how Christ has renounced the divine form that was properly his own and thus renounced his substance (in the Aristotelian sense). This desubstantialization, this "notting," meant at the same time the gift of the Name above all names—the Name that makes knees bow on and under the earth. That the notting is a naming—let us call this "God."

To save the honor of the name means to rehabilitate the singular event, to revitalize it by breaking the hegemony of the system—insofar as that too is not one and the same process. That process, that event, is the postmodern. Postmodern*ism*, then, is total control of the postmodern, which is an absurdity—not a contradiction, since postmodernity is not bothered by that. Postmodernity leaves happening to the eventual and refuses to hand it over to planning, arrangement, the total scheme. We now come back to the metanarrative and along the way we have taken up meontology and kenosis.

Those who call Christianity a metanarrative only see its modern social form. Paradoxically enough, it is precisely to the extent that Christianity is not a metanarrative that faith is again given a chance in the "end" of the metanarratives. Now that faith has left those ideologies behind, it can turn to its only true source. Remember Nietzsche, whose autopsy of the moral and cultural God, the God of philosophical theism or metaphysics, barely affects the God of the Bible or faith.[22]

As a critique, therefore, philosophy still needs Christianity precisely as the other-of-the-world that disrupts the closure of discourses, of narratives. Just as the sale of indulgences marks the beginning of modern Christianity, the human rights discourse marks its end. Indeed, it is claimed that the Universal Declaration of Human Rights closes off Christianity, spells its end. This declaration, some say, makes God and Christianity superfluous. But that is not only a serious misconception as to the finality of Christianity—by reducing it to its modern version—but also an underestimation of the "role" of the name (of) God. If the human rights discourse, like all others, is not "kept open," the Declaration is in danger of becoming dead letter. This is true of many such declarations, by the way. It is not just coincidence that at the moment the United Nations launch their sustainable development goals, much attention is paid to the visionary encyclical *Laudato si'*.[23]

We also should not read the finality of Christianity, its end times, in the same register as the eternal achievement of the world, such as the 1000-year *Reich* of the Nazis or the worker's paradise of the Leninists. Terms like "fulfillment," "messiah," "promise," and "judgment" keep eschatology away from the necessary factual realization of an ideal. It remains curious that Lyotard did not have anything to say about the Last Judgment, given his interest in Kant's third critique.

12

Silent

Derrida

We end in silence. It could sound a bit cheap to add "deafening," yet that would not be unjustified. To Wittgenstein's inability to speak and Heidegger's better not to speak, Derrida adds the inability to remain silent.[1] From the Heideggerian expectation of new being, he subtracts hope. He deals with Russell via John Searle. He undoes Levinas's Face of its radical alterity and majesty. He dismantles the partitions between ethics and religion in Levinas and Kierkegaard. All that remains of Marx's *Communist Manifesto* is a ghost, without political ideology. He applies Freud's delayed gratification of needs to Nietzsche's drive for truth in metaphysics. He brings together Greek metaphysics (Heidegger?) and Jewish wisdom (Levinas?). But a theory of his own, no, none.

That would not be very consistent, since each new theory immediately falls "under deconstruction"—see below. Two titles of his main works show this in their tone. *De la grammatologie* and *Marges . . . de la philosophie*. The ambiguity is intended. If they are translated as *About Grammatology* and *Margins of Philosophy*, then these titles fit perfectly into the traditional philosophical bibliography. But they can also be translated as *Some Grammatology* and *Margins . . . Some Philosophy*. This already sounds more uncomfortable, at least to traditional ears.

Derrida deliberately refuses what philosophers did before him, which is to design a whole new system. He includes that design and its apparent evidence in his questioning. Why must thought necessarily be "system-designed"? In this sense, he takes Heidegger's version of philosophy seriously, namely to start thinking (about) philosophy from the unthought, to throw the unthought into philosophy, to explore the margins of metaphysics. Derrida reads and rewrites—we already heard that word with Lyotard. This reading does not "do" anything, such as prove a statement or theory, but rather undoes systems; in that sense it "works." It does not install Unmoved Movers and *Causae Sui* and Absolute Spirits and other capitalized Supreme Beings; on the contrary, it deconstructs, it undoes those very installations. Deconstruction sets thinking free, free from otherworldly anchors that Derrida calls "transcendental signifiers."

Richard Rorty once said that Hegel and Proust both wrote literature but only Proust realized this. Hegel still thought that philosophy had its own access to truth, opened the *via regia* to it—and he himself was then the *autostrada regia*. Now, Derrida would join Rorty along another path, I think. There is not, first, philosophy and a professional practitioner of it who could then only write and talk philosophy. No, there is writing and talking going on and we can only wait and see in what "discipline" that ends up—if such categorization is at all necessary or desirable.

There is thinking, speaking, and writing going on. That does not sound like a classical divine "origin," like an Idea or Creation. In traditional metaphysics, consciousness conceives of an idea that afterwards can be converted into language, speech, or text. Text then lies outside pure thinking, belongs in a world that lies opposite consciousness, a material "outside" that does not affect the spiritual "inside." Text is inferior, contaminated by materiality—Derrida calls this "écriture."

Derrida brings to mind Jacques Lacan's famous "ça parle." The "I" takes or receives the word, but never founds or owns it. The words and their play were already at work before I open my mouth or my laptop. Even what I want to say, my intention, is strange to me because it is unconsciously motivated, as psychoanalysis demonstrates. Speaking never starts from a purely reasonable, spiritual intention, from consciousness present in and to itself.

Derrida erases all philosophical—and other—zero-points such as Descartes's subject, Hegel's Spirit, Aristotle's Unmoved Mover, and the like. These do exist, as "philosopheme," but no longer enjoy the status of pure origin, unnegotiable principle, or absolute norm.

This makes many philosophers feel very uncomfortable. They fear that this way, the whole construction of metaphysics, philosophy, yes, even thought itself will collapse. There were even unfortunate "incidents." For example, when Derrida had written an extensive review of John Austin's *How to Do Things with Words* (lectures from 1955, published in 1962). Austin's colleague Searle, who clearly did not understand what Derrida was talking about, declared that review meaningless in his "Reply to Derrida: Reiterating the Differences." Derrida then wrote another response, *Limited Inc.*, also the title of the collection in which the English translations of both his texts were included. Searle refused permission to include his text in that collection. Or when Derrida was nominated for an honorary doctorate at Cambridge and the whole Anglo-Saxon world turned purple. He was awarded it anyway, in 1992, and subsequently at several universities around the world.

Initially, Derrida's work was considered highly "speculative," so much so that his critics hardly reacted at all. After all, according to them it didn't make any sense, so as long as Derrida did not receive any academic recognition, his writings could not cause any real harm. But then suddenly the Nazi party card of Heidegger, his teacher, and the anti-Semitic war pieces by Paul De Man, his student, came up and threatened to ruin his fragile reputation. Suddenly Derrida was thrown into a suspiciously neo-conservative right-liberal pseudo-fascist camp. Yes, apparently that's how it goes. Nevertheless, this had a beneficial effect, because it encouraged Derrida to give his thoughts more ethical and political, even theological relevance.

Like many other philosophers in this book, Derrida spent some time in prison, more specifically in Prague. He had chaired a colloquium there for which the communist authority had not given permission. While Derrida was visiting Kafka's grave, the state police shoved some drugs in his underwear and he was jailed. Fortunately, president Mitterrand got him released—the second time in this book where a French president "liberates" philosophy.

Deconstruction

Derrida launched the word "deconstruction" with which, to his distress, he remained associated for life. After all, just like postmodernism, deconstructivism soon became a hype in America. It was supposed to be a new epistemology to replace the traditional one—which it is certainly not. Others reacted with horror. To them, deconstruction was supposed to be a strategy that rejects all epistemology. It decrees the end of truth, understanding, logic, meaning, in other words of philosophy and thought as such—again, which it most certainly does not.

Deconstruction belongs not to planning but to happening—since Heidegger and Lyotard we are familiar with the difference between those figures of thought. It also has no subject—which would only threaten to turn deconstruction into a modern project. Deconstruction is not humanism—and this makes it already suspect in the eyes of many. There is no "I" that deconstructs, or humanity, or metaphysics. Deconstruction is what happens to metaphysics, to thinking itself. In late modernity metaphysics finds itself under deconstruction, at least according to Derrida. It is the old magician who does his tricks and at the same time explains how he does them. It is still impressive, but more as a parody. Tommy Cooper, but not all that funny.

"What is deconstruction? Nothing! What is deconstruction not? Everything!" Derrida exclaimed in an interview. Well, we are not going to ask him again. Incidentally, he makes the same claim elsewhere about "differ*a*nce"—I will come to that later. You may think that this is easy, that you can do this too. But that is not the case.

Deconstruction belongs to the critique of metaphysics, that is, to metaphysics that includes its own evidences and limits in its reflection. And indeed, we find a first sample of such thinking with Nietzsche, more specifically in his brilliant critical reading of Descartes' *Cogito ergo sum* in *Beyond Good and Evil* (§16–17). You know the story. Descartes has had enough of inflated scholastic theology and wants to return to a pure zero point of thinking. His doubt chops away at all traditional knowledge until only doubt itself remains as what cannot itself be doubted. Doubt is thought, so when and where this happens, there is necessarily such a thing as a *res cogitans*, a thinking being. That thinking needs a subject, a carrier, a conscious being, an "I" or *ego*. In my consciousness I find the idea of perfection, which must necessarily exist outside my consciousness—primo, because it is more perfect than my finite consciousness it cannot be a product of it; secundo, because it would not be perfect without also existing. And because it is perfect, it will not deceive me if I arrange my thinking according to the necessary hygienic requirements. From all this follows the fact that I really exist and that the rest of reality must indeed correspond to my clear and well-defined, clean ideas.

Nietzsche points out that this whole reasoning is anything but pure but is weighed down by a lot of presuppositions that are implicit and not declared, let alone elaborated. These presuppositions include those that precede the installation of thought at the alleged "origin," namely about what thinking is, how logical argumentation proceeds, what the ideas or contents of consciousness are precisely, how consciousness and methodical argumentation work, what the position of "subject" implies, what it means to exist, how the principle of truth as correspondence works, etc. The well-known *Cogito ergo sum* alone unavoidably hinges on vocabulary, grammar, and logic. Thus, all these determinations are already decided upon before Descartes can install his allegedly pure zero point. Prior to the origin, therefore, everything that is supposed to be produced by the origin is already in operation. In the case of the *cogito*, the determinations that precede it are ideas that come from that *cogito* and therefore cannot precede it. Derrida calls this sort of instability or ambiguity typical of metaphysics. I will elaborate on this instability later, with Anselm.

Gramma

A message cannot be separated from its bearer. There will always be tone, volume, handwriting, font, facial expressions. These contribute to the message. If someone is raging in Chinese, I don't have to pull out my Chinese–English vocabulary to know what the message is. Meaning is not preferably purely spiritual. Every meaning unavoidably has its material side. And this materiality, this "flesh" cannot simply be "subtracted" from meaning to keep it purely spiritual. That is a metaphysical illusion.

The great linguist Ferdinand de Saussure already taught in his *Course of General Linguistics* (1916) that such a thing as purely spiritual meaning does not exist, cannot even exist. His contribution to the critique of metaphysics consisted in defining the sign as the union of one element from the domain of the signified, the ideas, and one element from the world of the signifier—let us refer to the latter as "word" for the sake of convenience. A word in itself means nothing; it is a series of letters that can only be said to differ from all other series and thereby to be able to acquire meaning. This is called a differential system: all elements differ from each other without carrying an inherent "positive" meaning of their own.[2]

Once a word is connected to "its" signified, namely the notion or concept or idea, a (relatively) stable sign with positive, no longer differential meaning emerges. To acquire positive meaning, spiritual meaning must be connected with a material carrier; otherwise it cannot get signified at all. Thus a concept in itself means nothing, just as a sound in itself means nothing. Because there is no such thing as a pure, purely comprehensible meaning, concepts on their own also form a differential system.

Derrida famously deconstructs the sign. He wonders, primo, how the sign is exempted from all difference and becomes "positive"; secundo, why an arbitrary distinction is made between two domains, spiritual signifiers on the one hand and material signifiers on the other.

Signifier and signified, idea and word belong together as "gramma"—hence grammatology—or trace. We already encountered this notion of trace with Freud and Levinas. Signified and signifier do not really come together as in the sign. We must not forget that the sign is not a thing; that is a wrong superficial reading. It is a relation between word and idea. This relation is much more stable in classic semiotics than in Derrida's. After all, according to him, word and concept do not fit together perfectly as in the ideal of *adaequatio rei et intellectus*. When a word evokes an idea, it silently expresses more than just that idea. On the other hand, a concept is always somewhat broader than "its" word, which cannot contain the full concept. One always and persistently flows over into the other—and this never stops. The epistemological accounting never balances out. When a word captures an idea or vice versa, when there is reading, speaking, or writing going on, this process does not neatly move from idea to word, from theory to text and back again. It goes back and forth simultaneously each time. There are all kinds of associations, connotations, which precisely create new and unexpected meanings and insights each time. Every crystallization into concept is always already at the same time a dispersion toward other words and ideas. Thinking (and speaking etc.)—the message—does not start from a "pure" idea in a pure consciousness—the sender—and never arrives as such in another pure consciousness—the receiver—as the classical model of communication would have it.

Thinking draws traces that cannot be traced back to an original pure ideal intention. To say that the trace is the absolute origin of thought, as Derrida does, is tantamount to saying that there is no origin at all. Nor will traces ever converge definitively in, say, a final and/or total explanation—as implied in the abovementioned persistency of the mutual overflow that never stops. This total explanation, like the Grand Unifying Theory, is science's favorite metanarrative—remember Lyotard. One day science, that is the modern form of metaphysics, will be able to explain everything and religion (and myth and poetry) will become superfluous, claimed Freud and Russell. But that moment will never arrive. We will never reach the one, stable, definitive truth. "Il nous faut la vérité," says Derrida. We need it, but it will always be lacking. Every meaning, every truth, every insight is always transitory because at the moment it presents itself, another already lies in the offing.

Derrida calls this: "delay"; it afflicts and haunts full and ultimate truth. Metaphysics considers this a mere marginal perturbance but for Derrida it is precisely this subordination or suppression into irrelevance that is arbitrary. Delay marks thought. Delay affects the purity of thought, infects it. It indicates that thinking never becomes "purely" spiritual; it can never shed its materiality (completely). There will always remain a "rest" (*restance*) that offers resistance (*résistence*) to being fully "absolved" in the absolute, pure idea. This is what Derrida means by the well-known "Il n'y a pas de hors-texte." Thinking nowhere never fully escapes its texture, its materiality.

Because this line has been misunderstood, as if only (additional) characters and numbers existed, Derrida "clarifies" this formula with another, "Il n'y a pas de hors-*con*texte." All reference is always also "proference." Meaning can never be lifted out of an untraceable network of reference, never be exempted from trace. A text does not refer to a spiritual content or to a world of ideas, but always to other texts. In that reference, which is completely unpredictable, meaning emerges. However, this is never definitive, full, eternal, or intact. No meaning escapes the effects that contaminate the "original" meaning as further reference. That play—Derrida calls it "dissemination"—cannot be epistemologically controlled or managed. It is an illusion to think that people are in charge of the production of meaning.

A text, then, is a dynamic entity that is never finished. The traditional format of a text, "book," is no longer the standard model for the presentation of meaning. In any case, every author has read, heard, seen, experienced, and gathered a lot of insight before starting to write. A book always quotes and therefore refers to other books, implicitly or not, and is itself quoted, discussed, and reviewed in several leading journals. It has a layout and a publisher that is never neutral. A debate at a Book Fair is organized. There will be a reprint, because it appeared in a bestsellers list, or even a completely revised reprint because a real author never stops thinking; there might even follow a sequel. It gets burned, or thrown on the index, so it will be distributed "underground" among those who are always enchanted by forbidden fruit. The author dies, but the text remains. Someone replies to this book with another one. Both books are compared, end up in various bibliographies. Reading groups gather, conferences take place. And so on. It seems like it is all about the book, but actually the book is a momentary "condensation" hiding in a very complex thought texture that is also "book"—book as event, not as a thing.[3]

That whole process is text-in-context. The book is a temporary crystallization, the tip of the iceberg if you will, the excuse for the event of the text that was always considered by metaphysics to be unimportant, incidental. But this whole process has become the format, the measure of thought. Thinking is not limited to the mental process that precedes the writing of a book. A "book" as an object may be "finished" at a certain point; the book as an event, as text, never is. Text is always haunted by delay. Text *is* delay, actually. But this should not be read literally or logically, as a proposition.

Delay implies that every conclusion of any discourse always concerns a deliberately concealed strategy, is always ideologically motivated, invariably results from a decision concerning thinking. It is like yielding to a preference that is subsequently presented as evidence. The decision, the preference, then applies as a metaphysical dogma that can or may no longer be questioned—the metaphysical imperative that Heidegger violated.

Is delay then the new format or determination of truth that replaces the previous model, that of correspondence? Such an assertion would get Derrida in trouble. Delay is not a model or a theory, but a mark. The moment that metaphysics decides that we must work on a total explanation based on objectivity, correspondence, and conceptual hygiene, thought is irrevocably tainted, infected by a delay that this same metaphysics frantically tries to marginalize because it would frustrate its ambitions. Delay cannot be a concept since it is beyond the reach of metaphysics. That is, metaphysics tolerates it within its reach only when it diminishes itself into side effect, and thereby suppresses its own "truth." Delay is only considered secondary and provisional within metaphysics. Precisely in such margins hides the most interesting philosophical challenge—recall the title *Margins of Philosophy*, but also feel free to think of Heidegger's Nothing. There slumbers what Heidegger still calls the "unthought" and what Derrida takes up as the "unheard." It remains unthought because it is unheard-of to think such things.

So deconstruction is still not about a (new) theory or even a revolutionary concept, because these philosophical items never end up in the margins of thought. It is not about a content; delay is not a principle from which anything can be derived. Delay haunts and traces through the dark, impenetrable, resisting materiality of thought. There is no point in calculating how long delay will or can last, because then it would be thrown back into the teleology of metaphysics.

Différance

This materiality is inaccessible to traditional metaphysical approaches. When texture is admitted and included in philosophy, it turns out that ideas no longer seamlessly fit "their" words and that a full, stable truth is haunted by delay.[4] It turns out to be impossible to reduce the traces of thinking (and writing, etc.) to an original unity, like a Creator or a *cogito* or *Geist*.

Derrida calls this impossibility differ*a*nce. This is not even a word, but marks and affects thought, which remains marked and affected by this impossibility as long as metaphysics lasts. It does not want to say anything but keeps the game of differences—hinging on the non-matching of word and idea—and delay "alive."

What is obvious to metaphysics, for example that thinking should result in "total explanation," is questioned by Derrida. It is not so much this total explanation itself that he doubts, since it was never achieved so far, but rather this evidence. He recognizes the structure of a decision behind this evidence, which is based on a preference that itself has no reason outside itself and can therefore be considered arbitrary. There are more such evidences, such as the preference for concepts over metaphors. Differance produces both, without itself being the original and full unity of concept-plus-metaphor. Differance, then, is certainly not the sum or original *Aufhebung* of concept and metaphor. It is neither; both sprout from it. More than that, therein also lies the metaphorical effect of concepts and the conceptual potential of metaphors—pure horror in the eyes of epistemology. Metaphysics, however, decided to install a relation, to perform a double operation on thought, namely opposition+subordination, so that within the space of this decision it could continue to install a system, a logic that would merely consist of pure concepts. Throughout its history metaphysics found it obvious that more truth could be extracted from concepts than from metaphors.

Differance insists—if it is at all possible for differance to insist—that essentially neither is there such thing as a concept *versus* a metaphor, nor is there anything like an original unity that dialectically unites the two *a priori* into the most original and truest unit of meaning. So, to be clear, it is not differance that causes the concept and the metaphor and their relationship. The decision to gather concepts in a logic "at the expense" of metaphors entails its own inefficiency, injustice, and arbitrariness until today, when it comes into view at the "end" of metaphysics.[5] Then it even turns out that metaphysics owes its longtime existence as well as its secure future precisely to the covert operation of metaphoricity behind the conceptual screens of metaphysical epistemology.[6]

The decision for this double operation, opposition and subordination, has been pushed outside the field of vision of metaphysics and has to remain there. "Inside" is the domain of those evidences of which, according to metaphysics, there is no further need to think through. Deconstruction is the insertion of that outside in metaphysics—that is no longer "traditional." Outside thus "avenges" itself (from) inside the system.[7] Every metaphor has something intelligible; every concept thrives on some form of imagery. That is the play of differences, of the system of stable signs being broken open into a rhizome of traces, of the imperfect matching of signifier and signified, of word and idea. Every notion can temporarily precipitate into a concept and at the same time refer to other notions through its metaphoricity. That referral cannot be analyzed or controlled. That play of differences, then, is what Derrida calls "differance."

Differance, according to some, is a kind of vanishing point in thought, a black hole that sucks up all meaning. But then that word is read metaphysically again, as a deliberately planned epistemological operation. It is not that at all; it was not even a word when Derrida proposed it. It reveals, by the way, a wordplay that is all but innocent. The "-a-" in "differance" marks the difference with the word "difference"; it is visible but not audible. Differance is unheard-of, *inouï*. It shows itself only in its mute materiality of signifier. Again, it is not a thing but the tension of the play that keeps world and thought open. Differance is not a concept and does not even want to say anything itself, but makes all thinking and speaking and writing possible because it "gets to work" where the sign breaks open: gramma. If it does not want to say anything, it also cannot mean anything. That which does not want to say anything itself and does not mean anything is also that from which all meaning emerges. In spite of all "differences," this very much resembles Heidegger's Nothing, which does not mean anything within metaphysics; it also reminds us of what Wittgenstein wanted us to remain silent about because, although it produces all meaning, it does not mean anything itself.

Something recognizable as or comparable to a desire works through in differance, so that wants-to-say-nothing produces cannot-not-say. We all emphatically want to experience the world as meaningful. Remember: "Il nous faut la vérité." We must accept that the sense of it all depends precisely on truth being wanted *and* lacking. This does not relieve us of the "need" to signify. We cannot not mean anything. Thinking can go on endlessly without the illusory risk of Hegelian suicide of a philosophy that has already thought everything through.

God, Trace of a Trace

We already saw with Heidegger that being cannot be identified with God, despite apparent similarities. With Derrida, the same is true: differance cannot be identified with God, although it is tempting. After all, differance is the element or the state of the trace "par excellence." With Levinas, God is the name of the trace (of traces), but not for Derrida—even though we will find that there are great similarities, even a rapprochement on the part of the latter.

Derrida calls metaphysics theological because it constitutes the time of the sign. God in Christian metaphysics is the agency that stabilizes meanings, that orders creation into a system. This, by the way, is what Nietzsche meant when he said that we will never get away from theology as long as we keep using the word "is." But Anselm already demonstrated, probably unintentionally, that the Supreme Sign that is supposed to guard the stability of all signs is itself broken open. In his famous *Proslogion* he states that on the one hand God is the greatest that can be thought and on the other hand God is greater than all that can be thought. On the one hand, then, God is the highest that can be thought, the Supreme Being within the order; on the other hand, God can be thought of as beyond the reach of thought. God is not one *or* the other. This tension is extremely significant because it shows thinking as an excessive event that can never be definitively encompassed, totally understood—not even by itself. Thinking is thus at the same time an excess and a deficit. It exhibits its own openness where the epistemological balance is overthrown and cannot be made conclusive. God is a possible, or perhaps rather an impossible name, the name of an impossible God. As Supreme Being, God is the most powerful concept conceivable; as metaphysical excess, God is a name that cannot be conceptually appropriated and disrupts thought as a system and turns it into an open event. It is clear that metaphysics cannot think these two perspectives together, that it does not know how to reconcile this "double God" theologically or philosophically. Positively formulated, this non-relation, this oscillation or contamination only comes into view and is discussed within differential thought, i.e., at the "end" of metaphysics.

Like Heidegger and Levinas, Derrida does not develop a coherent theology or philosophy of atheism. Like Heidegger and Levinas, he does call his philosophy atheistic.[8] The "problem" with Derrida, as with both other thinkers, is that he cannot be read and understood in the traditional register. That register, as we have already seen, hinges on the system of objectivity and deploys some fundamental operations to that end—remember opposition and subordination. Once these operations are at work, they are classified as self-evident and thus inaccessibly intertwined with metaphysics. I already mentioned the installation of the Supreme Being, which is yet another operation. Deconstruction questions that installation—and undoes it without rejecting it.

When we follow the trail of Derrida's thinking about, or toward, or away from God, we must be aware that we should expect neither a theology nor a Judeo-Greek-Christian metaphysics—insofar as there is a great difference between those two. That is why Derrida does not ask about God, just as Heidegger does not ask about being *as such*. After all, in that case the latter would emerge with yet another traditional ontology, which answers the question "What is being?" only with "That is being." That is why Heidegger asks about the forgetting of being in order to find in this forgottenness the trace of being as being-forgotten and not as fully present, as Supreme Being. Similarly, Derrida does not ask the question "What is God?" because that question can only generate a theology. Rather, his question is "What happens when we think (pronounce, write, read, hear, etc.) the name (of) God?" We must consider this in light of the foregoing. There can be no pure origin, no original word, no original creating consciousness. After all, in that case God would remain meaningless. God also cannot escape the materiality of signification—hence revelation. Still, to connect the dots: Derrida does not claim that this being named "God" is material, but rather that if that name is to have a philosophic relevance, it must arrive through materiality and not from out of some pure spirituality. If God is not touched by the world, he cannot get into the world—into thought, speech, etc. If the world is not touched by God, it is just a Cartesian thing.

However, the whole metaphysics hinges on such pure ideas—what Derrida calls "transcendental signifiers." Transcendental, because they are stripped of their materiality and temporality. We have not only God, but also Man, Consciousness, Origin, End, Spirit, Cogito, Substance, Idea, etc. These strong concepts are supposed to spiritualize thought, to stabilize meaning, to suppress trace, and to cancel out differences. This total indifference, however, would mean the death of philosophy. All meaning would be clear and completed, forever wrapped up in concepts, hanging in thin air. These concepts would be assumed to correspond to a reality that lies in perpetual wait for those adequate and stable meanings. Thinking would find itself reduced to deciphering and calculating. The fact that philosophical thinking still occurs, currently as (under) deconstruction, shows at least that those concepts do not perform well and do not accomplish the tasks for which they were installed.

Until modernity, God was the exclusive Supreme Being, both as thing and as concept. In God, "thingness" (substance) and "ideaness" (concept) came together perfectly. This gave him the power to guarantee this perfect adequacy also with regard to all the rest of reality. From the concept God automatically followed his whole being, including his necessary existence, and his complete beingness could be considered as contained in his concept. In firmer terms, his existence is contained in his conceptual essence. Not so with us and all other things, because our and their existence is contingent rather than necessary. This does not imply that we (can) know God completely, but at least this suggests that God could not be thought of as lacking anything that could or should yet become real. From the God-concept, for example his creation plan, the whole meaning of reality could further be derived, right down to morality. It is this system that finds itself under deconstruction. Metaphysics now understands that this system is its own product, with the help of some heavy theistic levers that were installed on a rather arbitrary basis. The motive for that installation, for the decision to install a system, is to be discerned in the preference, namely for pure concepts, for system, for ground, for unity, for stability, and so on. Deconstruction relieves God of that system—without abolishing him, because there is no ground for that either.

Actually, in this connection the foregoing mainly means that God can no longer be thought within metaphysics because he is dead and metaphysics has come to its "end." God can no longer occupy the position of Supreme Being, not because something else does—the mistake "flat" atheists make—but because that position no longer exists since Nietzsche.

Back to the question concerning what happens when we say "God," now that we know that God arises from differance, that differance produces the name God and all (other) holy epithets. The way in which difference occurs can also be approached or articulated in another way. I return to this metaphysical preference and subsequent decision. Thus, as demonstrated, there does not exist any unambiguous and evident ground or reason for this "preference." The question concerning the ground cannot be answered because there is no philosophical position outside of thinking from where its dynamics can be evaluated or (re)directed. Thinking happens. The notion of preference now appears as the vanishing point of (the evidentiality of) logic, objectivity, the Supreme Being, and the concepts. In principle, then, another preference or indeed a preference for the "other" would be equally legitimate. This would of course still be a preference, but one that would not deny this. Rather, it is actually a preference to undo the previous preference—a counter-preference, if you will. This is undeniably a feature of metaphysics criticism.

It is not that alterity was imposed on philosophy. It arose within it and was taken up first in Germany (until Heidegger and World War II) and then in France and the Balkan states (thereafter, together with psychoanalysis and linguistics), and finally in the United States. The other has left traces. It has "split" philosophy at its very root, in the sense that the gap between, on the one hand, continental (i.e., primarily French) differential thinking, and, on the other hand, Anglo-Saxon analytical thinking has become a philosophical issue that demands of every scholar to take a position.

Implicitly, Heidegger and Levinas take their stand in that "other" preference—Heidegger on ontological, Levinas on ethical "ground." French contemporary philosophy is "preferably" the place where the other has irreversibly and irreducibly made its appearance. Because some were not sympathetic and supportive *re* this encroaching "other"; they feared that this was no longer proper philosophy, but rather theology. Dominique Janicaud devoted a book to his concern about this outsourcing of philosophy, which he called *Phenomenology and the "Theological Turn."*

Actually, the reverse was true. Rather, it was theology that took advantage of that openness to the "other" to sail into philosophy. This openness disarmed modern resistance against such intrusion. Modern philosophy had worked its way up from being the "maid" of theology to being its "master" and its representatives were afraid that postmodern thought would chase philosophy from this position, to be parceled out and end up in theology, literature, cultural criticism, or worse.

God is a trace of a trace, not a trace of/toward a thing, and it cannot be fully brought into the world, into the element of the "same." Whereas Levinas calls God the "Tout Autre," with Derrida it becomes "tout autre est tout autre," each other is totally other, and further "tout autre est Dieu est tout autre." How can Derrida now criticize Levinas's "tout autre" by coming up with something even more powerful himself? It has to do with Levinas's capitals. The latter finds God outside the world, even though he also speaks of the trace that is God. Derrida also follows God's trace without any direct access to a God-self, but that trace does not lead out of the world. Levinas's God seems to be a trace that leaves the world, that lends majesty and glory from outside to absolute vulnerability—absolute, from the Latin for "absolving," cleansed of all egology, redeemed from the laws of the world. Levinas considers each one responsible for *any*one. In the eyes of Derrida, I am responsible for *every*one, not in the Sartrian sense, but in the sense that the election of one implies a betrayal of all others, no matter how understandable and psychologically acceptable.

Derrida takes up (Kierkegaard's and) Levinas's reading of Abraham's sacrifice of Isaac (Gn 22:1–18) and sees a possible refusal to comply with

God's request—a test, incidentally, not a command—and thus to give priority to the life of his son, as a betrayal of the individual, the "singularity of God," in the name of a universal ethics that decrees that one does not kill one's own child. The refusal would imply a choice for the prevailing, universal ethics and go against the singular, personal demand of God. God then, with Derrida, is not the name of the majesty of the appeal, as with Levinas, but the name of the individual who is simply different, and can only present himself in his irreducible singularity. Derrida writes in *The Gift of Death*, "I cannot respond to the call, the request, the obligation, or even the love of another without sacrificing the other other, the other others."[9] If every other is wholly other, this does not mean, as some claim, that there is no similarity between two people (and animals? things?) and that therefore all ethics or politics or religions are declared invalid. What it does mean is that election is not transferable through moral, political, or religious channels, institutions, rules—here is a clear echo of Kierkegaard. There is no universality in this, no law or duty to which an exception is made. By electing one person, I betray every other as a singular other, not as a category. I cannot justify this election, certainly not by means of an ethical argument, because the latter makes me equally responsible for every other. The "why" of the murder of Isaac therefore remains secret and is given the name "God." The sacrifice of Isaac is the sacrifice of ethics in the name of the divine. Now I can hear Antigone approaching. The biblical passage wants to know if you are willing to set aside law and ethics for this singular other who evokes the name God, without probing for any reason why.[10] There is a why, but it remains secret. Something can only be your secret when at least someone else knows it is there, but that someone just does not know what it is. It hides in my deepest "inside," near the name "God"—ever since Augustine.

But in whose name, then? Not of an otherworldly God, but of a God who is the name of every other and *only as such* completely other *and* all other others. God is the name that carries me away from every (ethical, political religious . . .) system, without destroying that system. God therefore works in differance—without coinciding with it or being its (only, true . . .) name—by declaring every ethics to be an effect, an effect that can never assume any fullness or completion. God is older than all ethics but frustrates any ethics only in retrospect by showing its inadequacy, appearing where ethics fails, erodes, and stumbles upon its limits. Should God do so *a priori*, God would be the Principle of Evil or its personification: the devil.

My responsibility is always in oscillation, in the sense that it must obey the law, our duty, and at the same time dare to go beyond the law for this one totally other that we mark for the moment with the name God. God always remains the name of a dispossession—an echo of Levinas. When we call the other by a proper name, the system already appropriates the other and undoes alterity.

I summarize the scene with Abraham and Isaac again from Derrida's interpretation. God is the wholly other, the singular and anonymous other, who calls upon me. The question is whether Abraham understands that this means he must sacrifice all others, signified by Isaac, and thereby violate the ethics of equality and universality. This is not what Levinas reads. To him, God is the majesty that "amplifies" the call of the defenseless, gives it its absoluteness. But apparently Derrida considers the upgrade to such a transcendent God unnecessary.

If a difference between Levinas and Derrida has to be indicated, then it could be—with some exaggeration—the following: for Levinas every other appears in the Face, it does not matter who, as long as it is the other who appears to me and not I to myself; for Derrida, God is the name for the appearance of one concrete other, only this particular other and no other other. For Levinas, God is the name for the groundless coercion emanating from the other in all vulnerability; for Derrida, God is the name for the expulsion from any (ethical, political, socioeconomic . . .) system.

Another divine name is "justice." It does not coincide with any concrete legal institution or legal text or honorable practice. In its name, every concrete right must be permanently and persistently questioned. But God also has other names. Promise, for example. Differance leads thought beyond calculation, i.e., beyond possibility. The impossibility is something else here than the declaration that something is impossible. It is about an event that cannot be explored as a possibility, that lies beyond what we can conceive of as possible. God no longer works as a guarantor, but rather in the register of the promise. Only the impossible can be a promise. Nothing is promised by anyone. But thinking from differance always leaves open an element of promise in the future—however still under the sign of calculation. Derrida points to the messianic character of such an element of future, of advent; only: there is no messiah. This cannot be understood in a strictly Jewish way but certainly all the more in a philosophical way. It is about thinking openness, or philosophical hospitality—thoughtfully receiving the other, welcoming the other and wondering over and over again whether we are doing it "right" or "just."

Yet another name came up. Hospitality presupposes total alterity of the other. This does not mean different as in a well-defined relation, for example opposition (e.g., white–colored) or complement (e.g., man–woman) or subordination (e.g., lord–slave) or comparison (e.g., laborer–civil servant). The other may remain irreducibly other. On the other hand I have to look for channels of reduction or precipitation—if only to be able to communicate, to offer food, to open my house to this other. Let us move on from the impossibility of hospitality to the impossibility of the gift. After all, any gift is already contaminated by the slightest expression of thanks. Indeed, the moment something is returned, if only a suspicion of gratitude, the gift is no longer pure but has become an economic transaction.

Perhaps I can put it this way: just as concepts like Idea, Substance, Cogito, etc., along with God, belong within metaphysics on the position of Supreme Being, names like hospitality, impossibility, promise, etc. belong in differance.

Only the undecidable demands a decision, only the unforgivable can be forgiven, only the impossible offers possibilities.[11] In any case, God is impossible and the question concerning (the existence of) God is undecidable. God is impossible not because science proves it to be so, but because God lies beyond the possibilities that can be conceived and explained by human thought and imagination. But the undecidability of the existence of God still does not erase the name.

God is the name of the ambivalence or the oscillation emerging from difference. It is the name of absolute hospitality that nevertheless also has to become concrete, "worldly," and will incarnate in politics, law and economy. Whereas with Levinas ethics is primarily a matter of discarnation, with Derrida it becomes the oscillation between discarnation and incarnation, the same effect as that which breaks open the sign: spiritualization that immediately is always already also materialization and vice versa. With Levinas, although God is the Totally Other, God is completely absorbed in motivating an ethics. God draws a trace through the Face, along the ethical decentration of the subject. On the other hand, according to Levinas, God has no valid meaning outside the ethical interactions with the other.

The ambiguity and opacity at the roots of hospitality that Derrida divulges should be accepted and acknowledged as inescapable. They should be endured and embraced. If they are denied, then all that remains is system and law, control and calculation. Not that ambiguity and opacity are a logical necessity; rather the opposite: they can never be completely cleaned up. We have to live with it. At least that is what Derrida learned from his own reflection on Levinas. Initially, after all, Derrida was very critical. In "Violence and Metaphysics," one of the first major studies of Levinas's work, he argues that the infinite (the majesty) carries with it precisely the risk of violence that Levinas wants to avoid. Afterwards, Levinas would call this critical study a "murder under anesthesia." At the latter's funeral, Derrida delivered the speech *Adieu* where he almost entirely agreed with Levinas. Levinas is right, ambiguity does run the risk of violence—even if at first he did not see it in the same way as Derrida did; and Derrida did not yet accept the risk he discerned.

If God is a risk beyond calculation and control, then hope and trust enter the philosophical stage. Just as the "end" of the book does not mean that there are no more books but that "book" is no longer the standard text format and from now on becomes a provisionally stable crystallization within the texture of thought, so the "end" of calculation means not that there is no more calculation but that it is a crystallization within the texture of thought that has become open and hopeful. In this way, differential thought became a religious matter—not as a magisterium of a religious institution, for these are inclined to exempt certain truths from the materiality and precocity of the world, of philosophical texture.

If God and being "diverge" beyond metaphysics without finding any relation by which they can be understood and stabilized, could not God be the name of that divergence, of that particular difference that is the opening of the world, this alterity that marks the world as opening, which we experience as promise?

Negative Theology

We cannot leave Derrida without a brief digression on the relationship between him and negative theology, or rather the accusation against Derrida that he forces negative theology back upon the philosophical and theological agenda.

Derrida easily refutes these allegations by reminding his critics that, unlike himself, negative theology still thinks of God as a supra-essentiality outside text, unaffected by the texture of the world, even as not contaminable by textuality—uncontaminable because language cannot reach it. Thinking is denied all access, but God [is] [there]. Derrida does not make it easy for himself, and for us, by arguing that God cannot be thought apart from the fabric of thought, but then again, God is not a thing that is being "explained" by that thought.

Negative theology still clings to traditional thought to such an extent that it states that the approach to God must at the same time be an exodus away from the world. This exodus can be forward or backward. The latter means that we can never trace back or appropriate divine provenance. That from which Trinity arises, which at least still has a word, remains closed off to all human thought and speech. The exodus forward is a dialectical event. It is produced by every theological speech, by every positive theology, in which we spontaneously confess God in terms that are familiar to us. This terminology must always at the same time be denied because God can never be completely grasped by these terms. For example, when we say that God is good, as Christ says in Mt 19:16–26 (and Mk 10:17–27 and Lk 18:18–27), we must immediately recognize that this does not mean that human thought can develop an ethical model or moral theory in which God's goodness is totally divulged, presented, explained, determined. When Christ duly says that "Only God is good!" this also means that this goodness cannot be derived or (re)constructed from the laws of the world. Calling God good immediately urges us to call him "ungood" as well—but not "evil." So it is not God who is denied in negative theology; he has completely withdrawn from the world. And this makes no sense, according to Derrida.

We do honor to the name of God, says Levinas, by not pronouncing it. Perhaps that is also what Lyotard means by saving the honor of the name. But we cannot remain silent about God, replies Derrida. The desire for truth, theologically motivated, never peters out. This desire, the hope for a new arrival of being, was also a core theme of Heidegger's. But is that justified? Does not this awkward prefix "post-"—see Lyotard—in fact mean that metaphysics, modernity, "ends" endlessly? Can we say more than that? If modernity is thought that recognizes itself for the first time as history, as contained in time, should not postmodernity open up a way of thinking that lifts itself out of time-as-history and becomes "adventual"? Actuality as promise?

Extroduction

In this last chapter, I want to pick up the threads and traces that I hid in my tendentious exposition of the twelve philosophical apostles. I read these threads and traces through the death of God and an old Christ hymn. For me, this is where philosophy and theology "touch" each other emblematically. From that point arises a philosophical atheism, significantly different from the "flat" or shallow version. The former moves beyond theist metaphysics and metaphysical theisms. Looking back in the mirrors of God's autopsy and kenosis, flat atheism appears as hyperreligious theism. The latter is nothing less or more than a variant of theism, having replaced God as Supreme Being but hanging on to the structure and logic of traditional metaphysics. Philosophical atheism thinks along with the erosion of this structure and is enchanted to meet a purified theology on this path. This renewed friendship promises to become one of the most fascinating adventures of our times, since these times are called crisis or mutation—at least, these are names of the world today. In this case, there is no harm in peering beneath the surface and questioning the obvious. This is precisely what philosophy and theology are going to do, together. Here hides the relevance of the question concerning their collaboration, including politics. Reflecting together on the circulation and publication of the name "God," we inevitably enter another, as yet still unfathomed relation to what occurs and arrives. This relation cannot be thought through in traditional metaphysics.

Archiving or Exploring?

These twelve philosophical apostles certainly gave us enough food for thought—as do, of course, all great philosophers. Now, thinking can either re-flect or pro-spect, archive or explore. These are two faces of philosophy. The archivers try to re-construct what Feuerbach meant by "mirror," Heidegger by "Nothing," Sartre by "freedom," and so on. When the re-search is completed, the re-sults are re-cited at a conference, and that's about it. The explorers try to think through the work of Feuerbach, Heidegger, and Sartre, gathering what sounds promising and challenging underway, and then embark on unchartered paths, lightened by newly acquired and daring insights. These are two ways of receiving tradition—literally: what is handed over to us—and of accepting the world that we find ourselves thrown into. Those two ways are intimately intertwined; they cannot exist without each other. They are like two ends of a stick: no stick has only one end. But one stick is thicker on this end; the other is heavier on the other end. Archiving without exploring only reveals dead mummies; exploring without any archiving only results in speculation and lots of thin air. This chapter starts on an exploration, slightly reshuffling the archives of twelve thinkers.

I will not try to refute their alleged atheism and end up in a dead-end yes/no game. One good reason for this is that I do not recognize atheism as argument (or contention or conclusion) but rather consider and treat it as a container term for many pertinent questions concerning the idols that traditional Christian metaphysics has woven around God. Besides, it was only by liberating their thoughts from any argumentative motivation that I was able to discern the nuances on the thinking paths of these twelve scholars. In other words, these nuances reveal another atheism than the flat version.

Refraining from argumentation was not really a matter of truly free choice; I find it is contained in the critique of metaphysics. Indeed, arguing against metaphysics still remains metaphysics. Those who fear that it aims at the abolition of philosophy and thought as such suffer from a severe misunderstanding about this critique. They do not realize that this abolition would constitute nothing less than the greatest metaphysical maneuvers in history.[1] Fortunately, it never came to that. Its history consists almost entirely of protagonists that push each other off the philosophical stage. It is what Aristotle did to Plato, Thomas to Augustine, Hume to Descartes, Hegel to Kant, and Nietzsche and Heidegger to anyone else.

Furthermore, by refraining from argumentation I liberated myself from the need for clear and well-distinguished concepts, the way Cartesian thought likes them. Modernity has thought God "to death," so late modernity has no other option than to think God as dead. I will no longer conceive of God as a concept but I call him by the Name that has survived God's death. This is one reason why the Name is holy—and therefor written with a capital N, if only to avoid the possibility that yet another Supreme Being would hijack this capital again.

I do not prove anything, I do not contend anything, and I do not refute anything. All I do is follow a path that I did not lay myself. I notice that Christian themes are more and more articulated in philosophy, that philosophy is becoming more and more religious itself, that this process is keeping pace with the critique of metaphysics, and that the partitions between philosophy and theology are eroding. But I also notice that many philosophers reject and deny this trend.

Humiliation/Exaltation in God and Death of God

I discern a connection between philosophy and theology that, unfortunately, I cannot elaborate on in depth since this book still declares itself a philosophical exploration, meeting theology "by the way."[2] But perhaps this connection does not (yet) lend itself to elaboration, analysis, conceptual treatment. I quote from a letter of Paul in which he himself quotes an ancient Christian hymn:

> His state was divine, yet he did not cling to his equality with God but emptied himself to assume the condition of a slave, and became as men are; and being as all men are, he was humbler yet, even to accepting death, death on a cross. But God raised him high and gave him the name which is above all other names so that all beings in the heavens, on earth and in the underworld, should bend the knee at the name of Jesus and that every tongue should acclaim Jesus Christ as Lord, to the glory of God the Father. (Jerusalem Bible, Phil 2:5–11)

I am trying to read this text philosophically here, more thoroughly than I did earlier in his book. In the first part, Christ leaves the traditional determinations from metaphysics behind—whether that is Substance, or One, or *Causa Sui*, or Supreme Being, makes little difference. Most secularization models only take that first part into account and conclude from this that divinity implodes massively. They ignore the important second part, which reveals that humiliation and exaltation are inextricably linked. At least it says this: in the Name all determinations disappear, become invalid. This event obeys the monotheistic principle: only God is divine. We can search the whole world; among all things, never will we encounter God. No one has ever seen God (Jn 1:18). The Name does not refer to anything at all. This is the second reason for calling the Name holy.

Moreover, this hymn is not about a dialectic or a strategy. Exaltation is not the necessary consequence of humiliation. Nor is exaltation the stake of that humiliation, as if the latter were the price of the former, or the former the reward for the latter. Christ did not empty himself in order to be exalted. In Christianity, the divine strips itself of every (metaphysical) form and content without there being a reason for this—*ex nihilo*. This "stripping" does not imply a loss; on the contrary, it purifies and liberates the Name and saves its honor. The kenosis or self-emptying is thus not a simple abolition but an event that transcends such factuality, even any occurrence.[3] Here we have a third reason for calling the Name holy.

The attentive reader has noticed that this humiliation/exaltation does not concern God *as such*, but only Christ. The person of the son obeys the loving father. It is crucial not to consider this event a "zero-operation," as if exaltation outbalances humiliation, as if the divine barely touched the world and remains unaffected by it. That would completely devalue the message of Christ. This is about an event of enormous complexity and ambiguity that cannot be grasped by pure logic. This event is divine—theologians call it a mystery—without any divinity appropriating this event as sacred fact or strategy. Kenosis reveals a weak rather than a strong divinity.

This hymn seems to me just as crucial as Nietzsche's parable of the madman. It is no coincidence that Girard, provokingly, calls Nietzsche the greatest theologian since Paul. My discourse hinges on the hermeneutical potential of kenosis as well as of the death of the metaphysical God. These are not mere concepts that refer to things or facts in a transparently descriptive way. These are names of strong experiences, so strong and deep and large that no coherent conceptual system can contain and explain them. Here, philosophy and theology intertwine and, in that vortex, lose their modern oppositions.

The Concept Became Name

In a traditionally treated concept, nothing happens. It is supposed to remain forever stable and sterile, in eternity. This used to be the attractive feature of ideas; they seemed immune to treacherous change. This Platonic appreciation of an idea is not wrong or bad as such, of course. Meaning has to "precipitate," "crystallize" in order to be taken up again. Where this never happens, only absurdity sprouts. But to petrify meaning forever, and thereby actually push the ideas outside the event of thinking, goes too far. Then meaning is no longer thinking, but a substance that thought can go and collect by means of the correct method. Meaning then remains unaffected by thinking but just lies there, waiting to be collected and finally recomposed into the one total explanation of reality. Then we can stop thinking—*o metaphysical horror*.[4]

Traditionally, meaning is supposed not to "move," not to writhe and fester; on the contrary. Concepts are finished, perfect. Each dissemination should be suspended and stopped. But however accomplished each concept deems itself, when Nietzsche taps them with his diagnostic hammer, they sound hollow.[5] Critique of metaphysics, continental tradition, differential thought allow this writhing and festering, if only because it simply cannot be stopped. The huge conceptual edifice of metaphysics collapses under the weight of its own mobility and unmanageability. Logic and method are clearly unable to keep the structure erect.

In the Name, anything happens—unfortunately not only what is true and good and beautiful. What resounds in that Name in the writings of the twelve? This is what I want to explore as the religious register of modern philosophy.

Each thinker in this book did launch a direct attack, not against Christianity but rather against metaphysics as the cultural format that integrated Christianity. This integration jeopardized the critical distance to the world that is so essential for Christianity's opening toward the alterity of this world. This is why it is unclear which "part" of Christianity is criticized in modern philosophy: its worldly aspect (the institute, solidarity, morality . . .) or its essential, divine aspect (bible, mystics, charity . . .). This may remind of Derrida's formula "religion without religion" as thought that has eliminated what obscures this alterity. This thought is carried by that "other" philosophy and theology that upsets traditional metaphysics.

The history that is called metaphysics has produced many philosophical but also many theological giants. The latter were able to give theology, faith, and the church momentum each time they needed it. Now that metaphysics is getting exhausted and the world is being liberated from rigid structures, this alterity reappears almost as a natural phenomenon. Because we are dealing with true alterity here, it cannot be identical to earlier versions and exclusively belongs to actuality—still in the sense Foucault gave it (see chapter 11, note 3). There is another reason for this. If God would be the name of an alterity where thought becomes hope, trust, and openness, there is no sense in engaging in the past. The past is opened together with actuality, as is the future. They are opened *in* actuality to avoid the past becoming archive and the future remaining utopia. If the world is opening, it is opening toward a future that arrives and that is not "deployed." If the world is opening, then also the past arrives, not as a closed box full of meaning but as "food for thought." Tradition is not what needs to be closed off, but what is handed over in the sense of: entrusted to us, to thought. Since thinking never starts from a zero point, there is only that food and it needs to be reheated.

Unlike before, that alterity no longer appears *per se* as wrong or bad, as a situation that needs to be remedied. Formulated more philosophically: the "other" is allowed to remain "other"—which is arguably a major achievement of twentieth-century thought. Not everything must be appropriated or grasped as a concept and posited in a total system—as in a file. That is not at all the sole challenge, determination, or experience of thought. Philosophy opens up to what resists integration by undoing the imperative of integration. The rise of psychoanalysis has to do with this, together with other forms of research into narrativity, like mythology. Psychoanalysis and mythology, two study domains thriving on metaphoricity, where hermeneutics plays a crucial role, urge philosophy to question all metaphysical imperatives like unity, logical consistency, pure conceptuality, and the like. These are all principles that metaphysics introduced as self-evident. It is those evidences that make metaphysics the way it is. Part of the philosophical world no longer resists ambiguity and opacity of thought and courageously questions these alleged evidences.

Traditionally, philosophy had to clean up these dark spots in thought. They had to be made intelligible, turned into concepts or they had to be rejected. Only primitive cultures would endure, even celebrate all things dark, illogical, and plural—you may notice how nowadays, polytheism also finds its way into philosophy. Metaphysics considers itself "better," hygienic, pure—in other words, "sterile." Thinking should be a purely spiritual matter. To acknowledge equal—or any—truth value of metaphors is simply unheard-of. Each idea starts from the mind of the speaker or writer and arrives in the mind of the listener or reader exactly the same.

But this is not the case—or at least: an ideal case. The critique of metaphysics—especially Nietzsche and Derrida—shows convincingly that the event of speaking or writing is not something accidental, the effects of which can easily be neutralized. All speaking and writing, all hearing and reading, all looking and understanding have their own autonomous, resistant, recalcitrant, untraceable traces. They are not accidental and not "dirty." On the contrary, they preserve thought from suicidal sterility. Should the self-image of metaphysics be correct instead of the effect of suppression, then there would be no more thinking, only cleaning up and stacking away: archive.

The workings of metaphors are, of course, less controllable and manageable. They escape the clutches of logic. A metaphor will not bear any definition but "speaks for itself." A name is not a metaphor. When Mary has many names, this is not about definitions. It concerns a cluster of images that make up a name, that acquire the character of a name. In the case of Mary and Jesus, we are dealing with historical persons; in the case of Abraham and Antigone, to name but a few, not. Yet all these names still refer to beings in the world, even when fictional. Fictions are also beings. This does not apply to God; only that Name is holy, divine.

How does this Name work? How can something happen in a Name?[6] Take Christ's famous "For where two or three meet in my name, I am there among them" (Mt 18:20). Where people are together in the Name, i.e., of Christian Love, then there you will find heaven, i.e., where God is supposed to dwell. This is not about behavior that fits a definition of charity, because there is no definition—remember Mt 19:16–17; Mk 10:17–18; Lk 18:18–19. But "love" happens, God gods. How do we know this? Because every act of love is always immediately questioned *in the name of that love*. This is an endless vortex of a Name without definition that meddles with all forms of "implementation" or "incarnation" without ever declaring them wrong, but also without declaring any one of these the ultimate true form.[7]

Hyperreligious Theism and Religious Atheism

The chapters in this book have shown how an atheist discourse that reaches beyond academic philosophy often moves in a religious register and follows Christian schemes. This will certainly not always have been the intention of each modern thinker in this book. Nevertheless, their alleged atheism is certainly much more nuanced than the versions presented in standard introductions and handbooks. That these nuances allow for a religious register to be heard and Christian themes to appear is not all that surprising. The whole Western culture, including its philosophy, is and has always been radically motivated by Christianity—among other influences, of course. However hard this culture tried to "emancipate" from this source or provenance, it has not succeeded—and maybe these emancipation attempts belong to the "Christian message." Philosophy cannot keep on ignoring this provenance as well as its suppression. Only a shallow, flat atheism separates reason and religion, philosophy and theology from each other. Such atheism does not even deserve the title "philosophy." This philosophical, religious atheism I have in mind does not fall in the trap set up by Enlightenment and does not recognize the sense of that suppression—or indeed of any suppression, without contending that critique of metaphysics is completely exempt of any form of suppression; at least it tries not to suppress suppression.

Reading the twelve philosophical apostles as I did suggests a path toward a new religious atheist philosophy that reconnects with theology—this connection being "other" than the premodern version. Actually, the term "philosophy of religion" sounds misleading, which is typical of modernity. It allows philosophy to treat religion, religiosity, hope, trust and openness, hospitality, etc. as objects, as themes. Reason proclaims itself justified in evaluating, even censuring theology, faith, etc. where the genitive in "philosophy of religion" is used solely in the objective sense. There is also a subjective sense that reveals how philosophy, thought, and reason belong to the religious register or sphere. This kind of "philosophy of religion" no longer formulates proofs of God's existence, stops drawing maps of an outer-world, and does not try to reconcile a divine substance with the evil in the world anymore.

As I already announced in the introduction, I will start from the simple and reliable observation that the Name circulates and that neither modern Enlightened reason nor postmodern indifference has erased the Name. Even biologist Richard Dawkins, not at all bothered by any unfamiliarity with theological matters, largely contributes to this circulation, more than the average theologian. Although the Magisterium of flat atheism keeps preaching that God does not exist, Dawkins cannot deny the circulation of the Name without at the same time denying the sense of a large part of his public appearance.

I do not want or need to formulate a full image of God or present an ultimate, absolute, substantial Godhead; on the contrary. Instead of polluting the Name with a definition in order to search for the one Supreme Being that obeys this definition and noticing to everyone's devout joy that "existence" is an unalienable part of that definition, I search for what happens "in that Name" beyond all definitions and determinations. This search does not require the Name to refer to a being but to arrive in thought. This is what makes thought religious: hear what the event has to say. To allow the event to speak to thought in a divine Name, I think that is what makes thinking theological—this is somewhat more specific than religious, though not all theology is religious and not all theological thought is theology. When philosophy turns theological, that still does not mean that philosophy becomes theology. Theological here means "reaching out to theology." This is possible now since the partitions are becoming more and more porous. Modernity, again, tried to separate philosophy and theology by identifying the former with reason and the latter with faith. It did not realize that reason and faith cannot be separated—only distinguished up to a certain degree. Thought and faith, reason and trust presuppose each other; they both belong to the same element. Philosophy and theology work like two "regions" on one and the same plane, namely religious thinking.

The event in the Name is of the order of arrival, promise, gift, mercy. It will never be planning or claiming or storing. The latter are human initiatives; the former require an answer to an appeal. Without such answer, the promise remains empty, the gift false, and mercy hollow. Nothing arrives. There is no advent, only extrapolation, which is a totally different time frame. Extrapolation calculates every "now" into a next "now." Advent opens up to what arrives and that is always-already, no matter how subtly, the "other" in the sense of unexpected and impossible. Indeed, expectancy and possibility are both modes of the "same." These modes construe a future that is function of the present. This is, of course, not radically wrong. It helps us to keep daily life on tracks but it is useless in any serious philosophical exploration, in what Heidegger called "ek-sisting": the transcendent, religious vector of our existence.

The event stems from a transcendent moment, beyond or before any human grasp. The event *is* this transcendent moment that unhinges the world. We are called upon to respond because the promise, although without concrete content, is always a promise of "better." No one knows exactly what this "better" entails, contains, means. This trust belongs to what is called the eschatological reserve or *caveat*. Humanity is not the norm. This is why signs and winks are so important, despite—or indeed thanks to, since a promise can never be its own fulfilling—its poverty in meaning.[8] This is very risky since in the Name, all kinds of horrific things may occur—but always on human initiative. The *caveat* offers no guarantee. Signs can never be arguments. Yet it is easy to separate the "good" responses from the "evil" ones—if only because the latter respond not to signs but to natural urges like egoism, materialism, identitarianism, etc. The "compassionate society," living well together, has always been one of the primary aims of (especially ancient) philosophy.⁹ Remember that where people join together in the Name, i.e., of Christian Love, heaven happens (Mt 18:20). This event within the world does not itself belong to the world but leaves a divine trace.

This is why the Name names a trace and not a plan, as on a map with <depart> and <arrive>. The trace that carries the Name never fully arrives. Or more precisely: the trace keeps calling—in the sense of both addressing and visiting—without ever arriving. The trace never loses the mark of a promise. It keeps calling on us to forsake egoism and exclusion, to abandon hereditary sin, without accomplishing this abandonment itself. Redemption always remains dwelling at the horizon, but is never and nowhere realized, let alone guaranteed. Redemption is a matter of appeal, not of causality.

What renders the Name holy in philosophy is not the power and the glory and similar categories that tradition came up with to decorate—or perhaps rather disfigure—God. Many passages from the Bible can be used to criticize not only the pharisees but also just as many episodes from the history of the church and her theology.[10] As already mentioned, what makes the Name holy is the absence of any referent—the condition or an effect of the absence of God "himself." The trace keeps referring without ever "landing." Though the Name persistently circulates, the Name never sticks to any being, to a thing or a fact. The trace remains endless—which is something else than "eternal." The eternal is always-already there; the endless never arrives.

On the other hand, humanity has stuck innumerable names to the divine. I once heard a self-confessed Catholic declare enthusiastically that to her, God was a big ball of white light. Now, I cannot call this contention false. If someone called me a big ball of white light, I could easily disprove this contention. I am obviously and manifestly not a ball of any kind. But apparently, we can propose anything about God—as long as we keep in mind that all we propose about God is in a very important way invalid, as we learn from negative theology. We can declare anything about God, it will never be completely true—even this sentence. It needs to be noted, however, that we can only negate what has been posited. Negative theology, it will be remembered, does not claim that we must remain silent about God. Derrida adds: How to avoid speaking?—the title of an essay of his from 1986.

It seems as if the Name pushes all connections and institutions out of their temporary and local evidence. Each system is carefully constructed of, on the one hand, things and, on the other, ideas. Each thing has its very own idea and vice versa. The epistemological books balance—at least, so they are supposed to do. But suddenly the Name appears without any "on the other hand." The Name seems frictionless, or rather, the Name *is* friction, resistance, discomfort, discontent. Each time a system threatens to close itself off, the Name appears and breaks the epistemological files open.

The Name does not mean anything, does not offer any content. All it does is prevent any discourse from petrifying into a "total explanation"—this could be a scientific one; remember the Grand Unifying Theory. Once the world is locked up inside a total explanation, thinking just stops. Philosophy is closed down. All that is left, is applying, implementing, and extrapolating. All thinking becomes planning and management. Logic has become logistics, Heidegger said.

Now something remarkable happens here, something that I already touched upon but did not really develop. Metaphysics, this wonderful—in all its senses—marriage between Athens and Jerusalem, strived to "stabilize" everything and used the Name as the label of the capstone, of the Supreme Being. The trace of the critique of metaphysics leads away from closure, from exclusion, inclusion, seclusion, etc.[11] Whereas traditional metaphysics appreciated stability in terms of trustworthiness, now it is considered rigid, dogmatic, and totalitarian. Dis-enclosure is now experienced as threat and demise; then as liberation, hope, and promise. In these times, when Aristotelean mentality, understanding for the sake of control, has reached its summit—and therefore in the eyes of Heidegger a transition—the critique thereof gradually undermines each faith in that stability. The metaphysical rock that supported faith as well as scientific reason—depending on what held the title of Supreme Being—is eroding. Thought is pushed over the abyss. Some fear a crash landing; others look forward to a free flight and the promise of a horizon. The latter are those philosophers and theologians that think through the death of God and take the Christ hymn seriously. The rock upon which was first built the *scriptorium* and later the *laboratorium* has now become a stumbling rock of offense—in Greek: *skandalon*. It resists every religious, epistemological, and moral accountancy. Not only that, it subtly undermines these accountancies.

The twelve scholars in this book have each dug so many wells and tunnels in metaphysics that a subsidence became unavoidable. Each of them spooned pieces out of metaphysics and threw over a pillar. The ground opened up and became an abyss. But this abyss is still called "God," just as the ground before. The Name now names an *opening*—verbal tense. This is not a hole in the ground but the "other of the world," as Nancy called the contribution of Christianity to the world. Here, this alterity stands for the arrival of meaning, for the event of sense. The Name therefore also names *meaning*—again, verbal tense. God, that is, the Name, cannot mean anything itself since it is the name of the gift of sense. "It makes sense." This "it" is the same one as in "it is raining" or the "il" in "il y a," or as the "es" in "es gibt." "It" is not the thing "world," standing in and on itself and possessing intrinsic and unalienable signification that can only be divulged by scientific reason. World is not a thing but an event, the event of sense. World is the shared experience that "it makes sense."

God is the Name that names the world as the event of *opening* and *meaning*. God is not an opening; God does not cause or create meaning. Sense is an event in the Name, not in a concept. In a concept, nothing happens; it is hollow. It sounds too absurd to contend that the meaning of God has been closed off at the definition "opening." The concept "God" has succumbed under the many brave efforts to fill it with meaning in the sense of signification.

But if the concept of God is exhausted, what then does the Name really do? Would the Name not prefer to disappear as well? No. Derrida was probably right when he toned down Heidegger's hope for a new understanding of being to arrive. If Heidegger's exhausted being is capable of promising and indeed producing a new being, if only in the hope that we will not be exposed to the experience of total absurdity, then this schema perhaps reveals a metaphysical trait. Not that there is a taboo, but if it is there, we should be able to recognize it as such. If we will detach openness, hope, and trust—as figures of a thought that contains faith, again: 1 Cor 13:13—from that metaphysics, if we prefer the word "mercy" over dialectics, then "God" is a better name than "being."

Neither "being" nor "God" is a word or name that refers to a thing. Philosophically, they belong to differance. Each carries its particular metaphors with it. Who reads a "better" future in the name "being" confuses the names because "better" belongs to the metaphoricity of God, to theopoetics. Being teaches us about the world and still sticks to beings, but does not open the promise of a "better" world. Each eschatological reference belongs to the Name "God." This is not the property claim over which philosophy and theology have fought for ages. It is just about fair play in the language game. This fair play is interpreted by metaphysics as changing sides and moving from philosophy tot theology. Actually, it is almost the other way around. Philosophy has learned that openness, hope, and trust have also become philosophical categories, figures of thought. I will go further: thought *has become* openness, hope, and trust. Therefore, the Name can no longer be ignored by philosophy.

We already hear about this eschatological reference in the first creation narrative (Gn 1:1–2:3). God does not create all things, only *living* things. And only human beings are created in his image and likeness. All other things are not created but ordered, by separation and differentiation. This order stands for a world were humans can live in.[12] When we turn away from this divine gift, the order disappears. Then our faithlessness undoes the division of the waters above and the waters under the vault. The waters "close" again: the Flood. God could be the name of the deferral of the Flood, of total absurdity. In the Name we confess our hope for sense and we trust it will arrive, that it keeps arriving. Taking Derrida's reservations about Heidegger's ontological hope a little further, I do not recognize "being" as a valid term for that deferral. Hope reaches beyond a philosophy that has not yet reconciled itself with theology. Being is the event of world; that is correct. The contention that the modern world is mutating is strictly philosophical; that another world will arrive, a "better" one as promised, is no longer strictly philosophical but stems from a philosophy that has befriended theology without becoming theology. Here the Name resounds. I can hear Levinas who reproached Heidegger for not qualifying being ethically. I do not hear an ethical theory that has integrated ontology, but an event beyond ontology.

It is impossible and certainly undesirable to construe or formulate a theory about the Name. The Name is surrounded by all kinds of theories, models, aphorisms, metaphors, allegories, etc., without the Name ever becoming a center or core. It is rather the vanishing point of all this; it is their abyss. The Name does not offer firm, stable calculation and full total explanation. That is only about what we count, and not about what counts. Thinking that is open to what arrives, that answers to the call and accepts the invitation of the wink, applauds the abyss. The reason is obvious: if every theory, etc., is finite, imperfect, and always remains unaccomplished, then the vanishing point is at the same time also the point where new meaning, fresh sense comes in.

This "other" atheism that I mentioned in the introduction is announced as follows. "God" is no longer the name of a substance or entity that either exists or not. God is not a being, let alone a Supreme Being. God does not belong to the world, though the Name circulates persistently. The Name keeps the world "open"; it is the event of world as opening. This way, the

Name leads philosophy beyond logic and calculation without, of course, abolishing or expelling those—an act that would require an enormous amount of logic and calculation. Thought becomes hope, trust, and grateful reception. In these three terms, previously exclusive property of (moral) theology, philosophy (re)connects with theology. This connection pulls down the (modern) partitions between both. Yet this still has nothing to do with common, superficial atheism.

To continue. The atheism that is promised and as such arriving—in this text as well as in the world—obeys a certain monotheism. It says that only God is divine. It says nothing about there only being one God—(see chapter 11, note 16). It claims nothing about the existence of God. Again, it just contends that nothing in the world carries the name "God," that nothing corresponds to that Name, that the Name does not "refer." The Name reveals its metaphors, which enlighten thought.

Being is not divine; only God is. Divine could mean "better" without knowing what "better" implies or contains. It cannot be calculated, only hoped for and trusted in. Being is not holy because it clings to beings, each apart and as a whole. Ontology is the choreography of things, which is still not theology. Both are exempt from being-in-the-way-of-a-being—this we learn from ontological and now also theological difference.[13] God does not direct anything—on the contrary. The difference between ontology and theology is not simply ethics. Modernity understood the difference in terms of moral qualification, but "better" cannot be determined by any conceptual model or theory. This "better" can only be the religious echo of a modern legitimation of religion.

Then what could the prefix "a-" mean in this "other," religious, philosophical atheism? Superficially, as we know, the prefix is supposed to claim the non-existence of God. But the "other" atheism does not engage in the debate about the existence of God. It agrees with flat atheism that God does not exist in the way of a being—there the agreement stops. Philosophical atheism is concerned with the critique of the promotion—or demotion—of the divine as Supreme Being. It has learned from Nietzsche that each such promotion is from then on declared invalid. This promotion is labeled "theism," and the prefix "a-" now disturbs, deconstructs theisms. It is where the erosion of theisms is gratefully thought through. Flat atheism is nothing but a variant of theism, the version that simply replaced God as Supreme Being with Reason. Each theism carries the same structure: a Supreme Being is appointed and needs to supply meaning to all beings that are gathered in its name. It indexes all beings that are allowed to have meaning—in our case, technoscientific meaning—and arranges them into a world, a coherent network of signification—in our case, a file. It then closes off the totality—at least in principle, since no metaphysical system has ever survived (metaphysics' own) history, except as archive. Flat atheism is a variant of theism; religious atheism takes thought beyond each theism. In this sense, "a-" goes against the theistic grain instead of being a variant.

The prefix "a-" harbors the workings of the Name. God no longer dwells in premodern theisms, in Christian metaphysics, but in this "a-." In the Name, all metanarratives, petrified principles, eternal structures, logically rigid systems, unnegotiable norms, undebatable truths, are shamed (1 Cor 1:27), defused, and undone. They are not abolished and replaced, because that strategy is a continuation of metaphysical dynasties. Philosophical atheism recognizes the erosion of theism as an exhausted format of thought. It freely collaborates with this erosion. This is not about what happens to each metaphysical paradigm, but with (not to) metaphysics *as such*. It takes this erosion seriously instead of marginalizing and ignoring, even rejecting it.

This "new" atheism answers Eckhart's prayer to God to rid us of God. It is certainly not the metaphysical determinations that make the divine adorable; on the contrary. God cannot at the same time occupy the position of Supreme Being, exercising all the omnipotence and omniscience and omnipresence that goes with that position, and also be with those who are excluded from society, expelled from the world, and where thought is closed off. But when God may be opening and meaning in philosophy, then theological metaphors as Father, Shepherd, Creator, Savior, Lord, etc., do not sound that far-fetched anymore.

World, Crisis

The world is not "in" crisis; the world *is* crisis. What we are living now is not a crisis that we can remedy by means of current models and institutions. If the world itself is (the event of) crisis, than these models and institutions are also "contaminated" by it.[14] Reality is leaking out of a dying modern world into "another" one. This image, the "leaking," refers to Zygmunt Bauman's notion of "liquidity" as an epithet for (late) modernity. Lots of his books have "liquid" in the title. In *Liquid Love* (2003), he ponders "on the frailty of human bonds" (the book's subtitle). This melting process, modernity's models and institutions becoming liquid instead of remaining solid, is consistent with the erosion of theism. The world is liquidated, is becoming event instead of structure. Nancy prefers the term "mutation," which sounds very Heideggerian. Actuality is mutation.

This is not about a system of definition and deduction. Mutation is not the new determination of a world that can be appropriated by current, tried and proven strategies. This goes much deeper, broader, huger. This is precisely what worries many scholars, those that are still convinced that current strategies, i.e., models and institutions, are the best, even the only valid ones—modern *hybris*. They fear that if we leave current strategies behind, we do not prepare ourselves to receive another thinking, viz. thinking the other *as other*, but we will leave thought itself. I, on the "other" hand, string along with that alterity. To paraphrase Nancy once more: I am not looking for the other *than* the world but for the other *of* the world. I have joined the "eventure" of theological philosophers and philosophical theologians who refuse to recur nostalgically to the "old" world and open their minds to the arrival of what is "new." Crisis is not negative or pejorative but promising. Remember Hölderlin's "Wo aber Gefahr ist, wächst das Rettende auch" (note 3).

This promise has to be "picked up." I cannot prove that the world is crisis without contradicting myself. Proof is a metaphysical notion that has lost its power. I can only suggest signs that try to guide us. It is quite "sign-ificant" to notice how political thought reverts to this philosophy that has reconciled itself with theology since it turns out that the political—which refers to what underlies concrete, manifest politics—can only be fully understood from traditional theological schemes. *Homo Sacer* (2017), the *magnum opus* of Giorgio Agamben, meticulously investigates this path.

This is all but coincidence. Something very interesting is going on here. Political thought approaching and consulting philosophy/theology means that the former also "discovers" the alterity of the world. Politics, the political complex, politicians do not recognize this—not out of malevolence, but because of institutional inertia and basic survival instinct. They deploy a vast administration in order to postpone each insight that would only jeopardize fast decision making. Do not talk to politicians—or industrialists and financers, for that matter—about long-term vision. It is not they who will change the world, but philosophers and theologians who are concerned with the political.

༄

We have come a long way from the old guy with the long white beard at the Great Switchboard to the Name where world is the event of opening and meaning. If anything remains of the old divine majesty, then it is about what lies on the knees of the gods and not about what we have in our hands, to speak theopoetically. We also reached beyond the God of metaphysics, the Supreme Being that had to close off the world in a total representation but could not itself be adequately closed off—remember Anselm. Instead of ignoring this ambiguity at the very top of the epistemological and ontological order, I placed it at the very core of my research, inviting my readers to prevent this preliminary study from becoming archive, prematurely, by joining me and others on this fascinating track. There is no longer anything to keep us from doing this. By undoing the taboo that a flat atheism imposed on thought, the Name can resound (again), with every promise that this entails. This promise hides in the wink of an "a-" that does not do or mean anything on and in itself, but marks the erosion of the edifice of what was once the pride of thought and has now become exhausted.

Hear the Name, and say "Yes!"

(Philosopher and theologian cordially shake hands—"À-Dieu!")

Notes

Introduction

1. Perhaps God is history, in the sense that history can be perceived as a modality of revelation. That God must obey history, and hence modernity, is itself a purely modern notion. It would be more accurate to say that God became historically determined during modernity. Nietzsche, however, has declared that determination invalid and the modern God dead. The God who went through his own death and maintains that direction is therefore not the modern God who obeys history, but the God who shows himself in all history. A pre-modern God is still the modern God of history, only in reverse. This, however, is no longer acceptable. Now, what had to be called obsolete during modernity may now become interesting again. That explains, for example, the vast interest of contemporary postmodern thinking in Paul and Augustine.

2. Erik Meganck, "Church and World: Philosophical Exploration of a Mutual Approach," *Acta Comparanda* 33 (2022), 19–26.

3. Unless otherwise specified, "science" does include all sciences, the philosophy of science that legitimates the truth claims of science, and the scientific way of thinking or its "reason." It does not refer to scientific practice, the lab jobs from 9 AM to 5 PM.

4. Lobbies have succeeded in keeping God out of the European Constitution, whereas many nations still mention God in their Constitution. If the American president failed to end his speech with "God bless America!" he would have a big problem. If the president of France ended his speech with "Que Dieu bénisse la France!" then he would have a big problem . . .

5. They both turn out to be atheists in the philosophical, religious sense, not the flat one.

6. There are two basic models of secularization. In the first, God withdraws *from* the world in total transcendence. In the other, God totally immerses *into* the world. I call these models one-sided when they refer to the Christ hymn in Phil

2:6–11 to defend a massive immersion of the divine in the world and deliberately leave out the exaltation.

7. Philippe Goodchild in *Continental Philosophy and Philosophy of Religion*, ed. Morny Joy (New York: Springer, 2011), 163.

Chapter 1

1. The term "projection" is not Feuerbach's own; he used the word "reflection"—in German, *Reflexion* or *Spiegelung*. But since that first term became so ingrained in Feuerbach's reception, we chose to retain it.

2. The devil would then be omnipotent, omnipresent, omniscient, and anything but all-good. According to contemporary thinkers, here we have the Internet, or rather, *Baphonet*.

3. Heidegger calls it "onto-theo-logy." See later.

4. Phenomenology wonders how anything can manifest itself in a world at all. Heidegger calls this *Offenbarkeit* (manifestness). They presuppose the existence of a *world*, a "domain of meaning" where a revelation or manifestation can take place. This manifestness is somehow obstructed and obscured since our world has become technoscientific. Some claim our world still is; others read postmodernity as the experience that technoscience is losing its dominance over other forms of rationality. I will come back to this when we come to Lyotard.

5. This sounds very Platonic. The great philosopher was truly amazed by the experience of meaning and communication. He reflected on what everybody found evident, namely that we understand things, that we can exchange meaning. To him, this gift was truly divine.

6. In models like this, secularization is often identified with modernity as such, and therefore understood as progress, evolution, and emancipation.

Chapter 2

1. Nietzsche definitely refuted that idea in his eternal return of the same. If Kierkegaard accepted a historical teleology, then that would lie outside the aesthetical and ethical world. Teleology left the world when the organic, Aristotelian worldview transformed into the mechanical, Cartesian one. Science can only yield a world without finality. Philosophically inclined scientists who, like Leibniz against Descartes, want to infuse "soul" into nature, like Rupert Sheldrake, find themselves isolated from the scientific academy.

2. See "Introduction," *Marxists.org*, www.marxists.org/archive/marx/works/1843/critique-hpr/intro.htm.

3. The prototype of this dialectic goes back to Paul, the thirteenth apostle, who wrote the manifesto of an entire political theology in just a few letters. In 1 Thes 2:6–7 he mentions the *katechon*, a mysterious force that withholds or postpones the outbreak of lawless chaos. But this lawlessness is the situation that will bring forth the Youngest Day, the Final Judgment. Could this dialectic have inspired Marx, with capitalism as *katechon*, revolution as the state of lawlessness, and ultimately the Last Days where there is no more history because there is no longer any class struggle, which is the motor of human history; or is this just another tendentious Christian reading of Marx's prophesy?

4. There are similarities with the way Giorgio Agamben elaborated on this theme in his momentous *Homo Sacer*. These similarities, however, have to be treated with such great care that I find it impossible to do this here. In any case, Agamben himself does not seem to encourage the comparison, since in his 1,300-page omnibus *Homo Sacer*, he mentions Marx only seven times.

5. This lack of interest was not new, of course. Who will not remember the famous words of French queen Marie-Antoinette when they reported to her that the people had no bread to eat? "Well, why don't they eat brioche then?" We are not sure about the historicity of this anecdote. Jean-Jacques Rousseau, who coined the phrase, mentions a princess. In any case, this anecdote speaks volumes, apart from of the historical accuracy of the quote itself.

6. Not that there is such a thing as a "true" self-image or a full consciousness that is always totally present to itself. Psychology, always prepared to drop its ontological aspirations to be taken seriously as a science, will rather study the way a self-image functions.

7. Scholars like Jacob Taubes, Carl Schmitt, and later Alain Badiou, Giorgio Agamben, and Slavoj Žižek, while not quite examples of Cristian devotion, have disclosed this intimate connection between Christianity and (modern) politics, especially after reading the letters of Paul.

8. Therefore, it has been said that there is a "crisis of the crisis" because it is not a crisis *within*, but *of* the world. We then live in a world that *is* crisis—with all the hope that entails. Indeed, if the world, if actuality itself is crisis, then the future can no longer be extrapolated from current (political, economic) models, from the laws governing the present world—i.e., by means of the laws by which we understand the present world. In this sense, we no longer dispose of a self-image that can lift us beyond the crisis. The future becomes advent.

9. This requires some nuance. On the mount, Christ asks his disciples to be the salt and the light of the world (Mt 5:13–16). Salt does not change the recipe, but only the flavor. Light does not change the arrangement of the room but allows us to move through it without bumping into the furniture. In this sense, heaven is not another world but the "salted" version of this world. It injects love into the world without changing its laws and ways.

10. Lyotard's search also arrives at this impossibility, albeit by another path.

11. French journalist Jean Birnbaum wrote in *Le Monde* that politics is doomed, at every crisis or exhaustion, to return to its original reference, which is Paul (my translation of "En Occident, à chaque fois que la politique est à bout de souffle, dès qu'elle connaît un passage à vide, il lui faut repasser par la case départ—c'est-à-dire par la station saint Paul." "'Paul ou les ambiguïtés,' de Jean-Michel Rey: Paul, la révolution en bégayant," *Le Monde*, December 4, 2008, www.lemonde.fr/livres/article/2008/12/04/paul-ou-les-ambiguites-de-jean-michel-rey_1126681_3260.html).

Chapter 3

1. In the preceding chapter, I discredited the idea that Marx was a purely systematic thinker. He was much too subtle for that and did not consider himself a Marxist.

2. Starting from a thorough and original reading of Sophocles's tragedy *Antigone*, rejecting Hegel's interpretation hereof, Kierkegaard reopens the tension between ethics and religion. An elaboration would, however, take us too far. Antigone will return in the company of Abraham when we read Derrida.

3. This reminds us of the "rich young man" (Mt 19:16–17; Mk 10:17–18; Lk 18:18–19). When he asks Christ what to do to become a good person, Christ cites the Ten Commandments. Then, when the young man asks what *more* he can do, Christ tells him to leave everything behind. The young man confesses himself incapable to do this. Christ, however, does not mind. In terms of the Sermon on the Mount (see chapter 2, note 9), a dish that would consist solely of salt would be no less than a culinary disaster. To follow Christ into the world by getting away from it is too much for most of us. A world inhabited exclusively by saints would be pure hell—especially considering their sometimes rather unyielding characters.

4. To say the least, because apart from the philosophical and theological objections, the term shows a blatant lack of respect for each one who takes care of someone else without any thought of self, as evoked in the parable of the merciful Samaritan (Lk 10:25–37).

5. As we know by now, "in but not of this world" does not imply any reference to an "other" world, nor to the "other-than-the-world." It refers to the "other-of-the-world" and marks the non-(en)closure of the world.

6. By the way, the sacrifice of Isaac as well as Iphigenia is each time suspended by a deity and an animal is slaughtered instead. Anthropologists have speculated whether this did not mark the transition from human to animal sacrifice. Others think that this happy end was supposed to curb the cruelty of the scene. Most likely, however, the gods did not really demand the death of a loved child but the

assurance of the humans involved that they knew whom they had to thank for their blessings.

7. Kierkegaard even refers to a manual for lovers, where they can find quotes to ensure a successful engagement.

8. Maybe we can replace "world" with "culture," in the sense that Oswald Spengler used the word. He distinguished a Chinese, Indian, Babylonian, Egyptian, antique, Arab, Mexican, and western culture. These "worlds" are, according to him, not translatable into each other—at least not completely. This reminds of how Heidegger thought about world. There, it refers to a consistent network of sense where all things receive their meaning. Things do not own their own intrinsic meaning, but become manifest within a world. This view does not allow for intrinsic, eternal, or universal meaning.

9. How faith remains independent from reason is expressed strongly in "Credo quia absurdum," "I can only believe because it is absurd." This does not mean that I have to believe all that is absurd. That would itself be absurd. It does suggest that some of the revealed—a crucial term in some religions—truths cannot be understood and can therefore only be believed. Question remains: how do we know they are true?

10. One of the most beautiful and poignant texts that evokes this is without any doubt the dream of the grand inquisitor in Dostoevsky's *The Brothers Karamazov*.

11. This is the famous protestant baseline: "sola fide, sola gratie, sola Scriptura," sometimes competed with "solus Iesus Christus" and "soli Deo gloria."

12. Maybe we do not need Kurt Gödel to declare each discourse incomplete. Maybe philosophy can propose the name "God" as the *locus* of resistance against any sort of enclosure of a discourse, against any attempt to declare that discourse complete and true.

Chapter 4

1. In 1797, almost a century before the publication of *The Gay Science*, Jean Paul (Johann Paul Richter) had already reported a vision wherein Christ addresses the souls and boldly declares that there is no God. Paul's imagery in *Speech of the Dead Christ from the Universe that There Is No God* is very similar to Nietzsche's. Half a century later, Gérard de Nerval made the same declaration in his *Christ on the Mount of Olives*, a poem from the cycle *The Chimeras*.

2. Friedrich Nietzsche, *The Gay Science: With a Prelude in Rhymes and an Appendix of Songs*, trans. Walter Kaufmann (New York: Penguin Books, 1974).

3. Once, Derrida dedicated a whole presentation to one sentence from Nietzsche's *Posthumous Fragments*, namely "I forgot my umbrella." Let me suffice with the report that the reaction of the public was "mixed."

4. This dismantling, including the dismantling of the dismantling itself, runs out into what Caputo calls hier*an*archy.

5. Also this notion has been so misunderstood. The Nazis in particular turned this will to power, together with the notion of overman—perhaps *the* most misunderstood term in Nietzsche's oeuvre—into a pseudo-Darwinist "racial law of the strongest." Nietzsche, like Heidegger, found everything that smacks of mass, structure, system, and every kind of -ism repugnant. Of course, he linked this repugnancy to a not completely unsuspicious heroism, as did Heidegger. The problem with the Nazis is a simple translation error. In the German languages, "fit" tends to mean well-developed, so strong, whereas in English, it means well-adapted. In evolution, it is not always the strongest who survives, but the fittest, the living being that adapts best to its environment.

6. Indeed, some passages point in one direction; others suggest a different view. If we read Plato's metaphors *as such*, as didactical attempts to express a completely new insight instead of illustrations to his theory, then dualism retreats from Platonic thought. Anyway, it is still completely different from the hard boiled version of Descartes.

7. Friedrich Nietzsche, *Twilight of the Idols: Or, How to Philosophize with the Hammer*, trans. Richard Polt (Indianapolis: Hackett, 1997), 23–24.

8. Friedrich Nietzsche, *The Will to Power* (Penguin, 2017), §481.

9. Initially, Nietzsche went along with the unmasking by science, following Auguste Comte from afar. Later, he unmasked this unmasking itself. Unmasking of one truth always takes place in the name of another truth that hides behind what then becomes the unmasked lie. This notion is precisely the main lie of Christian metaphysics. Truth as well as lie belong to the mask of metaphysics. From behind the mask, beyond truth and lie, *incipit* Zarathustra.

10. This perspective switch can be understood in terms of the Sermon of the Mount (Mt 5:1ff). Whatever is seen as pure misery in the plains can appear as blessing on the Mount. What counts as loss of meaning in metaphysics can appear from another angle, that is not an opposite angle, as gain of sense.

11. This has nothing to do with transhuman phantasies—cyborgs and the like. This sort of posthumanism aims at a technological improvement of the human race. They consider this a "natural" effect of an evolution away from "nature," that is no more than a nostalgic anachronism, and also away from evolution itself because the achievement of the transhuman project would make any further evolution redundant. Once humanity has overcome itself, cultural history can be thrown away as the ladder that has become superfluous.

12. Surprisingly, *Why Is the Christian Legacy Worth Fighting For?* is the subtitle of one of his books.

13. Mt 21:12–13; Mk 11:15–17; Lk 19:45–46; Jn 2:13–25. In the gospel according to John, this passage appears much earlier than in the other, synoptic

gospels, which probably means that the author of this gospel considered the antireligious insight much more important than the others.

14. This needs nuance, since Mary's "Fiat!" can hardly be understood as *amor fati* in its antique sense. It can, however, perfectly well be read in its "naked" sense, without any connotations from antiquity. Again, we cannot identify the God of the Christians with the *fatum* in antiquity.

15. It is important to note here that this is not about the installation of an "external reference." I have elaborated on this "divine invasion" in Erik Meganck, "Modern Violence: Heavenly or Worldly—or Else?," *Human Studies* 43, no. 2 (2020): 291–309.

Chapter 5

1. Psychology is mentioned here in its broadest sense. Strictly speaking, Freud was not a psychologist but a neurologist. Nevertheless, he can even be read as a philosopher.

2. Newtonian physics became a special case of relativity theory where the relative speed of two inertial systems remains so low that the Lorenz transformations become negligible.

3. Leaving aside the excesses, of course. How many pets have not succumbed to an overdose of chocolate? Belgium knows of a case where a rich widow visited top restaurant *Comme chez Soi* almost every weekend and ordered for her pet dog whatever she was having herself.

4. Ignoring the phenomenon of domestication, noting that this would only complicate matters by obfuscating the relation human–animal. Far be it from me to avoid obfuscation, but in this case there is nothing gained by going into it. It would certainly not change the argument, so there it is.

5. In a totally different register, we also found this tension reduction in the thoughts of Marx, that other "master of suspicion." Coincidence?

6. This is what bothers those psychologists who reject Freud. They are proud to have succeeded in giving their profession a more or less scientific stature by removing the medieval concept "soul" from their textbooks and opening a laboratory for empirical or experimental psychology (William James in 1875, and Wilhelm Wundt in 1879). The *psyché* became measurable, the soul a "black box."

7. In order to be allowed into town, Oedipus had to solve the sphinx's riddle: what moves on four feet in the morning, two feet at noon, and three feet in the evening? A human being. As a baby, it crawls on hands and knees; as an adult, (s)he strides as a biped; as an old person, (s)he uses a cane. By solving this riddle and blowing the sphinx off its feet, Oedipus entered Thebes to conquer the most tragic throne ever.

8. Carl Gustav Jung introduced this mirror version of the Oedipus complex. Electra assisted her brother in the murder of their mother Clytemnestra because she had killed their father Agamemnon—well, seemingly because he had tried to sacrifice their daughter Iphigenia, but probably also because she had started dating her husband's nephew. Yes, once those Greeks started slaying each other, only a few remained alive: just the choir. This is also a basic element in tragedy: killing only provokes more killing, a fate that never rests.

9. This is why psychoanalysis seems so *unheimlich* in a technoscientific world that has been thinking in terms of causality since Aristotle. The talking cure can perhaps afterwards trace back what repressed desire provoked the symptom, but never the other way around: predict from the repressed desire what symptom it will produce.

10. In his *Untimely Meditations*, §3: "Schopenhauer as Educator," Nietzsche writes, "if the hare has seven skins, man can slough off seventy times seven and still not be able to say: 'This is really you; this is no longer outer shell.'" Nietzsche, *Untimely Meditations*, ed. Daniel Breazeale, trans. R. J. Hollingdale (Cambridge University Press, 1997), 129.

11. Sigmund Freud, *Totem and Taboo*, trans. A. A. Brill (Routledge, 1919), 124.

12. As it is, in some cases religion will become the language of the pathology. These patients will express their problem in terms that they borrow from, for example, Christian liturgy. Some imagine themselves to be Christ; others are satisfied with Caesar or Napoleon. But to conclude from this that every person who believes in God suffers from a similar psychopathology is exaggerated, to say the least. If not, then we should never follow the example of saints; on the contrary, we could then only deplore their lack of psychiatric treatment. This said, saints were not really nice people. Were Father Damian to be treated by Freud for his lack of social skills, Freud would in all probability have interested himself in this obsession with leprosy and tried to find Oedipal troubles.

13. This will only be recognized as valid as long as the monotheist premise is taken seriously. If only God is God, then God avoids all worldly systematics and becomes a metaphor that is not necessarily bound to any conceptual connotation.

14. In *The Natural History of Religion*, David Hume had already pointed out that there exist areligious cultures. This notion allows for a future Europe to become one of these. Anthropologists like René Girard are rather inclined toward the view that the root of every culture is religious.

Chapter 6

1. We have this fascinating evolution theory, launched by Charles Darwin and continuously refined, recently by Richard Dawkins, among others. We also have this evolution paradigm, a typically modern nineteenth-century legacy where the

notion of evolution (progress, growth, accumulation, expansion, etc.) is translated into other sciences like sociology, economy, cosmology, even theology. Finally, we seem to have an evolution ideology, an evolution*ism*, that serves as an excuse to abuse this notion of evolution in a very unscientific way in discussions that are purely socio-politically motivated.

    2. You will find the text at users.drew.edu/~jlenz/whynot.html. The quote can be found in the 2004 edition (Routledge) on pp. 18–19.

    3. Bertrand Russell, "Letter (1958) to Mr. Major," *Dear Bertrand Russell: A Selection of his Correspondence with the General Public, 1950–1968* (Houghton Mifflin, 1969), 41–42. The first part of this well-known quote has been regularly cited, by Nobel prize winner (physics, 1979) Steven Weinberg, among others.

    4. This has sometimes—and unduly—been called "negative theology." It abuses God as explanation for anything that has not yet been given a scientific explanation. The name of this phenomenon is rather unfortunate, since in theology it means something almost completely different, as we shall see when we get to Derrida.

    5. As if science does not thrive on imagination! The famous physicist Richard Feynman was bragging to a colleague about a brilliant student of his. When this colleague later asked about this student, Feynman replied, "Oh, that one, well, he lacked imagination and became a poet instead."

    6. It is clear that the Bible is crammed with nonsense, at least when read through scientific glasses. How about this star that suddenly appears in the sky, virgin birth, a king that enters his capital city on a mule, a mite that is worth more than all the money in the world, etc. Fortunately, thought has other registers that make these phenomena sound very meaningful.

    7. This reminds of the growing interest in what is called re-enchantment, as a response to Max Weber's disenchantment as a category that describes modernity.

    8. Oxford philosopher of religion Richard Swinburne has applied classical statistics to calculate the probability of Resurrection; he came up with a surprising 97 percent. I am surprised not at the score but at the fact that intelligent people waste their precious time with this. An Italian math professor wasted his retirement by trying to calculate where Mary ended up after her assumption. Then there is the American couple Zohar that during their research on spiritual intelligence found a lump in the brain with electromagnetic activity of the same amplitude as the background radiation of the Big Bang. They concluded that this has to be God's dwelling place in humans. Whereas the horsemen of the Apocalypse can count on my indignation, this only brings embarrassment.

    9. By the way, the Hebrew word for "death" hides inside the Hebrew word for "sea." In the same way, the Hebrew word for "unconditional love" hides inside the Hebrew word for "daddy," which is "abba."

    10. Evolution theory is not correct because it is true, but because it fits into the modern project. During modernity, the evolution paradigm is valid because it is modern.

11. Teleology has been thoroughly explored by Aristotle and belongs to an organic world view. It looks for the purpose of things and processes in nature. Later on, this became the Creation plan. During the seventeenth-century transition into a mechanic world view, the explanatory potential of teleology became suspect. Current science, apart from people like Rupert Sheldrake, does not recognize any teleology in nature.

12. Are you familiar with the hilarious sitcom *Big Bang Theory*? At a certain moment, Sheldon snarls at his mother, "Evolution is not an opinion, it is a fact," whereupon his mother replies that that is his opinion.

13. Postmodern thought has discovered the seeds of a perversion here. What exactly does "new" mean in this context? Nietzsche already warned us about the danger that hides inside "innovation" as an autonomous motif. The modern "new" has become a goal in itself, an absurd obsession. In museum leaflets on contemporary art exhibitions you may read sales talk like "No other artist has ever done this before!" When I visit that exhibition, I can only remark that there has always been a very good reason for this reticence. However, notions such as "retro fashion" show us the limits of this imperative of "new." The same limits can be discerned in economics, where the notion "growth" undermines itself when it becomes a goal in itself. I read a negative review in a newspaper about a firm that was "growing," only its growth was not growing . . . Where is the long-term vision in this exponential disaster? A blatant lack of vision, is this not another symptom of "crisis"?

14. This makes Descartes the father of modern thought. In the name of certainty, he threw out everything that was "primitive," all that preceded him, all tradition. What remained turned out to be scientific thought.

15. Erik Meganck, "'World without End': From Hyperreligious Theism to Religious Atheism," *Journal for Continental Philosophy of Religion* 3, no. 1 (2021): 65–89.

16. It should be noted that this hard-boiled atheist scientist/philosopher seems to tend toward a moral version of Schleiermacher's romantic religiosity that stems from the emotional experience of belonging to the greater enveloping whole of Creation. Already Freud taught us about the "oceanic" feeling. And we learned about human innate egoism from Kierkegaard, telling us about the esthetic stage in human existence.

17. It is highly significant that thinkers of such caliber will ultimately admit that the laws of the world could never produce a satisfactory ethics. Even Sartre will recognize this problem—see there.

18. I specify "Enlightened" modernity because there is also such a thing as romantic modernity. Romanticism is more than just an art movement; it can also denote every thought that resists rationalization, from Aristotle onwards. It would, however, be naïve to "identify romantic" with "religious." In fact, modern Enlightenment and ditto romanticism should rather be treated as entwined.

19. There actually exist scientific studies that (try to) show that people with faith are "happier" than the faithless. Now, not only does this research raise serious questions in terms of scientific validity, the terms involved not being measurable and the results not repeatable; one can also doubt the value of these studies as "faith arguments." People who acquire a faith *in order to* be happier tend to end up disillusioned. To me, it still looks more sensible to see faith as a form of grace rather than as a project. But then again, who sees life as a project, like Sartre, will not easily open up to the grace of faith.

20. Erik Meganck, "'Spem in Aliud . . .': What May I Hope For?" *Ethical Perspectives* 23, no. 3 (2016): 473–498.

Chapter 7

1. This is the only sentence of the final chapter of his *Tractatus Logico-Philosophicus*.

2. Logic, said Heidegger, is the result of opposing what initially belongs together, namely "being" and "thinking." He rereads Parmenides's famous "Being and thinking are the same." Scholars have broken their heads over this fragment. Heidegger suggested that the same is the element that is shared by being and thinking alike. This way, the old familiar quote becomes the baseline of twentieth-century hermeneutics.

3. We already saw this strategy at work, but here is a footnote for advanced students. Kant never really and definitely spoke out on the question concerning the unity or plurality of reason. Is there only one reason in many different states or modes, such as a scientific one, a moral one, and an esthetic one? This rhymes with the triple basic concern of metaphysics: truth, good, and beauty. Kant posed the question without ever answering it—which might be considered suitable for a critique of metaphysics. Anyway, Hegel was not amused . . .

4. In a similar vein, Ivan Karamazov (in Dostoevsky's *The Brothers Karamazov*) cries out that if God does not exist, everything is permitted, in a moral sense, that is. I will return to this when we read Sartre.

5. Let us not exaggerate this "canonization"; "Le vert est ou" returned 3,780 hits on Google on December 10, 2021.

6. This chasm may be said to have become explicit in its current version after the debate between Heidegger and Carnap about . . . nothing. I refer to the chapter on Heidegger for this.

7. Levinas, whom we will meet later, has elucidated the experience of meaninglessness, of absurdity by means of the metaphor of sleeplessness.

8. This raises the pertinent question whether (religious, political, economic . . .) terror is also a language game. Lyotard seems to think not, since ter-

ror—and therefore probably also totalitarianism, extremism, fundamentalism, maybe even populism—seeks to destroy the free play of language games.

9. The reader may discern a parallel here with the free play of differences that do not submit to any central coordination of super-difference. Derrida calls this "différance."

Chapter 8

1. Emmanuel Levinas, "L'intention, l'événement et l'autre. Entretien avec Christoph von Wolzogen, le 20 décembre 1985 à Paris," *Philosophie* 93, no. 2 (2007): 12ff.

2. It seems to me that the relation between the world of science and the world of (aesthetic, moral, religious, etc.) experience is a rising topic on the philosophical agenda, mainly in debates that concern the question concerning re-enchantment of the world, such as in the work of Charles Taylor—the Canadian philosopher, of course, not the Liberian president and war criminal.

3. I will go into this problem of legitimation when we meet Lyotard.

4. Arab culture had already mastered algebra and experiment for more than eight centuries, but since that culture was not motivated by this combination of control and progress, they never arrived at what is called modern science.

5. Heidegger considered this metaphysical obsession with control a violent way of thinking. I will go into this when we meet Levinas.

6. Yet Heidegger cannot be called a traditional metaphysicist because he pleads a non-metaphysical way of taking up metaphysics as a tradition, as what is handed over to us. This is precisely the step back. Until then, all thought was metaphysical, apart from Nietzsche—though even Heidegger at one time considered not Hegel, but Nietzsche the summit of metaphysics. Therefore, philosophy cannot do otherwise than take up metaphysics; there is nothing else. So Heidegger looks for what remained unthought in metaphysics. This is the forgetting of being.

7. Between these great thinkers, who both laid out the philosophical agenda of the twentieth century, more than just one parallel can be drawn. The proposition that thought does not fall out of the skies but springs from our being-in-the-world is one of the main theses in Heidegger's *Being and Time*—his best-known but not necessarily most intriguing work. He had planned a third part but he renounced this project because the whole book was not really written from the viewpoint of being itself. It clung too much to subjectivist thought. So he threw away his first book like the ladder he no longer needed, as did Wittgenstein. In both cases, their first *magnum opus* was more of a philosophical—or anti-philosophical?—clean sweep.

8. This now-here is not the "nowhere" in Nagel's "view from nowhere." That view refers to a transcendent point where the whole objective reality could be examined.

9. Let us call facticity the existentialist and phenomenologist purport of Heidegger's thoughts. It is inspired by the mystics, by Luther's critique of Aristotle, by Schleiermacher, and by Kierkegaard. They planted the seeds of critique of the "metaphysicalization" of Christianity, according to the earlier Heidegger. As was his wont, Heidegger added his own connotations to the term.

10. One of Heidegger's disciples, Hans-Georg Gadamer, is considered one of the founding fathers of philosophical hermeneutics, or perhaps better of philosophy *as* hermeneutics, since the publication of his *Truth and Method*. He explains how Heidegger taught us that thinking has become interpreting and that objectivity as a system is no longer valid. There no longer exists a reality apart from thought, as an object opposed to a subject. Remember Nietzsche's hermeneutic contention that there are no more facts, only interpretations.

11. This is not a matter of identification, as in A=B, but of an early Greek inspiration. Remember Parmenides's proposal that being and thinking are the same. This is not a logical proposition, because the split between *physis* and *logos* comes after Parmenides.

12. One could, of course, consider looking for a connection between Heidegger's nothing and the "mé on" in (Pauline) meontology, but that would lead us too far without producing insights that are relevant to this book.

13. Which is fortunate, because otherwise Dawkins would have all the evidence he needs and faith would become science, theology.

14. That is also the basic contention in Oswald Spengler's *Decline of the West* (1918).

15. This is the cheapest accusation that science formulates to whoever brings up the unthought and unheard-of, namely that it is nothing more than a fleeting fancy of philosophy, a ripple in the otherwise pure surface of metaphysics. It is, however, precisely this unrippled surface that remains a persistent illusion.

16. 1 Thes 5:2, and also Mt 24:43.

17. "Ontological" is concerned with being and therefore only refers to Heidegger's philosophy; "ontic" means concerning beings and therefore refers to sciences. This includes theology since to Heidegger, God has also become a being. Metaphysics deals solely with the ontic since it thinks even being in the way of a being.

18. Nietzsche is talking not about theology as a science here, but about the way thinking and being are organized around this Supreme Being.

19. In German: "Nur noch ein Gott kann uns retten." In German, all written nouns start with a capital letter, so the text itself does not divulge whether Heidegger meant a specific God or just any god. Scholars agree, however, that this is not the God of the Christians. It is the last god, who is in fact already dead.

20. This is where Peter Sloterdijk wonders what kind of God would want Heidegger to sing and dance for him . . .

21. His meetings with Rudolf Bultmann (and, of course, others) made Heidegger take a deep interest in Protestantism. His wife, Elfride, was Lutheran when they married.

22. The theological virtues from 1 Cor 13:13.

Chapter 9

1. Heidegger had actually already declared this in his comment on Nietzsche's death of God, explaining that the essence of *Dasein* lies in its existence. In scholastic thought—or faith—this was only the case with God. He considered his redefinition a true criticism of scholastics. He was not impressed by Sartre's accomplishment, though. In his *Letter on Humanism*, he simply states that a metaphysical contention turned upside-down still remains a metaphysical contention.

2. In his phenomenology, Edmund Husserl, who chose Heidegger as his assistant when Edith Stein decided to enter a convent, wanted to think beyond Cartesian dualism. The meaning of a thing in the world is determined not by its relation to an idea outside the world, but by the appearing of that thing to a consciousness that also finds itself in that world.

3. With Heidegger, "proper" (*eigentlich*) and "essential" (*wesentlich*) coincide; as far as Sartre is concerned, they do not.

4. Jean-Paul Sartre, *Being and Nothingness. An Essay in Phenomenological Ontology*, trans. Sarah Richmond (Taylor & Francis, 2020), 69.

5. Jean-Paul Sartre, *Existentialism Is a Humanism* (Yale University Press, 2007), 20.

6. Kant had already suggested that these three entities—the world as a totality of things and facts, the "I," and God—cannot be known by theoretical or scientific reason. Within practical or moral reason, however, we have to accept their existence, because without them we cannot understand why we should be happy to do our duty.

7. Jean-Paul Sartre, *Huis clos, suivi de Les mouches* (Gallimard, 1947), 93. This quote actually refers to something else, in another context, but it fits well here.

8. Jacques Lacan, too, has stated that desire is nothing other than the desire to be desired. Apart from such dialectical traits, left over from their study of Hegel, Sartre and Lacan have little in common. Sartre did not favor psychoanalysis, for that too was a case of the objectification of the *psyché*. After all, consciousness is hooked onto contents that are permanent and to which consciousness cannot relate because of the unconscious nature of those contents. Here Sartre makes the double mistake of understanding the unconscious from the absoluteness of consciousness and considering unconscious contents as an unconscious substance, as an unconsciousness.

9. In philosophy, love was considered to consist of three dimensions or elements: *eros, philia,* and *agape.* In real life, none of those three is ever present in its pure form. Love is always a mix of those three, but their respective dose may vary. The erotic refers to the egocentric dimension, which is not evil in itself—it is never wrong to enjoy love yourself. Love is also marked by reciprocity, which is denoted by *philia* or friendship. And finally, real or full love also contains an element of *agape*, which refers to the giving aspect in the sense of a self-giving. The latter may be a typically Christian form of love.

10. Friedrich Nietzsche, *Thus Spoke Zarathustra*, trans. Graham Parkes (Oxford University Press, 2005), 68.

Chapter 10

1. A short note on terminology here. Levinas calls his ethics metaphysical because its appeal reaches beyond ontology. Heidegger's ontology reaches beyond metaphysics. To reduce this complexity, we should remember that what Levinas calls ontology refers to what Heidegger means by metaphysics—without these ever becoming straight synonyms. The common substrate of both terms would be Western philosophy since Aristotle.

2. Fortunately, he had already cured his friend Maurice Blanchot of anti-Semitism. The latter showed himself trustworthy by keeping Levinas's wife and daughter from the clutches of the Nazis and offering them sanctuary in a convent of the sisters of Saint Vincent de Paul.

3. Like also Marx's father and Wittgenstein's grandfather did.

4. Derrida plays with these words: *restance* and *résistence.*

5. Typically Heidegger, the meaning of this expression becomes ambiguous. On the one hand, being gives itself to thought; on the other hand, being means that there is "to-think."

6. It is interesting to note how Levinas's Greek reflection on egology acquires a typically Jewish register. The Face must be discerned with proper, "other" eyes. Since Plato—especially his well-known allegory of the cave—philosophy distinguishes between seeing shadows and perceiving the true nature of things in the light of an initially blinding sun. In Western metaphysics, thinking is about seeing, about in-sight. Jewish thought is provoked by listening—"Hear, Israel!" Beyond merely seeing a Face, in the transformation from ordinary seeing to seeing-through, the decentered "I" hears the call of those who in the Old Testament are known as the stranger, the widow, and the orphan.

7. This may seem peculiar in the case of someone who explicitly situates himself within the phenomenological tradition. Usually, these philosophers study what happens when the world appears to a perceptive consciousness. Thinkers like Levinas (and Jean-Luc Marion to name but one) try to break open this scheme.

Though Levinas would certainly not appreciate this, some are even setting up a phenomenology of the mystic experience. What Levinas did try to do was, in the wake of Heidegger, to disconnect the appearance of meaning, the sense, from the Cartesian subject or the Kantian categories. This appearance, this revelation would not, like it still did with Husserl, be determined by an intentional consciousness, but should rather be understood within the register of a receiving or, more theological, a form of mercy.

8. Levinas loved this quote from Dostoevsky's *The Brothers Karamazov*: "Each of us is guilty before anyone for anyone, and I more than the others." His open admiration for the great Russian novelist was found to be suspicious by Jewish intellectuals, who considered Levinas too Christian because of that.

9. Levinas compares the egological Odysseus, Greek figure of totality, with the faithful Abraham, Jewish figure of infinity. Odysseus starts from himself and only arrives back to himself. Underway, he thought of nothing or no one else but himself. Abraham answers a call from the Other, leaves all his possessions behind and goes where God leads him, without any guarantee other than the promise of the Other.

10. The almost-nothing is an important theological theme. Christ places the "mé on," the barely-being, what remains invisible to the eyes of society, what is systematically neglected, in the center of the world. Remember the widow's mite (Mk 12:41–44; Lk 21:1–4). Theologically speaking, this is much more relevant than the large sums of money that are offered in plain view.

11. Derrida says more or less the same when he declares that hearing without seeing is a scandal to Western metaphysics. Thought without in-sight is "unheard-of." This has a moral connotation: renouncing total in-sight in the other—which is a form of violent annexation—is considered philosophical treason.

12. Girard understands religion in terms of a *do-ut-des* deal between people and gods. In religion, gods are petty, arbitrary, and revengeful and must therefore be placated with (sometimes very cruel) sacrifices. Christ has rejected this salvation strategy—see the passage of the temple cleansing (Nietzsche).

13. Kenosis is the incarnation and the obeyance up to the cross, the humiliation and self-emptying that is *at the same time* exaltation, as it is sung in the Christ hymn that Paul cites in Phil 2:5–11.

14. I distance myself emphatically from the superficial contention that religion only generates violence.

Chapter 11

1. I will avoid the term "postmodernism" since this has a modern ideological connotation that hardly befits the matter at hand.

2. This is also the title of the second chapter of *The Inhuman: Reflections on Time*.

3. Actuality, as understood by Michel Foucault, is not just the present as the sum total of all facts now, but rather our (philosophical) relation to the present. It implies a critical, reflective distance from the present. In a certain way, Foucault's actuality replaces Marx's ideology. It is the present as it manifests and represents itself in thought—thought perhaps denoting here all cultural expressions.

4. This is all but a mere semantic matter. It implies that these fascisms are not relapses into barbarism but genuine modern projects.

5. This term "transcendence" is quite complex. The most simple version still maintains that immanence refers to "our" world and transcendence to another, "higher" world. It becomes already somewhat more complex—and intriguing—when I insert a Pauline element where "immanence" refers to the world, enclosed in and on itself—as for example in a scientific explanation offered by the Grand Unifying Theory—and transcendence refers to the world, the "same" world, opening up to an alterity that could be called divine. Insofar as this opening is read not structurally but "eventually"—not as a structure of the world but as its event—a Heideggerian element is added. Transcendence then becomes a verb, not a location or condition. It refers to the "ecstatic" emancipation or liberation from purely immanent (i.e., ontic) determinations—e.g., the human being as determined by the sum of all its scientific definitions—and delivering oneself thoughtfully to the event of being. Maybe I can even throw in a Lacanian aspect, where transcendence has to do with what consciousness cannot integrate, with the "real" that escapes all symbolization, all translation, and all cognition. All three transcendences can, by the way, be understood as so many fundamental criticisms of the Cartesian world model.

6. The "genius," by the way, is itself a typically modern (romantic) figure. He—or very seldom she—is then supposed to be exceptionally gifted by supernatural selection. Enlightenment holds that all human beings are endowed with the one universal reason and that only external factors (disability, madness, developmental issues, etc.) can diminish its potency. Hegel probably considered himself the synthesis of Enlightenment and Romanticism.

7. Equally unsettling as this debunking of scientific activity was Thomas Kuhn's groundbreaking study in 1962, *The Structure of Scientific Revolutions*. He shows how scientific enterprise does not depend on strictly academic criteria, but rather on psycho-social and economic factors. In order to protect scientific research from industrial and political concerns to a certain extent, the philosopher of science Paul Feyerabend proposed a "separation of state and science" along the lines of the separation of state and church.

8. In a certain way, the possibility of negationism testifies of the impossibility to integrate this event in history-as-salvation. Although condemnable in ethico-political sense, negationism points at Hegelian escape routes from difference, back into traditional overarching models. Remember how Hegel allowed his system to "precede" reality, implying that his system was more "real" than what we would commonly agree upon as reality.

9. This is, again, paradoxical, because it is now generally agreed upon that Nazism is actually not a fallback into barbarianism but a highlight, a summit of modernity.

10. This is what René Girard calls the "scapegoat mechanism."

11. *The Trial of God (as it was held on February 25, 1649, in Shamgorod)* is a play by Elie Wiesel, supposedly based on true "facts."

12. A striking example is the Vipeholm experiment in so-called progressive Sweden. Immediately after World War II, the Swedish government supported a joint program with the sugar industry and the dental syndicate, in which institutions for children with mental disabilities were supplied with masses of sugary foods to study their effects on teeth. This "A good mongoloid is one with caries" is a painful variation on "A good Jew is a dead, recyclable Jew." This (ab)use of people as research material, which Kant and Heidegger explicitly warned against, typifies a culture where human dignity is held in low esteem. Paradoxically enough, such regimes rely on dissidents and marginalized people, because they provide human material that can be used for free. Therefore, just as the Nazis did not hate the Jews, the USSR did not hate dissidents; on the contrary, they were put to good (cheap) use in the Siberian tin mines.

13. What else could "Not my Islam!" even mean? Do those Muslims not understand the Koran—or do they? I am convinced that terrorism has little to do with religion. I will come back to this.

14. This is why Nancy prefers the word "mutation." Transformation still contains the laws and lines along which the modern form translates into the other one, whereas mutation has the connotation of unpredictability, of the impossibility of an inference or translation.

15. Oswald Spengler already warned us of this in his *Decline of the West* (1918–1922). Democracy belongs to the decline of each civilization and the last episode thereof is populism.

16. Some terminological unscrambling. Strictly speaking, polytheism is not, as is commonly assumed, the opposite of monotheism, but of henotheism. Henotheism (from the Greek for "one") and polytheism (from the Greek for "many") are both a matter of counting. Monotheism is not a matter of counting, henotheism and polytheism are. Both of these latter end up with "one" and "many" respectively. Counting keeps the divine within human reach. Monotheism finds its antithesis in pantheism. While the latter (from the Greek for "all") means that everything is divine, the former (from the Greek for "only, alone") states that only God is God. The latter may seem trivial, but it is not. Thus, there is actually no statement in monotheism about the existence, quantity, etc., of the divine.

17. Why not "plural" rather than polytheistic differential? The latter indicates, and this is precisely what is crucial, that it is not about a manageable plurality. It is not about multiple positions that can be integrated in a logically coherent way in a "metanarrative." According to polytheism, I find myself in a narrative complex

that constitutes me—and not vice versa; I cannot even escape it. Its differential character reminds me that all I can say about the different positions is that they are not identical and also cannot be interconnected by means of other logical operations (opposition, subordination). These positions are not conceptual-theoretical constructs, but show untraceable traces that never lead to one single other-worldly origin. As narratives they cannot be used argumentatively, for example, politically, because they do not serve debate but inspire celebration.

18. As far as I know, Christ gets infuriated only once throughout the whole gospel, during the episode that is known as the cleansing of the Temple. This episode must be very important to theology, since it is told in all four gospels (Mt 21:12–13; Mk 11:15–19; Lk 19:45–48; and Jn 2:13–25). Whores, tax collectors, and any other outcast are not as bad as those moneychangers. The former can be molded, but whoever contributes to the bribery of God is really too far gone.

19. This is a misunderstanding of the famous "return of religion," as if the pre-modern God returns, after a short exile during modernity, in all his glory. This may be the plan of *Opus Dei*, but let us all agree that it is impossible to rewind history and deny modernity instead of wearing it out. We must not reverse history, but sit it through.

20. Remember the poor widow's mite (Mk 12: 41–44; Lk 21:1–4). This is about the smallest monetary unit, economically neglectable. Theologically and meontologically, however, it makes a huge difference. Christians evoke this difference by calling it "heaven on earth."

21. Erik Meganck, "Re-telling Faith: A Contemporary Philosophical Redraft of Christianity as Hermeneutics," *New Blackfriars* 99, no. 1079 (2018): 30–46.

22. Maybe Nietzsche meant his criticism to affect the God of the Bible, but faith cannot be refuted with blunt arguments. The other way around does not work either: faith cannot be installed with rational arguments. Kierkegaard and Wittgenstein were very convincing on that point. But maybe we should except deism here.

23. Contemporary French sociologist Bruno Latour, not exactly a devout Catholic, wrote a short text immediately after the publication of the encyclical letter, *La grande clameur relayée par le Pape François* (bruno-latour.fr/sites/default/files/P-176-LAUDATO SI.pdf). He considers *Laudato si'* anti-modern, like most encyclical letters so far, only this time not from a pre-modern but from a post-modern perspective, as modernity's self-critique. Enthusiastically—which means literally "visited by the divine"—he points at the radical originality of the pope, namely the intrinsic connection between nature and justice—between the stars above us and the moral law within us. This connection is evoked by the metaphor of the scream. He notes that before, no one ever explicitly entrusted nature with the ability to scream. The scream, by the way, does not come from environmentalists and social workers, but from the earth and from the poor themselves. The scream is therefore not a plan, a theory, nor a (scientific) given fact. A scream says nothing, has no content, but "shakes up," like Heidegger's wink.

Chapter 12

1. Derrida does not *conclude* that we had better be silent about God; he asks how we can remain silent about God. This "inversion" of the issue is analogous to Freud saying that the real question of psychology should not be how we can remember things, but rather how we are able to forget them. The analogy between deconstruction and psychoanalysis is neither accidental nor unfruitful. Unfortunately, a thorough comparison between the two lies beyond the scope of this book.

2. This "positive" is not about an evaluation; here, "positive" means that a sign presents its meaning from within and does not need anything from without, like in a differential system. The opposite of "positive" is not "negative" but "differential."

3. Gilles Deleuze calls this complex event "rhizome." This is not a clean process along clear causal chains, but an inextricable network of untraceable references.

4. Delay is not an ontological structure, entity, or institution, but a "hauntological" effect. This suggests that what is suppressed by metaphysics will always reappear in a ghost-like manner, as strange and intimidating. It comes from within but seems to be an attack from outside, like Freud's symptoms, including the dream.

5. Here is that "end" again, which we might compare to the afterparty of a happening. Officially it is not part of the program, but it is not completely separate from the happening. The theme is continued in a less stringent fashion with about the same people. And nobody has any idea how long it will last. It is usually a fairly informal and convivial ado.

6. Erik Meganck, "Is Metaphoricity Threatening or Saving Thought?" in *Metaphors in Modern and Contemporary Philosophy*, ed. Arthur Cools, Walter Van Herck, and Koenraad Verrycken (University Press Antwerp, 2013), 279–294.

7. This indeed resembles the way Freud described how suppressed content returns to consciousness as a symptom that cannot be deciphered by that consciousness. It is therefore perceived as outside.

8. In an interview, Derrida declares, "I quite rightly pass for an atheist." When someone asks him why he does not just call himself an atheist, plain and simple, he replies "Because perhaps I am not." Here's the full quote: "My religion about which nobody knows anything, any more than does my mother who asked other people a while ago, not daring to talk to me about it, if I still believed in God . . . but she must have known that the constancy of God in my life is called by other names, so that I quite rightly pass for an atheist, the omnipresence to me of what I call God in my absolved absolutely private language being neither that of an eyewitness nor that of a voice doing anything than talking to me without saying anything." "Circumfession," in Geoffrey Bennington and Jacques Derrida, *Jacques Derrida* (University of Chicago Press, 1993), 154–55.

9. He continues, "Tout autre est tout autre," which is translated as "Every other (one) is every (bit) other." *The Gift of Death* (University of Chicago Press, 1995), 68.

10. Jewish culture distinguishes itself from Greek thought by giving priority to the singular, the individual, the name, and the event over the universal, conceptual, substance, and fact.

11. After all, when there are good reasons to decide between two options, strictly speaking there is no decision but rather compliance with an argument. If there are good reasons to forgive someone a transgression, strictly speaking there is no forgiveness. Therefore, decision and forgiveness are extremely rare and always provocative. Should we forgive a serial killer, a child rapist, a camp executioner, etc.? And if so, can we, really?

Extroduction

1. This is why Heidegger considered Nietzsche now as summit of metaphysics, then as its transgression, sometimes as both.

2. I mean that this meeting was not scheduled; there was no agenda. Philosophy and theology are both moving on, having severed relations long ago. Suddenly, they meet. This meeting is actually (Foucault) destined (Heidegger). This means that, in hindsight, it will appear as senseful and then we will steadily get on to its meaning, but it was impossible to predict from an earlier destined actuality.

3. We find this non-dialectical play also in philosophy. In *The Question Concerning Technology*, Heidegger refers to Hölderlin's verse "Wo aber Gefahr ist, wächst das Rettende auch" (from the poet's *Patmos*).

4. This is the title of an interesting book by Leszek Kolakowski (1988/2001).

5. The subtitle of *Twilight of the Idols* reads *How to Philosophize with a Hammer*. Nietzsche did not, as many misunderstand, use this hammer to smash concepts, but to examine them—rather like when a physician taps your knee caps with a hammer.

6. John Caputo, the philosopher who became a theologian, learns from Deleuze (series XXI in *The Logic of Sense*) that an event takes place in a name, a concept, or a fact without ever being identical to it. Resurrection is an event, the empty grave is a fact. The event is what "shakes up" the world. God is a Name wherein much happens. Recently, Caputo started calling himself, among other labels, a "theologian of the event."

7. Freud thought Christian charity perverse. To be anyone's neighbor goes against the psychology of (s)election. But Freud also recognized this charity as the only force that could possibly be deployed against the threat of total self-destruction of humanity. Only, according to him, this charity does not really exist. I agree, it does not exist as a psychological faculty. But the total self-destruction of humanity did not take place either, even though it is still possible in principle. Perhaps the Name is capable of suspending principles?

8. It is this poverty that distinguishes these signs and winks from the signs that Paul denounces (1 Cor 1:22).

9. In her fascinating study *The Human Condition* (1958), Hannah Arendt relates how humanity has lost this focus on living well together and ended up in an each-for-himself survival mode.

10. This reminds me of the famous passage from Dostoevsky's *The Brothers Karamazov* about the grand inquisitor, already mentioned in chapter 3, note 10. In a dream, this grand inquisitor represents the institute that does not want to be disturbed by the "advent" of Christ. But again, Christ did not come back to unchain a revolution and overthrow the church, nor does he want to change the world according to its own laws. After the strong speech of the grand inquisitor, who even threatens to execute Christ, Christ rises, bestows a kiss on him, and walks out of the prison.

11. The first volume of Nancy's *Deconstruction of Christianism* is called *Dis-enclosure* (2005).

12. As a metaphor, it is the theological equivalent of Heidegger's thrownness (*Geworfenheit*), where we find ourselves thrown into a world, a coherent set of signification, that is already there.

13. Erik Meganck, "Philosophia Amica Theologiae: Weak Faith and Theological Difference," *Modern Theology* 31, no. 3 (2015): 377–402.

14. It is symptomatic of the crisis of the capitalist world that industry and finance are urging politics to impose on education, care, and culture those neo-liberal models with which they cannot sustain themselves, so that money that is meant for education, care, and culture goes to industry and finance.

Bibliography

Agamben, Giorgio. *Homo Sacer*. Stanford University Press, 2017.
Alexandrova, Alena, Ignaas Devisch, Laurens ten Kate, and Aukje van Rooden, eds. *Re-treating Religion: Deconstructing Christianity with Jean-Luc Nancy*. Fordham University Press, 2012.
Allen, Sarah. *The Philosophical Sense of Transcendence: Levinas and Plato on Love beyond Being*. Duquesne University Press, 2009.
Arendt, Hannah. *The Human Condition*. University of Chicago Press, 2018.
Bennington, Geoffrey, and Jacques Derrida. *Jacques Derrida*. University of Chicago Press, 1993.
Benson, Bruce, and Norman Wirzba, eds. *Transforming Philosophy and Religion: Love's Wisdom*. Indiana University Press, 2008.
Benson, Bruce, and Norman Wirzba, eds. *Words of Life: New Theological Turns in French Phenomenology*. Fordham University Press, 2010.
Bloechl, Jeffrey, ed. *Religious Experience and the End of Metaphysics*. Indiana University Press, 2003.
Blond, Philip, ed. *Post-secular Philosophy: Between Philosophy and Theology*. Routledge, 1998.
Boeve, Lieven, and Christophe Brabant, eds. *Between Philosophy and Theology: Contemporary Interpretations of Christianity*. Ashgate, 2010.
Burggraeve, Roger, ed. *The Awakening to the Other: A Provocative Dialogue with Emmanuel Levinas*. Peeters, 2008.
Caputo, John. *The Mystical Element in Heidegger's Thought*. Fordham University Press, 1986.
Caputo, John. *On Religion*. Routledge, 2001.
Caputo, John. *Philosophy and Theology*. Abingdon Press, 2006.
Caputo, John. *The Prayers and Tears of Jacques Derrida: Religion without Religion*. Indiana University Press, 1997.
Caputo, John. *The Weakness of God. A Theology of the Event*. Indiana University Press, 2006.

Caputo, John, and Gianni Vattimo. *God after the Death of God*. Edited by Jeffrey Robbins. Cambridge University Press, 2007.
Cimino, Antonio, and Gert-Jan van der Heiden, eds. *Rethinking Faith: Heidegger between Nietzsche and Wittgenstein*. Bloomsbury, 2017.
Crocket, Clayton, and Keith Putt, eds. *The Future of Continental Philosophy of Religion*. Indiana University Press, 2014.
Cunningham, Connor, and Peter Candler, eds. *Transcendence and Phenomenology*. SCM Press, 2007.
Deleuze, Gilles. *The Logic of Sense*. Continuum, 2004.
Deleuze, Gilles. *Nietzsche and Philosophy*. Columbia University Press, 1983.
Depoortere, Frederiek. *The Death of God: An Investigation into the History of the Western Concept of God*. T&T Clark, 2008.
Derrida, Jacques. *The Gift of Death*. University of Chicago Press, 1995.
Derrida, Jacques. "How to Avoid Speaking: Denials." In *Derrida and Negative Theology*, edited by Harold Coward and Toby Foshay, 73–136. SUNY Press, 1989.
Derrida, Jacques. *Limited Inc*. Northwestern University Press, 1988.
Derrida, Jacques. *Margins of Philosophy*. University of Chicago Press, 1982.
Derrida, Jacques. *Of Grammatology*. Johns Hopkins University Press, 2016.
Derrida, Jacques. "Violence and Metaphysics: An Essay on the Thought of Emmanuel Levinas." In *Writing and Difference*. University of Chicago Press, 1978.
De Vries, Hent. *Philosophy and the Turn to Religion*. Johns Hopkins University Press, 1999.
Dickinson, Colby. *The Postmodern Saints of France*. T&T Clark, 2013.
Dickinson, Colby. *Theological Poverty in Continental Philosophy: After Christian Theology*. Bloomsbury, 2021.
Dooley, Mark, ed. *A Passion for the Impossible: John D. Caputo in Focus*. SUNY Press, 2003.
Eagleton, Terry. *Reason, Faith, and Revolution: Reflections on the God Debate*. Yale University Press, 2009.
Falque, Emmanuel. *Crossing the Rubicon: The Borderlands of Philosophy and Theology*. Fordham University Press, 2016.
Francis. *Laudato si'. On Care for Our Common Home*. Encyclical letter, May 25, 2015.
Freud, Sigmund. *Civilization and Its Discontents*. Broadview Press, 2016.
Freud, Sigmund. *The Psychopathology of Everyday Life*. Hogarth, 1995.
Freud, Sigmund. *Totem and Taboo: Resemblances between the Psychic Lives of Savages and Neurotics*. Translated by A. A. Brill. Routledge, 1919.
Girard, René, and Gianni Vattimo. *Christianity, Truth, and Weakening Faith*. Edited by Pierpaolo Antonello. Cambridge University Press, 2010.
Goodchild, Philip. *Rethinking Philosophy of Religion: Approaches from Continental Philosophy*. Fordham University Press, 2002.
Gschwandtner, Christina. *Postmodern Apologetics? Arguments for God in Contemporary Philosophy*. Fordham University Press, 2013.

Gutting, Gary. *Talking God: Philosophers on Belief*. Norton, 2016.
Haar, Michel. *Nietzsche and Metaphysics*. SUNY Press, 1996.
Harasym, Sarah, ed. *Levinas and Lacan: The Missed Encounter*. SUNY Press, 1998.
Hart, Kevin. *Kingdoms of God*. Indiana University Press, 2014.
Hart, Kevin. *The Trespass of the Sign: Deconstruction, Theology, and Philosophy*. Cambridge University Press, 1989.
Heidegger, Martin. *Basic Writings*. Harper Colins, 1993.
Heidegger, Martin. *Being and Time*. SUNY Press, 2010.
Heidegger, Martin. *Identity and Difference*. University of Chicago Press, 2002.
Henry, Michel. *I Am the Truth: Toward a Philosophy of Christianity*. Stanford University Press, 2003.
James, Ian. *The New French Philosophy*. Polity Press, 2012.
Janicaud, Dominique. *Heidegger in France*. Indiana University Press, 2015.
Janicaud, Dominique. *Phenomenology and the "Theological Turn."* Fordham University Press, 2000.
Jonkers, Peter, and Ruud Welten. *God in France: Eight Contemporary French Thinkers on God*. Peeters, 2005.
Joy, Morny, ed. *Continental Philosophy and Philosophy of Religion*. New York: Springer, 2011.
Kearney, Richard. *Anatheism: Returning to God after God*. Columbia University Press, 2010.
Kolakowski, Leszek. *Metaphysical Horror*. Penguin, 2001.
Kuhn, Thomas. *The Structure of Scientific Revolutions*. University of Chicago Press, 2012.
Lambert, Gregg. *Return Statements: The Return of Religion in Contemporary Philosophy*. Edinburgh University Press, 2016.
Leo XIII. *Rerum Novarum. On Capital and Labor*. Encyclical letter, May 15, 1891.
Levinas, Emmanuel. *Existence and Existents*. Duquesne University Press, 2001.
Levinas, Emmanuel. *Otherwise than Being: Or, Beyond Essence*. Duquesne University Press, 1998.
Levinas, Emmanuel. *Totality and Infinity: An Essay on Exteriority*. Kluwer Academic Publishers, 1991.
Long, Eugene, ed. *Self and Other: Essays in Continental Philosophy of Religion*. Springer, 2007.
Löwith, Karl. *Meaning in History: The Theological Implications of the Philosophy of History*. University of Chicago Press, 1949.
Lyotard, Jean-François. *The Postmodern Condition: A Report on Knowledge*. University of Minnesota Press, 1984.
Lyotard, Jean-François. *The Postmodern Explained*. University of Minnesota Press, 1997.
Mannousakis, John. *After God: Richard Kearney and the Religious Turn in Continental Philosophy*. Fordham University Press, 2006.

Marx, Karl. *Early Political Writings*, edited by Joseph O'Malley. Cambridge University Press, 1994.
Marx, Karl. *The German Ideology.* Prometheus Books, 1998.
Meganck, Erik. "Church and World: Philosophical Exploration of a Mutual Approach." *Acta Comparanda* 33 (2022), 19–26.
Meganck, Erik. "Is Metaphoricity Threatening or Saving Thought?" In *Metaphors in Modern and Contemporary Philosophy*, edited by Arthur Cools, Walter Van Herck, and Koenraad Verrycken, 279–294. University Press Antwerp, 2013.
Meganck, Erik. "Modern Violence: Heavenly or Worldly—or Else?" *Human Studies* 43, no. 2 (2020): 291–309.
Meganck, Erik. "Philosophia Amica Theologiae: Weak Faith and Theological Difference." *Modern Theology* 31, no. 3 (2015): 377–402.
Meganck, Erik. "Re-telling Faith: A Contemporary Philosophical Redraft of Christianity as Hermeneutics." *New Blackfriars* 99, no. 1079 (2018): 30–46.
Meganck, Erik. "'Spem in Aliud . . .': What May I Hope For?" *Ethical Perspectives* 23, no. 3 (2016): 473–498.
Meganck, Erik. "'World without End': From Hyperreligious Theism to Religious Atheism." *Journal for Continental Philosophy of Religion* 3, no. 1 (2021): 65–89.
Meylahn, Johann-Albrecht. *The Limits and Possibilities of Postmetaphysical God-Talk: A Conversation between Heidegger, Levinas and Derrida.* Peeters, 2013.
Morny, Joy, ed. *Continental Philosophy and Philosophy of Religion.* Springer, 2011.
Nancy, Jean-Luc. *Adoration: The Deconstruction of Christianity.* Translated by John McKeane. Fordham University Press, 2013.
Nancy, Jean-Luc. *Dis-Enclosure: The Deconstruction of Christianity.* Translated by Bettina Bergo, Gabriel Malenfant, and Michael B. Smith. Fordham University Press, 2008.
Nietzsche, Friedrich. *The Gay Science: With a Prelude in Rhymes and an Appendix of Songs.* Translated by Walter Kaufmann. New York: Penguin Books, 1974.
Nietzsche, Friedrich. *Thus Spoke Zarathustra.* Translated by Graham Parkes. Oxford University Press, 2005.
Nietzsche, Friedrich. *Twilight of the Idols: Or, How to Philosophize With the Hammer.* Hackett, 1997.
Nietzsche, Friedrich. *Untimely Meditations.* Edited by Daniel Breazeale, translated by R. J. Hollingdale. Cambridge: Cambridge University Press, 1997.
Nietzsche, Friedrich. *The Will to Power.* Penguin, 2017.
Olthuis, James. *Religion with/out Religion: The Prayers and Tears of John D. Caputo.* Routledge, 2002.
Rorty, Richard, and Gianni Vattimo. *The Future of Religion.* Edited by Santiago Zabala. Columbia University Press, 2005.
Russell, Bertrand. *Dear Bertrand Russell: A Selection of his Correspondence with the General Public, 1950–1968.* Houghton Mifflin, 1969.
Russell, Bertrand. *History of Western Philosophy.* Routledge, 2015.

Russell, Bertrand. *Why I Am Not a Christian and Other Essays on Religion and Related Subjects*. Routledge, 2004.
Sartre, Jean-Paul. *Being and Nothingness: An Essay in Phenomenological Ontology*. Translated by Sarah Richmond. Taylor & Francis, 2020.
Sartre, Jean-Paul. *Existentialism Is a Humanism*. Yale University Press, 2007.
Sartre, Jean-Paul. *Huis clos, suivi de Les mouches*. Gallimard, 1947.
Sartre, Jean-Paul. *The Transcendence of the Ego*. Routledge, 2004.
Saussure, Ferdinand de. *Course of General Linguistics*. Colombia University Press, 2011.
Schrijvers, Joeri. *Between Faith and Belief: Toward a Contemporary Phenomenology of Religious Life*. SUNY Press, 2016.
Schrijvers, Joeri, and Martin Koči, eds. *The European Reception of John D. Caputo's Thought: Radicalizing Theology*. Rowman & Littlefield, 2022.
Shepherd, Andrew. *The Gift of the Other: Levinas, Derrida, and a Theology of Hospitality*. Pickwick, 2014.
Smith, Anthony, and Daniel Whistler. *After the Postsecular and Postmodern: Essays in Continental Philosophy of Religion*. Cambridge Scholars Publishing, 2011.
Stoker, Wessel, and Willy van der Merwe, eds. *Looking Beyond? Shifting Views of Transcendence in Philosophy, Theology, Art, and Politics*. Rodopi, 2012.
Taylor, Mark. *Deconstructing Theology*. Crossroad Publishing Company/Scholars Press, 1982.
Trakakis, Nick. *The End of Philosophy of Religion*. Continuum, 2008.
van Riessen, Renée. *Man as a Place of God: Levinas' Hermeneutics of Kenosis*. Springer, 2007.
Vedder, Ben. *Heidegger's Philosophy of Religion: From God to the Gods*. Duquesne University Press, 2007.
Westphal, Merold. *Postmodern Philosophy and Christian Thought*. Indiana University Press, 1999.
Wittgenstein, Ludwig. *Philosophical Investigations*. Wiley & Blackwell, 2010.
Wittgenstein, Ludwig. *Tractatus Logico-Philosophicus*. Routledge, 1961.
Wrathall, Mark, ed. *Religion after Metaphysics*. Cambridge University Press, 2003.
Žižek, Slavoj. *The Absolute Fragile—or Why Is the Christian Legacy Worth Fighting For?* Verso, 2000.

Index

Abraham, 46, 189, 204n2; Isaac's offer, 43, 176–178; and Odysseus, 204n9
absurd, 45–46, 83, 95, 118, 137–138, 158, 187, 194–195, 211n7
actuality (according to Foucault), 1, 34, 53, 58, 110, 147, 181, 187–188, 198, 203n8, 217n3, 221n2
Agamben, Giorgio, 198, 203n4, 203n7
Agamemnon. See Iphigenia
alterity, 5, 31–33, 140, 143, 163, 175, 178–180, 187–188, 193, 198, 217n5
Althusser, Louis, 34, 122
analytic thought, 8–9, 73, 92–95, 97–103, 111, 172, 176, 185
anti-religion, 63, 145, 207n13
Aristotle, 55–56, 65, 105, 108–109, 112, 160, 164, 184, 193, 202n1, 208n9, 210n11, 210n18, 213n9, 215n1
Aron, Raymond, 34, 121–122
Assman, Jan, 34–35
atheism, 2, 11, 17–19, 22, 37, 51, 54, 60, 126, 128–129, 189, 220n8; philosophical or religious, 2–5, 9, 156, 173, 183–184, 190, 195–196, 201n5; 'flat' or hyperreligious, 2–4, 9, 51, 60, 89–90, 117, 129, 175, 183–184, 190, 196–197, 199

Augustine, 4, 6, 8, 47, 138, 177, 184, 201n1
Auschwitz, 153

Bauman, Zygmunt, 197–198
Beauvoir, Simone de, 3, 37, 121, 124, 131
Bonhoeffer, Dietrich, 17, 78
Brecht, Bertold, 32

Caputo, John, 4, 6, 18, 45, 206n4, 221n6
charity, 19, 30, 41, 46–47, 60, 63, 77–78, 88, 187, 189, 221n7
Christ, 4, 32–33, 38–39, 43–49, 60–65, 70, 76, 83, 123, 141–142, 145, 157–160, 181, 183–186, 189, 203n9, 204n3, 205n11, 205n1, 216n10, 216n12, 219n18, 222n10.; hymn, 160, 183–186, 193, 201, 216n13
circulation (of the Name). See under God
Comte, Auguste, 16, 58, 206n9
Credo: quia absurdum, 86, 205n9; *ut intelligam*, 86
critique of metaphysics, 3–4, 7–8, 15, 21, 37–38, 45, 93, 96, 105, 133, 156–157, 166–167, 175, 184–190,

229

Critique of metaphysics *(continued)*
193, 196, 211n3, 213n9, 217n5, 219n23

Dawkins, Richard, 62, 89–90, 190, 208n1, 213n13
Deleuze, Gilles, 97, 220n3, 221n6
Derrida, Jacques, 4–5, 8, 42, 85, 95–98, 114–115, 122, 125, 135, 144, 155–156, **163–181**, 188, 192–194, 204n2, 205n3, 209n4, 212n9, 215n4, 216n11, 220n1, 220n8
Descartes, René, 14–15, 45, 82, 89, 93, 110–112, 136, 148, 152, 164–167, 174, 184, 202n1, 206n6, 210n14, 214n2
difference, 5, 8–9, 12, 16, 69, 111–113, 136, 143, 156–157, 167, 171–176, 179–180, 187, 196, 212n9, 217n8, 218n17, 218–219n7, 220n2
Dostoevsky, Fyodor, 130, 205n10, 211n4, 216n8, 222n10

Eckhart, *Meister*, 4, 106, 118–119, 197
Enlightenment. See *under* modernity
event, 93, 107, 112–117, 137, 153–155, 158–160, 164–170, 173, 186, 190–195, 197–198, 217n5, 220n3, 221n10, 221n6
evidence, 7–8, 34, 77, 82, 85, 89, 94, 109, 114, 129, 151–152, 163, 166, 170–171, 173–175, 188, 192, 202n5, 213n13
exaltation (of Christ). See kenosis
existentialism, 37–39, 40–48, 105, 121–123, 127–133, 213n9

faith. See virtues: theological
Feuerbach, Ludwig, 4, **11–19**, 21–22, 25, 39, 45, 48, 76–77, 87, 149, 184, 202n1

Feyerabend, Paul, 217n7
Foucault, Michel, 61, 187, 217n3, 221n2. See *also* actuality
Freud, Sigmund, 4, 13, 21–22, 40, **67–78**, 83, 88–89, 153, 163, 168, 207n1, 207n6, 208n12, 210n16. See *also* psychoanalysis

Gagarin, Yuri, 112, 138
Gauchet, Marcel, 34
Girard, René, 145, 186, 208n14, 216n12, 218n10
God: death of, 1–2, 51–54, 57–62, 65, 83, 96, 100, 107–108, 115–117, 123, 143, 156, 175, 183–186, 193, 201n1, 214n1; Name, 2–3, 5, 13, 15, 18, 43, 60, 64–65, 76, 84, 101, 132, 144, 160–161, 173–199; as meaning and opening, 15, 44, 115, 173–174, 180, 187–188, 193–199, 202n5, 217n5; circulation, publication of the Name, 5, 183, 190–192, 195–196
grace, 19, 47, 77, 89, 119, 138, 159, 211n19
gratitude, 56, 94, 103, 118, 196, 205n11

Hebrew. See Jew
Hegel, Georg Wilhelm Friedrich, 8, 16, 21–25, 34, 37–39, 44–45, 54, 61, 67, 81, 86, 109, 114, 123, 148, 164, 172, 184, 204n2, 211n3, 212n6, 214n8, 217n6, 217n8
Heidegger, Martin, 4–5, 44–45, 85, 92–94, 99, **105–119**, 121–126, 135–138, 143, 150, 155, 159, 163, 165, 170–176, 181, 184, 191, 193–195, 202n4, 205n8, 206n5, 211n2, 211n6, 212n5, 212n6, 212n7, 213n9, 213n10, 213n12, 213n17, 213n19, 214n1, 214n3,

215n1, 215n5, 217n5, 218n12, 221n1, 221n3, 222n12
henotheism. *See under* theism
Henry, Michel, 32–33
hermeneutics, 58, 68, 108, 110, 156, 159, 188, 211n2, 213n10
hieranarchy, 4, 206n4
hope. *See* virtues: theological
hospitality, 7, 158, 178–179
Hume, David, 103, 184, 208n14
humiliation (of Christ). *See* kenosis
Husserl, Edmund, 106, 124, 214n2, 216n7
hyperreligious. *See* atheism

immanence, 6, 37, 57, 217n5
Iphigenia, 41–43, 204n6, 208n8
Isaac. *See under* Abraham
Islam. *See* Muslim

Janicaud, Dominique, 176
Jew, 33, 46, 76, 83, 91, 105, 124, 135–136, 141–142, 145, 153–154, 158–159, 163, 178, 209n9, 215n6, 216n8, 216n9, 218n12, 210n10
Jung, Carl Gustav, 208n8

kairos, 45
Kant, Immanuel, 8, 39, 42–43, 82, 86, 95–96, 111, 121, 144, 148, 157–158, 184, 211n3, 214n6, 216n7, 218n12
katechon, 203n3
Kearney, Richard, 6, 18
kenosis, 1, 145, 160, 183, 186, 216n13
Kierkegaard, Søren, 3–4, 7, 21, **37–49**, 77–78, 86, 90–91, 102, 110, 135, 138, 163, 176–177, 202n1, 204n2, 210n16, 213n9, 219n22

Lacan, Jacques, 74, 77, 164, 214n8, 217n5. *See also* psychoanalysis

language game, 61, 98–101, 114, 194, 211–212n8
Latour, Bruno, 30, 219n23
Laudato si', 30, 161, 219n23
leap, 39–40, 43–48, 78, 90, 110
Levinas, Emmanuel, 3–4, 41–43, 105, 115, 123–126, 129, 131–132, **135–146**, 159, 160, 163, 168, 173, 176–181, 195, 211n7, 212n1, 212n5, 215, n1, 215n6–9
logical empiricism. *See* positivism
Löwith, Karl, 31, 149
Luther, Martin, 47, 54, 157, 213n9
Lyotard, Jean-François, 4, 85, 98–99, 123, **147–161**, 164–165, 168, 181, 202n4, 204n10, 211n8, 212n3

Marcel, Gabriel, 132
Marx, Karl, 3–4, 16, 18, **21–35**, 37, 39, 67–68, 75–77, 91, 123, 149, 163, 203n3, 203n4, 204n1, 207n5, 217n3
marxism, 24, 26, 32–34, 121, 129–130, 133, 204n1
Mary, 46, 189, 207n14, 209n8
meaning. *See under* God
meontology, 42, 159–160, 213n12, 219n20
metaphor (vs. concept), 8, 56, 68–70, 76–77, 87, 171–172, 188–189, 194–196, 206n6, 208n13, 222n12
Method Dispute (*Methodenstreit*), 86–87
modernity: as progress, 14–16, 34, 58, 62, 85–86, 108, 123, 149, 151–155, 201n6, 209n1, 212n4; Enlightenment, 2, 6, 8, 11, 89, 147–149, 158, 190, 210n18, 217n6; Romanticism, 68, 77, 108, 210n16, 210n18, 217n6
monotheism. *See under* theism
Mother Teresa (syndrome), 42

Mounier, Emmanuel, 37
Muslim, 155–156, 218n13
myth, mythology, 16, 77, 83–84, 119, 149, 168, 188

Nagel, Tomas, 81, 90, 213n8
Name. See under God
Nancy, Jean-Luc, 5, 31, 96, 193, 198, 218n14, 222n11
Nietzsche, Friedrich, 4, 6, 8, 21–22, 47, **51–65**, 76, 82, 84, 91, 96, 101, 106–108, 111, 115–116, 123, 133, 145, 156–157, 160, 163, 166, 184, 186–188, 196, 202n1, 202n1, 205n1, 205n3, 206n5, 206n9, 210n13, 212n6, 213n10, 213n18, 214n1, 219n26, 221n1, 221n5
nihilism, 54, 59–62, 103, 107

Odysseus. See under Abraham
opening. See under God
openness. See virtues: theological
otherness. See alterity

pantheism. See under theism
Parmenides, 211n2, 213n11
Paul, 30, 32, 45, 47, 65, 119, 141, 159, 186, 201n1, 203n3, 203n7, 204n11, 213n12, 217n5, 222n8
personalism, 18, 48–49, 133
Petrarch, 112
phenomenology, 106, 112, 124, 139, 202n4, 213n9, 214n2, 215n7
Plato, 43, 55–57, 65, 94, 144, 184, 186–187, 202n5, 206n6, 215n6
politics, 18–19, 22–34, 38, 41–43, 46–48, 54, 59, 62, 65, 77, 83–84, 99, 109, 122–123, 131–133, 136, 142, 148, 153–159, 165, 177–179, 183, 198, 203n7, 203n8, 204n11, 217n7, 219n17, 222n14
polytheism. See under theism

positivism, 57, 80–86, 91–93, 100, 114
proof. See evidence
psychoanalysis, 67–78, 133, 139, 158, 164, 188, 208n9, 214n8, 217n5, 220n1
publication (of the name). See under God

registers of thought, 5, 8, 17, 18, 39, 46, 58, 64, 70, 73, 76, 82, 84, 86, 90, 117–118, 127, 161, 173, 178, 187, 189–190, 209n6, 215n6, 216n7
relativism, 57–58, 100, 155
resignation (*Gelassenheit*), 106–107, 118–119
Ricoeur, Paul, 21–22, 82
Romanticism. See under modernity
Romero, Oscar, 30, 33
Rorty, Richard, 45, 147, 154, 164
Russell, Bertrand, 76, **79–90**, 91, 106–107, 122, 126, 129, 158, 163, 168

Samaritan (Good-), 64, 141–142, 204n4
Sartre, Jean-Paul, 3–4, 34, 37, 44–45, 48, 74, 88, 90, 110, **121–133**, 137, 140, 184, 210n17, 211n19, 211n4, 214n1, 214n3, 214n8
scientism. See positivism
secularization, 2, 6, 31, 48, 123, 149, 185, 201n6, 202n6
Sheldrake, Rupert, 202n1, 210n11
skandalon, 47, 158, 193
Spengler, Oswald, 205n8, 213n14, 218n15
Spinoza, 84, 109
step back (Heidegger), 44, 110, 117, 212n6
style. See registers of thought
supernatural, 6, 112, 217n6

Supreme Being, 4, 13–14, 19, 58–60, 89, 96, 106–111, 115–116, 132–133, 156, 164, 173–175, 179, 183–185, 190, 193–199, 213n18

Taylor, Charles, 212n2
terrorism, 130, 148, 154–156, 211n8, 218n13
Tertullian, 1–2
thanking, thankfulness. *See* gratitude
theism, 3, 14, 60, 86, 89–90, 96, 117, 127, 156, 160, 175, 183, 196–197; henotheism, 84, 218n16; monotheism, 14, 31, 43, 84, 117, 126, 142, 185–186, 196, 208n13, 218n16; pantheism, 218n16; polytheism, 156, 188, 218n6, 218n7
theopoetics, 118, 150, 194, 199
Thomas Aquinas, 6, 8, 109
transcendent, 6, 25, 40–41, 88, 99, 116, 118, 121, 124, 126, 129, 137, 149, 164, 174, 178, 186, 191, 201n6, 213n8, 217n5
trace, 9, 12, 72–74, 131, 138, 143–144, 146, 16181, 189, 192–193, 219n17, 220n3
trust. *See* virtues: theological

unmasking (Nietzsche), 6, 61, 96, 206n9

Vattimo, Gianni, 45
Virtues: cardinal, 65; theological, 2–3, 7, 17, 46, 65, 90, 118–119, 124, 141, 158, 178, 180–181, 188–191, 193–196

Wiesel, Eli, 153, 218n11
Wittgenstein, Ludwig, 4, 38, 82, **91–103**, 110, 163, 172, 212n7, 219n22

Žižek, Slavoj, 62, 77, 82, 203n7

www.ingramcontent.com/pod-product-compliance
Lightning Source LLC
Chambersburg PA
CBHW030648230426
43665CB00011B/998